Osage and Settler

ALSO BY JANET BERRY HESS

*The Art of Richard Mayhew:
A Critical Analysis with Interviews*
(McFarland, 2014)

Art and Architecture in Postcolonial Africa
(McFarland, 2006)

Osage and Settler

Reconstructing Shared History through an Oklahoma Family Archive

Janet Berry Hess

McFarland & Company, Inc., Publishers
Jefferson, North Carolina

LIBRARY OF CONGRESS CATALOGUING-IN-PUBLICATION DATA

Hess, Janet Berry.
 Osage and settler : reconstructing shared history through an Oklahoma family archive / Janet Berry Hess.
  p.   cm.
 Includes bibliographical references and index.

 ISBN 978-0-7864-9582-5 (softcover : acid free paper) ∞
 ISBN 978-1-4766-2117-3 (ebook)

 1. Osage Indians—Oklahoma—History. 2. African Americans—Relations with Indians. 3. Frontier and pioneer life—Oklahoma. 4. Oklahoma—Race relations—History. I. Title.
 E99.O8H47 2015
 305.8009766—dc23   2015014890

BRITISH LIBRARY CATALOGUING DATA ARE AVAILABLE

© 2015 Janet Berry Hess. All rights reserved

No part of this book may be reproduced or transmitted in any form or by any means, electronic or mechanical, including photocopying or recording, or by any information storage and retrieval system, without permission in writing from the publisher.

On the cover: Osage Indian dancers at Gray Horse ceremonial house, 1912 (Vince Dillon)

Printed in the United States of America

McFarland & Company, Inc., Publishers
 Box 611, Jefferson, North Carolina 28640
  www.mcfarlandpub.com

In memory of my Daddy and my uncle Everett Berry, Jr.
With respect for my ancestors and relations.
For Asa Hess-Matsumoto, so he knows.
For newborn Epiphany.
And for my Mama, Catherine Berry Hess—brilliant,
beautiful, and so beloved.

∼

"There was a woman here who was loved. She was good to look at because she was a quick and imaginative thinker. She liked the view of the peach orchard from the southern window and loved the turquoise earrings her mother had given her when she was married. Her life mattered, utterly, to herself, to her children, to the man she loved, to the birds she scattered crumbs to after the family had eaten. This was her house, and years later the house still remembers her, though it is almost gone and the woman's spirit has flown to the other side."
—Joy Harjo, "There Is No Such Thing as a Land Bridge"

Acknowledgments

I would like to thank Paula Farid for her unconditional support, kindness, hospitality, and friendship throughout this project. I thank the Childers family for welcoming me into their home, once my Grandmother's home, and for honoring the Berry family with their assistance. I am grateful for the delightful discussions with Arlena and Joe Trumbly of Pawhuska. I am also grateful to Lou Brock and Kathryn Red Corn at the Osage Tribal Museum, Daisy Njoku at the Anthropology Archives of the National Museum of Natural History/Smithsonian Institution, Holly Hasenfratz at the National Cowboy & Western Heritage Museum, Heather Shannon at the National Museum of the American Indian, Terry Zinn at the Oklahoma Historical Society, Linda Stone at the Woolaroc Museum, Tara Madden and Benny Polacca at the *Osage News*, and Michelle Maxwell at the Gilcrease Museum for their assistance with images in this book.

Michelle Manley Everson and Lisa Boyd Brashear's support and caring were critical to the success of this text, and I will always recall fondly my time with them writing this text. Maris Taulagan and Patience Foster read early drafts of this text, and I appreciate their caring and friendship. This book would not have been possible without the efforts of Veneta Berry Arlington, Ruby Berry Stallings, Camelia Berry, and particularly my beloved Uncle Everett Berry, Jr., who did research into the family in years past. Pbonchai Tallman offered the spiritual support without which this book could not have been completed.

Table of Contents

Preface   1

Introduction   3

1. Osage Culture and European Arrival: Culture, Trade and Imperialism   11
2. Embodied Anthropology: Settlers, Osage and African Americans   26
3. The Settler, the Trader and the Cowboy   39
4. Architecture: The Church of Immaculate Conception and the One-Room School   55
5. The "Invisible World": *Wa-kon-da*, Body Ornamentation and the Sacred Bundle   76
6. Turning the Century: The Land Run and the "Civilization" of the Osage   93
7. "Even poor varieties may be made sweet": Women's Labor and Constructions of Femininity   108
8. Family and Osage Extravagence and the Oil Boom   127
9. The "Empire of Vision": Exhibition, Photography and Pawnee Bill   139
10. "The View from Persimmon Hill": My Daddy, My Mama and Federal Policy in the 1950s   153
11. "The most beautiful blazing blue sky and emerald green fields": Memory and the Sense of Place   179

Conclusion	188
Appendix: Ross Hess's Writings	191
Chapter Notes	199
Bibliography	214
Index	219

"There is great good in returning to a landscape that has had extraordinary meaning in one's life. It happens that we return to such places in our minds irresistibly. There are certain villages and towns, mountains and plains that, having seen them, walked in them, lived in them, even for a day, we keep forever in the mind's eye. They become indispensable to our well-being: they define us, and we say, I am who I am because I have been there, or there. There is good, too, in actual, physical return.... I, too, happen to take place, each day of my life, in my environment. I exist in a landscape, and my existence is indivisible with the land."

—N. Scott Momaday, *The Man Made of Words: Essays, Stories, Passages*

Preface

Narrative accounts of settlement in America occupy a markedly different space than traditional histories and institutional representations. Settler/occupier histories are often homogenized or discussed solely in the context of the cultural erasure of, and centuries of violence perpetuated against, American Indian peoples. Older documentation and exhibition of the settlement/relocation experience provides a romanticized vision of occupants of "Indian Territory" which conclude with the "end" of American Indians, or accounts of white settlement that slight their personal experience and suffering. Such texts neglect rich intersections of cultural perspective—what cultural anthropologists have described as "embodied" or "sensuous" scholarship.[1]

The experiential, narrative emphasis advanced by Michael Jackson and Paul Stoller suggests the usefulness of an anthropological framework that examines lived experience, nuanced and intersecting relationships, and histories as they take place in specific work contexts and landscapes.[2] My family archives, and interviews with prominent Osage members, reveal parallel histories with strikingly different voices and perspectives. This text employs the theoretically provocative perspectives of "embodied experience"[3] and geography/place, and the anthropological perspective of intersubjectivity, to argue that Oklahoma settlers and the Osage had a mutually arising interaction. Their histories were dichotomous but also reciprocal, and African American history in the same period can similarly be contrasted and/or aligned in surprisingly complex ways, even in the face of the violence that characterizes interaction between majority and marginalized cultures.

This book argues that identity can be most deeply evoked in a narrative and experiential form, extracted from family archives and fieldwork. In an individual, personal, and reflective approach to history—including accounts of cultural interaction, gender, art, architecture, exhibition, and representation—the immediacy of individual voices emerges more clearly than in "objective," conventional scholarship. Individuals have the agency to transform, resist, and recreate the structures and spaces around them and frequently relate these transformations through accounts of their routines and environments. The resonance of narrative, this book argues, is most forceful in the individual's experience of space and landscape—in my case, the experience of a family property known as The Place.

Introduction

In *The Allure of the Archives*, Arlette Farge discusses the psychological experience of examining an archive, described as a "grouping of documents, whatever their form or their format, that were compiled organically, automatically, through the activities of a person or institution, public or private, and whose preservation in the archive respects this grouping and refrains from breaking it up."[1] Farge describes the exploration of the archive as a dive, submersion, or drowning, an immersion in an experience both unsettling and oceanic[2]:

> The archival document is a tear in the fabric of time, an unplanned glimpse offered into an unexpected event ... [it] captivates you, producing the sensation of having finally caught hold of the real, instead of looking through a "narrative of," or profound feeling of tearing away a veil, of crossing through the opaqueness of knowledge and, as if after, a long and uncertain voyage, finally gaining access to the essence of beings and things ... in a few crowded lines you can find not only the inaccessible but also the living. Scraps of lives dredged up from the depths wash up on shore before your eyes. Their clarity and credibility are blinding.[3]

The insights gained from an archive can pierce through official documentation into a greater "impression of reality,"[4] one at once more vivid and less subject to control. Against the understanding of Jacques Derrida, who initiated theoretical analysis with his discussion of archives as an expression of state power—echoing Michel Foucault's earlier exploration of "the question of the archive" in the Archaeology of Knowledge[5]—the archive can be seen as a disruption or break in the standard presentation and operation of power. As Ann Laura Stoler suggests in her discussion of colonial archives,

> What was written in prescribed form and in the archive's margins, what was written oblique to official prescriptions and on the ragged edges of protocol

Nineteenth-century roundhouse made out of brush for *I'n-lon-schka*, perhaps at Gray Horse. Hair roaches, eagle feathers and ribbon blankets are visible. Although many attribute flying the flag of the United States upside down to Russell Means and the American Indian Movement as a gesture of defiance and resistance, this photograph demonstrates that resistance to assimilation occurred as early as the nineteenth century. In theory the upside down flag signifies distress; here, it represents resistance to the distress caused by the United States. Photograph by G.W. Parsons, Pawhuska, Oklahoma (from the collection of Gilcrease Museum, Tulsa, Oklahoma).

produced the administrative apparatus as it opened to a space that extended beyond it.... Against the sober formulaics of officialese, these archives register ... movements of persons off balance—of thoughts and feelings in and out of place. In tone and temper they convey the rough interior ridges of governance and disruptions to the deceptive clarity of its mandates.[6]

The archive assembled by my family over the course of two hundred years constitutes neither official documentation nor a site for the exercise of state authority: it constitutes, as Stoler suggests, "a tear in the fabric of time," the feeling of "after a long and uncertain voyage, finally gaining access to the essence of things."[7] The quality of immediacy and sudden immersion into the essence of life emerges in family accounts, which serve as "disruptions to the deceptive clarity" of documented history.[8] Documents preserved from Kentucky, Kansas, Missouri, and Oklahoma offer the names of family members—Juliet, Eliza, Elida, Mattie, Isabelle, Lucinda,

Rose, Amelia, Dora, Aunt Bob, Louella, Nell, Grace, Nelita, Vida, Blanche, Ruby, Ophelia, Cora, Molly, Lelia, Avis, Addie, Jewell, Ruby, Elsie, Everett, Roy, Eugene, King, Jack—who evoke in their stories the sensation of living, rather than lived, experience. Family accounts of riding into what some called "Indian Territory" from Kentucky and Missouri, herding cattle, participating in the Land Rush into Oklahoma, and engaging in domestic patterns of life tied to a sense of place (our ranch was called The Place) are full of wonder. My Great Aunt Lesta Berry recounts her life with Papa, my Great-Grandfather:

> Since there was no running water in the house, it was necessary to make trips across the backyard to the privy. Until Pawnee could supply houses with electricity, we used kerosene lamps. When the wicks were turned down and the flames blown out, our house was in total darkness. Our first electric lights were light bulbs on electric cords dropped from the ceiling ... they filled the room with light. It seemed like magic[.][9]

Similarly, my Great-Grandfather George Madison Berry, who arrived in Indian Territory (the approximate region of present-day Oklahoma) to trade with the Pawnee, describes that existence with a delight and purity that feels just out of reach: "I have roped wild horses on the site of this town. My brothers and myself owned a ranch here before the country was opened for settlement—how I liked to ride a horse in those days and what hunting sport we did have in these hills and canyons!"[10]

Narrative accounts of white settlement occupy a markedly different space than textbook histories and traditional, institutional representations. Settler/occupier histories are often homogenized or discussed solely in the context of cultural erasure, and centuries of violence (although not sufficiently acknowledging the genocide) perpetuated against American Indian peoples; older documentation of the settlement/relocation experience provides a vision, partially romanticized, of Pawnee, Osage, Cherokee, and other occupants of Indian Territory which conclude with "the end of Osage hegemony,"[11] or accounts of white settlement that slight their personal experience and suffering. The Osage Tribal Museum in Pawhuska, Oklahoma, to name one, provides historical timelines, allotment roles, and photographs of nineteenth and twentieth century life that omit mention of interaction with settlers, while museums and displays addressing "local" and state histories invariably marginalize or romanticize American Indian culture.

Such texts and exhibitions neglect rich intersections of cultural perspective, and seem to be missing the breath of life, what cultural anthropologists have described as "embodied" or "sensuous" scholarship.[12] The experiential, narrative emphasis advanced by Michael Jackson and Paul

Stoller[13] suggests the usefulness of an anthropological framework that examines lived experience, nuanced and intersecting relationships, and histories as they take place in specific work contexts and spaces.[14] My family archives—accounts of the Berrys, Mullendores, and related settler families— and interviews with prominent Osage members reveal parallel histories with strikingly different voices and perspectives. Thus, while the Osage Chief Paw-hiu-skah, or Pawhuska, stated of the rush to acquire territory,

> [i]f their great American father wanted a part of their land he must have it, that he was strong and powerful, that they were poor and pitiful, what could they do? He had demanded their land and had thought proper to offer them something in return for it. They had no choice, they must either sign the treaty or be declared enemies of the United States.[15]

My Great Uncle Tom Berry stated of the same process,

> I was living with my parents near Stillwater, when my father and I decided to go to Arkansas City, Kansas, and make the run into the Strip. It was a long hot ride through the tall grass to reach Arkansas City, as we had to go clear around to the north side. We had two very good horses. Mine was called "Ginger." I could have gone much faster, but pa kept holding me back. I will never forget the excitement of that day. My heart was pounding … and I know everyone else's was the same.… I consider this the greatest horse race of all time[.][16]

The transgressed land claims, reservations, and ranches, and the trading posts, cities and dwellings of Oklahoma at the turn of the century, were thus the site of interactions, negotiations, and shared experiences, as well as violence on both sides of a cultural and "racial" divide. This divide is manifested not only in historical accounts, but also in literature, journalistic accounts and spatial and architectural arrangements, including the one-room schoolhouses of settlers, roundhouses positioned on land leased to ranchers, boarding schools, and institutional structures insinuated onto Osage land. The swinging bridge separating Osage reservation property from what is still described in hushed tones as "Colored Town" exemplifies yet a third "racial" division evident in narrative: occasional comments in memoirs are suggestive. "I felt sorry for the colored maid because Grandma kept her busy piecing quilts. As soon as she finished one she'd start another."[17]

This book examines the history of my family's experience as it intersects with American Indian and African American culture through the examination of a personal archive containing correspondence, interviews, journalistic accounts, photographs, illustrations and maps. My family, early settlers, participants in the Land Rush and among the framers of the Oklahoma Constitution, leased Osage land, negotiated mineral rights pivotal to the history of the Osage, and sheltered their own memories of political and cultural interactions, negotiations, and contractual arrangements. My Grandparents purchased The Place, the name given my family to a ranch near Pawhuska, Oklahoma, and dances were held on Osage property owned at the center of the property; a family member married the granddaughter of the Chief of the Osage, and the last surviving roundhouse for the central Osage ceremony, the *I'n-lon-schka*, stands within walking distance of what once was my Grandmother's house, in the Osage town of Hominy, Oklahoma.[18] Women also had distinctive interactions and occasions for the construction of identity, and this book examines moments of mutual recognition, resistance, and appropriation, embodying yet another historical and cultural "divide."

The archive preserved by my family addresses these interactions, occasions, and architectural arrangements in a strikingly fresh manner. "As soon as you begin to read," Farge states of private materials not conceived and constructed for publication, "you are struck by an impression of reality that no printed text, no matter how unfamiliar, can give."[19] Firsthand accounts of a centuries-long relationship between American Indians and a single settler ancestry are not only exceedingly rare, but convey this uncanny "impression of reality," avoiding the "euphemistic academic sterility" which often characterizes a generalized "master narrative."[20] The Western obsession with categorization, objectivity, origin, and order noted by Derrida[21] gives way in such an account to a more open, variegated, and ultimately more comprehensive historical perspective.

The Osage participated in centuries of negotiation, accommodation and warfare, expulsion, emigration, submission to control over their culture, education, religion, and political system, and triumph over adjacent nations, as well as the benefits and consequences of great wealth. Osage architecture, art, body ornamentation, sacred objects, religious ceremonies, and cultural performance—as well as exhibition practices—overlapped in complex and surprising ways with a dominant white culture and the culture of African Americans as well. Jackson argues that "plural societies are often born of tragedy and loss," and I examine the identities and perceptions that emerged as a consequence of great violence and oppression in the Indian Territory, as well as benign interaction and exchange. Material objects, structures, and even body practices reflect this interaction. Early twentieth century photographs of Osage men in ceremonial blankets alongside visitors in Western clothing—with ceremony houses and twentieth century homes visible behind the dancers—and the memories of my family adapting Osage culture in both respectful and essentialized ways illustrate this complex interaction. The adoption by white settlers of textiles, methods of food preparation, and romanticized

Osage elders in otter skin caps with eagle feathers, beaded adornments and neck and arm bands stand in front of an open air brush structure for *I'n-lon-schka* and a Western-style house, nineteenth century (courtesy National Anthropological Archives/Smithsonian Institution).

representations and exhibitions of American Indian culture illustrate the intersubjective nature of the formation of identity.

Scholars of cultural studies have argued that European American identity is inextricable from the identity of those marginalized, oppressed, and subjected to violence due to their characterization as "Other."[22] The Osage people too, I suggest, understood and characterized themselves in juxtaposition to those around them, in part due to the unique nature of their historical interaction with European Americans. I suggest that identity negotiation for American Indian nations and white settlers, including my family, was dichotomous but also reciprocal, and that African American history in the same period can similarly be contrasted and/or aligned in surprisingly complex ways, even in the face of the violence that characterized interaction between majority and marginalized cultures.

Some scholars suggest that landscape and a strong identification with "place" is deeply implicated in identity. A phenomenological, embodied approach to identity brings forward the deep implication of human involvement in "the world out there."[23] Landscape, and the individual's experience within it, may be generated and shaped by those in power, but identification with place can also be seen as a space of resistance, realized in "routine and repetitive social practices," often in gendered contexts.[24] When the Osage author John Joseph Mathews described the Osage land where "the curved blue sky met the undulating emerald on all sides among the rounded hills; the emerald becoming darker and softer, the blue becoming pastel as they merged,"[25] and when the settler Camelia Berry, my ancestor, describes "the most beautiful blazing blue sky, emerald green fields, and crisp breezes," and sleet storms that produced "the unearthly beauty of ice that glitters like crystal and diamonds in the innocent sunshine of early morning,"[26] they express not merely observation of the land, but as well individual experiences shaped by "particular historical, social and political contexts in which they themselves live and work."[27] For the Osage in particular, the landscape had a deeply spiritual meaning and efficacy. For settlers too, identification with the land acquired a powerful cultural and personal force.

In a poetic passage, Jackson states "that human culture, like consciousness itself, rests on a shadowy and dissolving floe of blue ice, and this subliminal, habitual, repressed, unexpressed, and silent mass shapes and reshapes, stabilizes and destabilizes the visible surface forms."[28] Cultural practices and histories, complex and multifarious, underlie much of what we understand as culture today. And this applies to identity as well, as memories and landscapes from the past shape our understanding of ourselves. As Roger Lloyd states of his childhood, "For me too Oklahoma stubbornly remains in some ways a landscape of the imagination, anchored in my personal experience thought it is. The power of some early memories is too strong to be drained by the dullest reality.... And the place itself has, to some degree, made me who I am."[29]

This book argues that identity can be most richly evoked in a narrative and experiential form, extracted from family archives and fieldwork. In an individual, personal, and reflective approach to history, the immediacy of individual voices emerges more clearly than in "objective," conventional scholarship. Bourdieu argues in his notion of habitus that "people experience and understand their place ... [through] routine and repetitive social practices."[30] Yet individuals have the agency to transform, resist, and recreate the structures and spaces around them, and frequently relate these transformations through accounts of their routines and environments.[31] Identities and meanings negotiated on seemingly opposing sides of cultural divisions resonate within and are carried through those who inherit and examine them. That resonance, this text argues, is most forceful in the individual's embodied experience of "Place."

1

Osage Culture and European Arrival: Culture, Trade and Imperialism

The Osage Indian Tribe Centennial Celebration of 1872–1972, published by the Osage Nation, is bound in thick red leather and sold only at the Osage Tribal Museum, the oldest tribally owned museum in the United States.[1] The text, commemorating the hundredth anniversary of the forced removal of the Osage from Kansas to the Osage Reservation in "Indian Territory," beautifully documents the chiefs, physical divisions of the tribe, and institutions and treaties associated with Osage history. Unlike other histories of the Osage people, the book is filled with personal biographies, photographs, commentary from local businesses, photographs of local buildings, and memorials to individuals who have passed away—Hayes Louis Little Bear, Osage Allottee No. 433; Agnes Buffalohide, Osage Allottee 601; Chief Charles Whitehorn, Osage Allottee 841; Rose *Wah-ko-ki-he-kah*, Osage Allottee 745.[2]

The accounts of the Osage Indian Tribe Centennial appear to those unfamiliar with Pawhuska and Osage County to be a curious representation of history—arbitrary reminiscences, renderings of buildings and other sites, with an emphasis on individual photographs. Entering the unique space of the museum, a dominating sandstone structure sitting high on the crest of a hill overlooking the town of Pawhuska below, the enclosed cases contain only family photographs of "Allottees"—individuals granted, under an amendment to the Dawes (General Allotment Act) of 1887, mineral rights to Osage individuals officially enrolled—and maps of these allotments. The museum, in this sense, serves as a personal and closely guarded archive.

Yet what is documented at the Osage Museum is more important than material objects, many of which were sold, stolen, confiscated for museum collections scattered throughout the country and beyond, or destroyed. The Tribal Museum in Pawhuska, in addition to marking a special space for honoring a unique history, contains the central memory of the Osage today—the survival and ancestry of those who comprise the tribe, who won an uncommonly rare victory among all other American Indians in surviving multiple removals, oppression and violence to attain collective allotment and the right to vast mineral wealth.

Scholarly accounts of Osage history—aside from the outstanding scholarship of Roger Hall Lloyd, Louis Burns, and Garrick Bailey, the riveting investigation of Dennis McAuliffe, and the work of John Joseph Mathews—have largely neglected the voices and histories of Osage individuals, and these individuals' interaction with white settlers and African Americans.[3] This academic neglect is particularly pronounced in the time after the outright genocide perpetuated against American Indian peoples,[4] and during the negotiation of oppression, land and resource acquisition. This chapter examines Osage history in the period prior to allotment as a means of framing the narrative and embodied history of the Osage, their art and architecture, interactions and sacred spaces, in the succeeding century.

Osage Scholarship

The Osage nation stands apart in historians' marginalization of its hegemonic power, and in the historical portrayal of Osage as either imprisoned on their reservation—"anonymous island remnants of the old"—or, conversely, as a people who were exceptionally fierce and violent.[5] Dependence upon French, Spanish and American accounts of the Osage—in the absence of written accounts by the Osage themselves—led to a historical and anthropological presentation of the nation as antagonistic and violent. As one French observer related in 1844, "They [the Osage] exercised cruel reprisals against the inhabitants of St. Louis, and many a French scalp has dried in front of the Osage wigwam."[6] McAuliffe describes the beheading of hundreds of Europeans who invaded Osage territory in the eighteenth century, and European reports "tended to be filled such adjectives as 'pernicious,' 'insolent,' 'despicable,' 'deceitful,' and 'perverse.'"[7]

One priest wrote, "It is a treacherous, cruel, audacious, robbing, wandering and very warlike nation."[8] Such accounts fail to acknowledge the experience of American Indians beset by the overwhelming force of European arrival, and the overwhelming context of racial eugenics and genocide.[9]

The absence of written records has recently been addressed by Willard Rollings, Louis Burns and Roger Hall Lloyd, who employ the methods of "archaeologists, cultural anthropologists, linguists, sociologists, biologists, and ecologists,"[10] as well as oral tradition and art ("material culture") to examine history in the absence of Osage voices. With the exception of McAuliffe, Burns, Lloyd, and Mathews, who are Osage, however, and the brilliant efforts of Garrick Bailey, historians have tended to slight the rich experience of the Osage following displacement onto "Indian Territory." Lloyd poetically personalizes and extends his outstanding scholarship beyond nineteenth century settler life, and McAuliffe's account of his own journey—investigating the dark side of Osage mineral rights in the twentieth century—is masterful. Yet their accounts address only one side of a dialectic emerging both from the perspective of white settlers and the Osage, originally the *Ni-u-ko'n-ska* (Children of the Middle Waters [the Missouri River]), misidentified by another American Indian group by their clan name, *Wah-sha-she*, and later Anglicized as Osage.[11]

To some extent, historian Alexandra Harmon argues, the failure of much history to accommodate twenty-first century realities is due to "normative generalizations about [all] Indian propensities."[12] The financial prosperity of the Osage in the mid–twentieth century produced an altered and disjointed historical record that largely neglects contemporary Osage life. The sensational wealth briefly enjoyed by the Osage seems to have, in a sense, put an end to Osage history: one American Indian reader wrote to the *Denver Post*, "many Americans seem to believe Indians must be poor and helpless in order to be Indian."[13] But the powerful persistence of art, performance, architecture, and community suggests that such perceptions are irrelevant to the experience of the Osage experience of their own embodied landscape.

Culture, Trade and Imperialism

Oral traditions of the Osage, and the closely related accounts of the Kansas, Omaha, Ponca, and Quapaw, allude to "a time when they were all one people living to the east on the banks of a great lake. This collective dissipated after a move across the Mississippi: "the last separation was that of the Kansas and the Osage ... the Osage moved south of the Missouri River and up the Osage River."[14] Some scholars identify Osage and related tribes as descendants of "the earlier Mississippian peoples who flourished during the period between A.D. 1000 and 1500 and constructed the great temple mound complexes of the central and southern Mississippi Valley,"[15] although this connection is contested.

In *Osage County: A Tribe and American Culture 1600–1934*, Roger Hall Lloyd describes in rich detail the history and culture of the Osage after their move west.[16] The Osage "took up a pattern of life which combined the settled habits of their eastern origins and the semi-nomadic life of the plains hunter."[17] Lloyd describes "the female genius of fecundity" in the Osage women's responsibility for tending crops, and beautifully evokes the image of their longhouses, "the spectacle" of travois migration, and

> ribbon applique work suggest[ing] a settled (feminine) culture in which trade is an important element ... [as well as] ceremonial objects of wood, skin, fur and feathers, almost evanescent materially, [that] were, like similar symbolic objects of the plains tribes, associated with masculinity, asceticism and war.... This duality in the Osage life pattern may be responsible for the complexity of Osage social organization, for which Osage mythology provided an explanatory account. This tribal story, since they had no written language, had to be lived out, ritually reenacted again and again.[18]

Lloyd suggests that the Osage origin belief involving explorers who descended from the heavens and subterranean peoples "reveals distinctive Osage cultural themes." Significantly, Lloyd indicates, the structure of Osage belief, the "inclination to tolerate alien social customs and to compromise in the interest of the entire tribe will recur in the history of the tribe's dealings with Europeans."[19] That the Osage never went to war with the Europeans or the Americans can be seen as an integral aspect of their spiritual and cultural customs.

One aspect of early engagement with Europeans was trade in furs, deer and buffalo hides, bear oil, buffalo meat, horses and slaves for guns and metal weapons such as knives, tomahawks, axes, and spearheads long before many American Indians had begun to engage in trade.[20] Although white trade led to sparse hunting for many Native peoples, the Osage were located along one of the main tributaries of the lower Missouri, the site of French settlements in the Illinois country, and their careful negotiation and trade with the French led them to become well armed.

> By the late 1700s ... we see the Osage trading furs, deer and buffalo hides, bear oil, buffalo meat, horses and slaves for metal goods, cloth and firearms in such quantities that the French considered it worth building a trading post and fort in the Osage country.... The Osage themselves, in time, profited from the [trading] contacts the French had made ... and in the next century would meet regularly with the Comanche to trade at what became almost a giant horse fair on the barren plains."[21]

After relentless warfare with the Pawnee and Wichita, the Osage "laid claim to a vast, rich hunting territory that stretched from the Missouri River south to the Red River and from the Great Plains eastward almost in Mississippi."[22] The intensity of the engagement with the Pawnee is suggested by the name of one chief—*Paw-Ne-No-Pa-Zhe* (Not Afraid of the Pawnees).

Chief *Shonga-Sa-Pa* (Black Dog), left, and Chief or Governor *Paw-Ne-No-Pa-Zhe* (Not Afraid of the Pawnee, also called Joseph), with bear medicine necklace, pierced ears, ribbon shirt and hatchet, 1874. Possible photographer Alexander Gardner (courtesy National Anthropological Archives/Smithsonian Institution).

The availability of different tools as the consequence of trade—"axes, saws, scissors, needles, and awls—as well as new materials such as cloth, ribbons, glass beads, and yarn that could be used to make or decorate goods"—would have a profound effect on Osage culture.[23] The perishable nature of materials formerly used by the Osage, as well as the lack of written records, has left little evidence of "pre-contact" Osage art. The earliest known Osage art, aside from archaeological findings, dates to the nineteenth century.[24]

Yet the quality of the art remaining is suggestive of what came before. Dazzling nineteenth and twentieth century beribboned blankets, ceremonial headdresses made of soft otter fur, sashes, velvety leather dresses, leggings, embellished cradleboards, bristled red and black hair ornaments, beautifully beaded bracelets and moccasins, and ritual implements—including carved stone pipes, wooden boxes, and other items—have highly specific, sacred meanings, although the objects are sadly now dispersed. Paula Farid, member of the Five Woman Council of the Osage Nation, still constructs headdresses, or roaches, worn in *I'n-lon-schka* dances; beribboned woman's blankets; and moccasins embroidered with patterns that carry significance in the tribe, much like the headdresses, blankets, and moccasins preserved in museums today.[25] When I attended an *I'n-lon-schka* ceremony in 2014, I was enthralled by the parallel between the brilliant costumes worn by female and male dancers, and illustrations of the Osage from the eighteenth and nineteenth centuries. The continuity in dress, drumming, circle dancing, and other aspects of performance reveals the continued existence of longstanding tradition.

Under the terms of the 1763 Treaty of Paris, France—which had enjoyed a relatively peaceful trading relationship with the Osage—ceded to the Spanish the territory of Louisiana, leaving the Osage "militarily the most powerful tribe in the newly created Spanish Louisiana."[26] Otherwise oppressive and even violent in their "civilization" of Native Americans, the Spanish were unable to implement an embargo on Osage trade,[27] and their military campaign against the Osage in 1793 was a failure.[28] As scholar Carl Chapman states,

> The Osage Indians were the most important of the tribes living in the western part of Spanish Illinois [Upper Louisiana] during the Spanish rule. They played several roles in the unfolding of the historical scene in the central Mississippi-Missouri Valley area and the prairies to the southwest. They were suppliers of hides and furs to St. Louis and Arkansas Post; they were barriers to overland travel and trade between the Spanish territory bordering the Mississippi rivers and that of Mexico and New Mexico; they were buffers against the English during the American Revolution. They were indomitable in their position of power.[29]

The inability of Spain to subjugate the Osage—"Hell's Angels on horseback," as McAuliffe describes them[30]—and the cost of the administration and defense of their "colony" led to a transfer of title in 1795 of Louisiana back to France.[31] After the failure of Napoleon's best general, Leclerc, to establish an operational base in Haiti, the reality of taking on the well-armed Osage in the Ozark mountains contributed to Napoleon's decision in 1803 to sell the land east of the Mississippi to the United States. The "inclination to tolerate alien social customs and to compromise"[32] is evident in the Osage's strategic refusal to go to war with the United States—not an option all American Indians possessed, but in the case of the Osage, cannily employed and critical to their survival.

Jefferson's purchase of the Louisiana Territory precipitated an influx of white settlers, along with previously present hunters and traders, on Osage land, as well as a national ideology that "treated cultural separation as a political threat."[33] In 1804 the Indian Agent for Upper Louisiana, Pierre Chouteau, arranged for his own benefit a trip to establish friendly relations with the Osage, and there spoke "approvingly of the power and wealth of the American republic."[34] The delegation, including Chief *Paw-hui-skah* (Pawhuska, or White Hair)[35] travelled to Washington, where Jefferson described them as "the most gigantic men we have ever seen" (Osage men typically stood six feet five, many seven feet tall), and "the finest we have ever" encountered.[36] In his message, Jefferson assured,

> I take them all by hand, that I become their father hereafter, that they shall know our nation only as friends and benefactors. That we have no views upon them but to carry on commerce useful to them and us; to keep them in peace with their neighbors, that their children may multiply, may grow up and live to good old age, and their women no longer fear the tomahawk of any enemy.[37]

Within a few short years it was clear that Jefferson's promise was worthless. The Land Ordinance of 1787

> [w]ith breathtaking arrogance, already envisaged a graph-paper-like overlay covering every unseen mountain and river on the continent. Each six mile square grid, subdivided into 36 sections, represented a "township," a community existing in a purely notional state as a part of the great plan covering land unknown to the surveyor. This was an expression of the mind of the Enlightenment—abstract, scientific, obsessed with measurement and categorization—but also a practical blueprint for settlement.[38]

The European longing for categorization and control during the Enlightenment was inextricable from colonization, including the colonization of American Indians. As I have argued elsewhere,[39] and as other scholars have noted,[40] obsession with order is linked to the division, alienation, and dehumanization of individual subjects, and has been imposed in spatial planning, "racial" categorization, and the destruction of unifying cultural practices, including such basic human practices as language itself. The numbering of Allottees, and the attempt to redistribute land parcels in distinct plots, was but one way to attempt to disintegrate the coherence and existence of the Osage people.

It would not be long before the obsession for colonization and imposed order intruded upon the Osage. In the years following the delegation to Washington, they experienced increasingly violent confrontations with white settlers and hunters. Osage access to guns and ammunition was cut off by the governor of Louisiana, and thousands of well-armed eastern Indians, themselves displaced, outnumbered the Osage on their own property: "in the north the Osage were being attacked by Sac and Fox and Potawatomie[;] in the south their hunting grounds were invaded by Chickasaw, Choctaw, Shawnee, Delaware and Cherokee."[41] The federal government did not include many prominent leaders in the negotiation over this situation, and "refused to allow the tribe's longtime and trusted interpreter, Noel Mongrain, to be present at negotiating sessions which ensued." The Osage ultimately ceded to the federal government 50,000 square miles of land in return for a mere $1,200 in cash, and once again the promise that the Osage could live in the remaining territory forever.[42]

Within the space of nine years white settlers poured onto designated Cherokee land and began to infiltrate Osage territory. "The roads into the Osage hunting grounds were 'literally swarming with emigrants.'"[43] Cherokee hunters, forced out of their land to the east, began to intrude onto Osage territory, often violently. The Osage responded with destructive raids, as described in a rare account by *Gra-to-moh-se* [Iron Hawk] in 1821:

> When he sent the Cherokees on this side of the great River and gave them Land we had sold him[,] he certainly did not give to the Cherokee all the Beaver, Bear, Buffalo and Deer on our Lands.... [W]hen the Cherokees hunt in our Land and kill our Game[,] we will always have trouble[;] they will steal our Horses and our young men will kill them.[44]

Cherokee retaliation against these raids was horrifying.

> In 1817, while the Arkansas Osage[] were on their autumn buffalo hunt, a 600-man eastern Indian war party, comprised mostly of Cherokee[], attacked their village, deserted but for 200 women, children, elderly and infirm. The warriors killed nearly all of the Osage women and elderly and many children—83 in all—and took 103 children captive, to be sold as slaves.... The United States ... declare[d] the Osage a defeated nation, and ... reward[ed] the Cherokee for their great military victory[.][45]

Using the captured children as leverage, the United States government, in the Treaty of 1818, forced the Osage to cede 1.8 million acres of

From left, Shunkamolah, Old Man Shunk (*Wa-sho-sha*) and Brokihekah, with otter skin hats, ribbon blankets and eagle feathers (courtesy Osage Tribal Museum).

land for nothing, and sold the right of passage through the land to the Cherokee for two million dollars.[46] In 1825, under threat of military subjugation, the Osage were forced to cede 96,800,000 acres—a quarter of Kansas (20,000 square miles); a quarter of Oklahoma, formerly known as Indian Territory (18,000 square miles); part of Missouri (6,000 square miles); and part of Arkansas (1,000 square miles)—in return for $7,000 annually for twenty years.[47]

Forced Exodus

In 1830, President Andrew Jackson defied the ruling of the United States Supreme Court in *Worcester v. Georgia* and ordered, in the Indian Removal Act, the forced exodus of almost seventy-five thousand Indians, including the Cherokee, Choctaw, Creek, and Chickasaw, from Alabama, Georgia, and Mississippi.[48] Thousands died along what has become known as the "Trail of Tears" to Oklahoma—including the crossing region operated by a Berry, "Berry's Ferry," Kentucky—conducted to "clear" American Indians from all land east of the Mississippi, "opening it up for the exclusive use and occupancy of Euroamericans and their black slaves."[49] Just four years earlier, President Monroe had stated that forced removal would be "revolting to humanity and utterly unjustifiable."[50] Although Jackson suggested in his first message to Congress that "the condition of the Indians made 'a most powerful appeal to our sympathies,'"[51] in private correspondence Jackon wrote, "I have longed viewed treaties with the Indians an absurdity ... [they are] mere tenants at will, subject, like the buffalo of the prairies, to be hunted from their country whenever it may suit our interests or convenience to take possession of it."[52]

Often overlooked in accounts of the "Trail of Tears" is the "ownership" by American Indians of African American slaves, who were also forced on the march. As Eliza Whitmere, from Estella, Oklahoma, recalled,

> The [black] women and children were driven from their homes, sometimes with blows, and close on the heels of the retreating Indians came greedy whites to pillage the Indians' homes, drive off their cattle, horses, and pigs, and even rifle the graves for any jewelry ... that might have been buried with the dead.... The trip was made in the dead of winter, and many died from exposure to the sleet and snow[.][53]

That enslaved African Americans were forced on the Trail of Tears alongside the Seminole, the Cherokee, Chickasaw, Choctaw, and Muscogee Creek adds to the depth and sweep of horror. The impulse toward "civilizing order" through exclusion and homicide thus must be understood as the overriding context of federal and American Indian relations in the nineteenth century. As my work and the research of McAuliffe and Lloyd document, that process continued well into the twentieth century.[54]

Resettlement had a devastating effect on those who were forcibly subjected to removal, as eastern nations and white settlers occupied the Arkansas Valley, the Ozark Plateau, and the Missouri Valley, including the region of the Osage (Indian Territory.)[55] Faced with a vanishing supply of deer, elk, and other game, the Osage were pressed against and thrust into competition with the arrivals, along with southern tribes, including the Kiowa, Comanche, Cheyenne, and Arapahoe.[56] The governor of Kansas' response to murders and threats against the Osage which resulted from this pressure and confrontation was an assurance to white interlopers: "[s]hoot the half-breed renegade and I will pardon you before the smoke gets away from your gun."[57] Indeed, it was rare that a white jury could be found to convict any man for killing a Native American.[58] In 1865, the Osage signed a treaty selling a thirty mile strip from the eastern end of their Kansas reserve; three years later, an estimated 12,000 to 15,000 squatters—including the author of *Little House on the Prairie*, Laura Ingalls Wilder—continued to swarm onto Osage land.[59]

In response to the violence, dying from typhoid and other diseases, compacted into increasingly small spaces for administrative convenience, and on the verge of starvation, the Osage agreed in 1870 to cede even more land—nearly 4 million acres in Kansas, and three years later another 8 million acres[60]—a total over twelve years of 98.6 million acres.[61] The voices of individual Osage speakers, suppressed in earlier accounts—Chetopah (*Tze To pa* [Four Lodges]), Hard Rope, *No-pa-wah-la* (No pa Walla [Thunder Fear]), Big Elk (*O-pon-Tun-ka*), *Wah-ti-um-ka* (probably *Wa-ti-An-ka* [Dry Plume]), *Kou-e-ce-gla* (unidentified), *Wa-ho-ta-she* (probably Loud Clear Voice), Drum, White Hair, Forked Horn, and *No-Kah-kah-he*[62]—indicated opposition to the treaty five years before which set the groundwork: as the Osage Chief Forked Horn stated, "[t]hey do not wish their chiefs to make any such treaty as they have made, and when you hand out the pen he don't want them to touch it."[63] According to one account, "[a]fter the signing of the paper, the [Osage] women sobbed their mourning songs every morning for days"[64]; Mathews writes that fifty Osage men travelled to the town of Independence, Kansas, "which they called Hay-House-Town on account of its thatched roofs," and, before leaving, changed into their dance regalia and danced,[65] likely a dance of mourning.

Motivated by his inauguration promise to settle "Indian Affairs"— and influenced by the first American Indian to head the Bureau of Indian Affairs, Ely Parker—President Ulysses Grant transferred in 1869 the administration of Indian Affairs from the Army to the Quaker Society of Friends. The Commissioner, Isaac T. Gibson, persuaded Grant to offer the Osage $1.25 per acre of land.[66] The Osage were granted "the opportunity to use their money to purchase a new reservation in Indian Territory," and the remainder of the money was placed in a trust account accruing five percent a year.[67] The most crucial provision in this final treaty—the provision that distinguished Osage removal from that of virtually all other American Indian peoples—was the ability of the Osage to hold their lands, which they themselves had purchased, in common.

The Osage made a pivotal move in obtaining this provision. While the Congressional Act of 1870 required the approval of the tribe, the Osage delayed their summer hunt until the delegation from Washington was frustrated waiting in the heat. "After the tribal leaders had signed the document of consent, [Joseph] *Pa-In-No-Pa-She* presented a list of proposed modifications.... Among these ... was the proposal that the tribe continue

to hold its land in community until the tribe as a whole should request a change. This was granted, at last, by a government delegation impatient to catch their train to the east [emphasis added]."[68] As Burns suggests, "[b]y asking and getting the right to hold their land in common until they requested individual allotment, the Osages gained an important right. Neither the Dawes Act (General Allotment Act [which forced individual American Indians onto allotted land, allowing the majority of the land to be sold to whites],) nor the later Curtis Act could be applied to them."[69] The importance of collectively held land is underscored in the administration's perception of the Act's purpose: "In his first message to Congress in 1901[,] Theodore Roosevelt remarked that the Dawes Act provided a 'mighty pulverizing engine to break up the tribal mass.'"[70] Because the Osage were not removed or assigned to a reservation, but purchased their land, they were able to initially reject the distribution of individual parcels of property that would place Osage property in white hands.

With compensation for their relocation, the Osage purchased 1,470,058,980 acres of Indian Territory in present-day Oklahoma from the Cherokee Nation for $1,099,137.41, with $8.5 million left over, held on their behalf by the U.S. Treasury.[71] The Osage novelist and historian John Joseph Mathews writes in 1932 that the Council view of what land was desirable was contested: *Paw Hue Skah*, descendant of Pawhuska, favored land in western Kansas; *Wah Ti An Kah*, the more charismatic and striking Osage leader, urged the Osage to select the stony, scrub timber-covered land of Oklahoma—a massive region stretching between the Arkansas River and the Kansas state line in the northcentral region of Oklahoma—believing no white settler would wish to farm there, and that it would therefore be to the Nation's collective benefit. As the Commissioner of Indian Affairs stated in 1872, "The reservation [is] poorly adapted for civilizing purposes, there being only one small valley of fertile soil, barely affording enough good farming land[.]"[72] *Wah Ti An Kah*'s view held, and would turn out to be prescient.

After years of oppression and starvation, with the federal government insisting that the Osage attempt to farm the unyielding soil, the nation "discovered that money could be had by renting their land for grazing

Opposite: Osage Council in Washington, D.C., 1895. From left, front row: Charles Prudom, Saucey Chief; second row: Tom Big Chief (*Tsa-mah-hah*), *Mo-sha-to-moi*, *A-she-gah*, *Ola-ha-wal-la* (Big Horse), Jules (Julian Trumbly); third row: Chief Clarence, *Wyo-Hah-Keh*, Joe Boulanger, Will Leahy, Black Dog; back row: Pete Bigheart, White Horn, Jim Bigheart, John Mosier, *Ne-Kah-Wah-She-Tun-Kah*. Photograph by Oscar Drum, Bartlesville, Oklahoma (courtesy Research Division of Oklahoma Historical Society).

Osage reservation with stony outcropping and blackjack trees (courtesy Research Division of Oklahoma Historical Society).

cattle, and in 1879, federal officials yielded to dogged Osage demands for quarterly per capita payments from the tribal trust account. After that, Osage families could count on cash income amounting to several hundred dollars a year," which was divided severally.[73] In a special amendment to the Dawes Act pushed through Congress due to pressure from the Osage, grass leasing and the right to all minerals was ratified.[74] Beginning in 1883, income came from leasing the west side of the reservation's pasture land, whose abundance of blue stem grass and its proximity to Kansas railheads made it attractive to trail drivers.[75]

Guided by James Bigheart, the Osage wrote and adopted a written constitution, and appointments were made to the new government.[76] In 1890, differential consideration of "full" and "mixed blood" alliances by the federal government led to conflict between the parties over allotment, although both ultimately emerged against dividing the land.[77] After negotiation and many trips by representatives of the Osage to Washington, frustrated that the "mixed blood" contingent whom he had supported failed to support allotment, the Secretary of the Interior abolished the

Osage government in 1900,[78] effectively removing from the Osage any right to control leasing on their own land.[79]

When the Osage finally were forced to subdivide their reservation among individual members after the Osage Allotment Act of 1906,[80] subsurface revenues from the Osage reservation remained common property. All members shared in the sale or lease of vast quantities of land, oil and minerals, divided among 2,229 "Allotees" (or original tribe members) into "headrights" (the right to profits). Many of the roughly 660 acre allotments—retained, and not reduced to 160 acres, thanks to the resistance of the Osage government—were leased or sold to white homesteaders. Oil rights to the entire nation were sold by Chief Bigheart for a nominal sum in 1896, producing millions for the white developer who founded the "Indian Territory Illuminating Oil Company."[81] But the corporate monopoly ended in 1916 after the federal government stipulated that one-sixth of the oil extracted from Osage property would be reserved to the Osage exclusively.[82] Between 1916 and 1932, grass and oil leases—sold at auction under a large elm tree by auctioneer Colonel E. Walters from Skeedee, Oklahoma—earned enormous sums for the Osage.[83] On eighteen occasions 160-acre tracts were auctioned for more than a million dollars; one auction drew $10,888,000 in a single day.[84]

The location of the "Million Dollar Elm," now gone, is marked by a plinth of sandstone with a plaque near the Osage Tribal Museum in Pawhuska, and commemorates the space where oil auctions were once held.[85] The tree's acknowledgement in the *Osage Indian Tribe Centennial Celebration of 1872–1972* reinforces the significance of the site, juxtaposed with former administrative, supervisory and boarding schools on the highest hill in Pawhuska. Buildings erected by the federal government to oversee administration of the reservation once institutionalized the effort on the part of the federal government to exercise surveillance, control, and erasure of Osage autonomy. Today, at the summit of this site, and in the pages of the Centennial, individuals like *O-Pon-She-Ni*, Allottee No. 276, Edith Ware (*Hum-Pah-To-Kah*), Osage Allottee 714, and Eves Tallchief, Osage Allottee 346, signify the Osage nation's greatest political achievement: survival.[86]

2

Embodied Anthropology: Settlers, Osage and African Americans

The archive of Osage photographs displayed in the Osage Tribal Museum and in the pages of the Centennial suggest that the government's effort to impose homogeneity was a failure. The images of individual Allottees, black and white, sepia toned, and color, reveal a captivating and even startling diversity. From the photographs gaze men in crisp collared shirts and dress pants standing next to fine cars (Joe Osage, Allottee number 37); women in small groupings draped with beautiful beribboned blankets marked with the symbol of the outstretched hand (May Rusk Red Eagle Freemont [*Me-tsa-he*], Allottee 10, and family); one man poses in a photographer's studio with leggings, embellished shirt, and an eagle feather and roach in his hair (John Wood, Allottee 337); several women pose in beautiful white flounced dresses, and Samuel Barker, Allottee 800, and Simon Henderson, Allottee 757, appear as if dressed for a ball. A man with a bow tie reads the paper in a rocking chair (George Baconrind [*In-gro-tah*], Allottee 746); another in a beaver skin cap (*Mo-sah-mum-pah*, Allottee 750) poses with his family, all in blankets; Elsie Big Eagle Rusk (*Wa-shah-hah-me*), Allottee number 793, and Bessie Rusk West (*Hla-me-tsa-he*), Allottee 2128, appear in flapper hair and elaborate fur collars. The sole characteristic they appear to share is their categorization by number.

The diversity in these photographs might suggest a tension between individual and group alliance, between total or partial cultural appropriation and/or the preservation of collective identity, or between minority cultures and those who seek to categorize and thereby dominate them. The anthropologist Michael Jackson, however, suggests that these tensions are characteristic of the formation of identity through a "social dialectic"[1]; the formation of a community between oppressor and oppressed, he suggests, can be seen as a "discussion of the relationship between the one and the many,"[2] regardless of political and cultural antagonism.

> In bringing home to us that plural societies are often born of tragedy and loss, with people driven from the place inhabited by their own kind and obliged to work out a modus vivendi with strangers, we are reminded that tribal worlds are no more insular than ours ... [and] that self has no reality except in relation to others.[3]

What Jackson offers is a means of understanding the necessary interactions and relationships between oppressor and oppressed, between those marginalized and those in the majority—white settlers and American Indians, including the Osage—as intersubjective, or "mutually arising."[4] This perspective does not deny the violence and suffering, and the efforts toward ordering, categorizing, and "civilizing," imposed upon the American Indian people, enslaved African Americans, and other marginalized groups, or the difficult labor and violence experienced by settlers. Jackson perceives intersubjectivity as a mode not of "shared experience, empathic understanding or fellow-feeling," but rather as a means of perceiving the human experience that embraces 'constructive and destructive extremes without prejudice."[5] By this view, "violence is a distinctively human modality" of interaction, as is compassion and the giving of life. Thus, American Indian, African American, and settler alike had a sense of self that arose from and was shaped by "embodied social interaction[.]"[6]

The Identity of Opposites

As in Jackson's anthropological method, reciprocity of identity in this text is acknowledged and located in "practical contexts of everyday life."[7] For white settlers and Osage, American Indians and African Americans, and men and women in each culture, it was in daily life and work and social interactions that identity and a sense of place was formed. The juxtaposition of Osage and European American cultures, settler and African American cultures, even the cultures of men and women, shaped complex perceptions of identity and place.

The nomenclature used in defining the dialectic of settler and Osage/African American culture is important. In stating that the American Indian/African American will be discussed alongside the culture of the settler, I address a relationship of dominant and non-dominant culture, majority and minority—that is, white and not white. Richard Dyer indicates,

> white people have had so very much more control over the definition of themselves and indeed of others than have those others ... the position of speaking as a white person is one that white people now almost never acknowledge and this is part of the condition and power of whiteness: white people claim and achieve authority for what they say by not admitting, indeed not realizing, that for much of the time they speak only for whiteness.[8]

Although my family is white, I do not wish in writing this text "to collapse whiteness into my own subjectivity."[9] Historians often fall into one of two diametrically opposed paradigms: ignoring the suffering of the American Indian and focusing on white history, or focusing upon the genocide of American Indians and the violence against African Americans, while denying the subjectivity of the individual white settler. I do not wish to fall into either paradigm, or consistently refer to my family or myself as white, as if this "racial" designation necessarily confines us within a position that denies the majority's historical position of power. The sweeping designation of my family within all institutional structures and individual decisions associated with white privilege obliterates their individuality in the archive, their choices and agency.

In wishing to avoid the term "white," do I escape into a longing to claim the "unmarked" category? As Dyer suggests, "[a]s long as race is something only applied to non-white peoples, as long as white people are not racially seen and named, they/we function as a human norm. Other people are raced, we are just people."[10] Yet are each of us not allowed to claim for ourselves our names, our authentic subjectivities? For the purposes of this text, I employ the terms "settler," "rancher," "homesteader," and the like, to separate my family's individuality from a hegemonic category which I here capitalize with the word "white." The overwhelming power and unstated privilege of what Dyer terms "whiteness," however, must never be forgotten.

The formative nature of juxtapositions between cultures is evident in accounts of both white occupiers and American Indians. Describing the 1868 Battle of the Washita, General George Custer relates his perception of the Osage man he encountered as a "tall, fine-looking warrior [holding] ... an entire scalp, fresh and bleeding.... [Custer] saw the Osage on the field, his face ... completely hidden under the stripes of yellow, black, and vermilion, the colors being so arranged, apparently as to give him the most hideous visage imaginable."[11] This perception of the Osage warrior—related in Custer's *My Life on the Plains*[12]—fails to account for the factors that drove Osage retribution (murder and violence against them, kidnapping of Osage children, the invasion and occupation of their property). Yet it would seem critical to Custer's sense of self, to what I would interpret as hypermasculinity, his "ontological security,"[13] that he understand the Osage in this fashion.

The American Indian poet Sherman Alexie describes in "Custer Speaks" Custer's role in this battle, the Battle of the Washita, and the poet speaks as Custer. The strange identification of Custer with Crazy Horse suggests what Jackson describes as a social dialectic. Alexie's depiction of Custer whispering Crazy Horse's name in his sleep, his construction of Custer as a man who perceives Crazy Horse as "his dear brother" who "created the universe"—all of these statements illustrate beautifully a dialectic in which identity is formulated through identification with individuals upon whom is inflicted tremendous violence. Despite the profound gulf between individuals and cultures, Jackson argues, "there is always some aspect of oneself, however well hidden, that corresponds, albeit obliquely, to the beliefs and behaviors one sees in others."[14] In Jackson's terms, the "self stands out momentarily against a background of otherness, only to become ground in turn for the figure of the other.... We have as many selves as there are others who accord us recognition and carry our image in their mind."[15] The social dialectic Jackson describes is not contingent on the absence of damage, conflict, or violence, which he maintains "must be accommodated in anthropological analysis as a distinctively human modality of intersubjectivity[.]"[16]

Evidence of the critical role of embodied experience and intersubjectivity, in all its "constructive and destructive extremes,"[17] emerges in my family's archival accounts about life in "Indian Territory." My Great-Aunt Ada Berry maintained that "[l]ong before the present prosperity of Stillwater was even dimly outlined in the minds of men, the name of William E. Berry [my Great-Great-Grandfather] was linked with the primitive conditions enjoyed by few but the roaming red man."[18] The sophistication and prominence of Berry is seen as enhanced by association with the "primitive insight" of the Indian. As Lloyd states, "[i]f the Indian imagination presents some sort of dark alternative vision to that of the white, by knowing the Indian[,] the white man [believes that he] might attain completeness in a psychological as well as historical sense."[19] For African Americans as well, the selfhood of the enslaver could not exist without those who were enslaved.

African Americans

The history of intersubjectivity in America is illustrated by the complexities and tensions in Thomas Jefferson's vision of "race" in America.

While he stated that Native Americans "astonish ... with strokes of the most sublime oratory; such as prove their reason and sentiment strong, their imagination glowing and elevated,"[20] he did not resist their forcible removal; Jefferson denounced "slavery on almost every ground, from moral issues to practical economics," and yet was capable of the grotesque statement that blacks have "a strong and disagreeable odor ... their existence appears to participate more of sensation than reflection," and that, compared to whites, "in reason [they are] much inferior."[21]

The perception by Oklahoma settlers of what was appropriate and submissive behavior from those formerly enslaved ("the good negro"), and the constructed fear of African Americans as criminals and renegades, demonstrates the same confusion of appreciation and destruction, identification and caricature, expressed by Jefferson. At the same time my Great-Aunt Camelia Berry, wife of Jack Berry, recalled stories of her grandmother (Nancy Jane Berry) such as these:

> She especially liked to frighten the slaves. One evening some slaves had gone to the spring to get buckets of water for the morning. It was just dusk so Grandmother slipped out of the kitchen door and ran down the path to hide behind some bushes. As the slaves came up the hill she jumped out with her dress and white petticoats turned over her head and ran at them. They were sure they had seen a ghost. The slaves spilled their buckets of water and ran to the house calling out, "Master Tom, Master Tom, we've seen a ghost." In the meantime, Grandmother had slipped in the back door and sat in the corner of the kitchen. Her father turned to her and said, "Nancy Jane, I have a notion to whip you." But he didn't.[22]

Camelia Berry also relates of Nancy Jane, "As a girl in her teens she had a personal slave girl, named Hannah, with whom she played. She and Hannah one time caught and butchered a pig by themselves."[23] This narrative of interaction is one of control and paternalism, but also mutual definition. Each is necessary to the other in this context: "as Hegel observed, no matter how great the social inequality between self and other, each is existentially dependent on and beholden to the other; the master's subjugation and negation of the slave is countermanded by their mutual need for each other's recognition."[24]

The "ownership" of slaves by my family provides a reminder that personal histories can be unforgiving. In the illustration rendered by my ancestor, Camelia Berry, of "The Berrys on Meadow Creek, Kentucky, 1857," African Americans are foregrounded—sewing quilts, carding wool, children playing happily. In the background of the illustration my ancestor Juliet Sophia Berry sits at a loom, and her husband and son arrive from a hunt. Such depictions—of enslaved individuals and their white "masters"

2. Embodied Anthropology   31

"The Berrys on Meadow Creek, Kentucky, 1857," by Camelia Uzzell Berry, in her *Oklahoma Prairie Plowed Under: The Story of Berry Bros. in Indian Territory* (courtesy Catherine Berry Hess).

at home together, rendered by a descendant of the slaveholder—are exceedingly rare, and therefore revealing. Archival accounts state that Nancy Jane Berry's husband "enjoyed being among and joking with the colored hired hands that worked for him and would dance with them,"[25] and that William Thomas Berry, "[w]hen with his colored hired hands who lived on his farms or who worked for him, was jolly and laughed and teased them, but they seemed delighted"[26]; another account of Mary Susan Berry states that "the only time they [the children] could play with the Negro children was when a baby was being born in the slave quarters."[27] My family may have treated enslaved blacks with particular kindness; however, the knowledge that enslavement is an aspect of my history is shocking. Nonetheless, as Ward Churchill argues, "the painful process of true self-recognition, coming to grips with realities rather than the myths of [Euroamerican] heritage," is the only "hope of a reforging of human relations."[28]

The complex choreography of intersubjectivity and interaction is evident in journalistic accounts of white settlers using one set of individuals categorized by "race" to control another. "Before 1889, when the agitation by the settlers (Boomers) and rail roads became serious, the Indians became dangerous and sided with the cattle men. Railroads and settlers meant towns and fences, whereas cattlemen left the land open, all able to move about with their herds. The Indians, Arapahoes, and Cheyennes became so unruly the army came in to keep peace. One book says they used black troops!"[29] The explanation point in this report signifies the reporter's astonishment at such a "racial" alliance.

An even more complex narrative of alliances is revealed in accounts of American Indians who "owned" enslaved individuals, a not uncommon practice. Robert Love, a Chickasaw, operated two plantations prior to the Civil War, and "owned" two hundred slaves; Robert M. Jones, a Choctaw, owned five plantations and enslaved over five hundred African Americans.[30] The slave codes under which these individuals labored were as restrictive as those imposed by whites, and blacks were forcibly segregated from American Indians, even to the extent of living in separate towns.[31] After the Civil War, freedmen were subjected to horrific violence by the Chickasaw, and to some degree, the Choctaw, although not by such tribes as the Seminole and Osage: as historian Nathaniel Washington states, "it was no disgrace to kill a Negro.... [Ex-slaves] were shot down [by the Chickasaw] like dogs by the dozens."[32]

WPA interviews of individuals once enslaved by American Indians reveal decidedly conflicted views on those who "owned" them. Eliza Whitmire, a former slave from Estella, Oklahoma, maintained,

> our Indian masters were very kind to us.... The slaves who belonged to the Cherokees fared much better than the slaves who belonged to the white race, for the reason that the Indian slaves who had left the states could come right back to the Territory, and settle on Indian land, and when allotment came, they gave us an equal right with them to land drawings. The United States government forced them to do this, I have been told.[33]

Similarly, Mary Grayson, from Tulsa, Oklahoma, insisted, "We slaves didn't have a hard time at all before the War. I have had people who were slaves of white folks back in the old states tell me that they had to work awfully hard and their masters were cruel to them sometimes, but all the Negroes I knew who belonged to Creeks always had plenty of clothes, and lots to eat, and we all lived in good log cabins we made."[34]

Not all former slaves shared this perspective. Chaney McNair, from Vinita, maintained,

> Most of the Cherokees was good to their slaves, but old Joe Martin wasn't.... You ask me, did I feel bad when my father was sold? I don't know if I did or not. I had to make the most of it. Most slaves did. They come and take you

sometime, maybe husband, maybe children.... I got free while I's in Kansas. We all knowed it was comin'. The colored folks never worried after they got up North. Which do I like best, the Northerner or the Southerner people? ... I like it the way I is, free.³⁵

Some African Americans enslaved by American Indians in Oklahoma turned their criticism to those designated "full blood": "When the Indians emigrated they brought their Negroes, just as they had their property or stock.... The only Negroes who had to work hard were the ones who belonged to the half-breeds. As the Indian didn't do much work, he didn't expect his slaves to do much work."³⁶

The tension between what were derogatorily termed "full blood" and "breeds" or "half breeds" was largely generated by the federal government. The General Allotment Act of 1887—what Annette Jaimes described as a "eugenics mechanism"³⁷—broke traditional systems of collective land tenure by dividing and treating differently individual nations according to "blood quantum," resulting in the appropriation by the government of approximately two thirds (one hundred million acres) of all American Indian-reserved land.³⁸ Additionally, "the government's policies of leasing individual reservation land parcels to non–Indians, increasingly 'checkerboarding' tribal holdings since 1900 ... has virtually ensured that a sufficient number of non–Indians would be residents in reservations, and that intermarriage would steadily result."³⁹ These policies, combined with the effect of the federal relocation program of the fifties, accelerated a process of "biological hybridization," fostering divisiveness as American Indian nations seek to "enforce the race codes excluding the genetically marginalized from both identification as Indian citizens and consequent [federal] entitlements."⁴⁰

The internal divisiveness created by the federal government is evident among the Osage as early as the nineteenth century, when the first National Council of the Osage was formed of two political parties: the Full-Bloods and the Mixed-Bloods.⁴¹ White "husbands, referred to as 'intermarried citizens,' composed, along with the mixed-bloods, a separate designation, 'the Half Breed Band,' in 1870 when the tribe was negotiating its removal from Kansas."⁴² The Osage Agent in the late 1890s, William J. Pollock, described the "mixed bloods" as "civilized and as competent to care for themselves as any community of white people ... while the large majority of the full-bloods still cling as near as possible to their ancient customs and traditions."⁴³

The determination of federal agents to regard "mixed" and "full bloods" differently profoundly influenced the internal dynamics and cohesiveness of the tribe in the 1920s, given the extent of intermarriage. As the scholar Francis LaFlesche stated in 1921, "the 1910 census showed that out of the 2,100 persons enrolled as Osages only 885 were full-blooded, and it was believed that many of those counted as full-blooded were in fact mixed-race. The 1910 census gave the entire population of the Osage Tribe as 1,373," with nearly half "full-blooded."[44] In 1926, the "full-bloods" and restricted members of the Osage tribe, concerned about the distribution of allotments and other issues, submitted a petition to the Commissioner of Indian Affairs, Charles Burke, protesting against "mixed breeds" holding office or voting in tribal affairs.[45] Divisiveness was only strengthened by the American eugenics movement of the 1910s–1920s, centered at the Eugenics Record Office at Long Island, whose directors—the Harvard-educated biologist Charles Davenport and his colleague Harry H. Laughlin—were awarded an honorary degree by Nazi biologists in the "science of racial cleansing."[46]

Differential treatment based upon "race" also became a source of dissension within the African American community. Despite their enslavement, many blacks in Oklahoma emphasized their tribal affiliation, perceived by some as "symbolic escape from the harsh rigidity of American caste boundaries"; yet American Indians were accepted "into white society only if they were willing to give up their unique customs and traditions and adopt Anglo-American traditions as their own"—in reality, they would only be accepted when they ceased to be Indians. Tension also existed between "freedmen, who had land allotments, tribal citizenship, and, in some cases, tribal wealth and leadership positions, and the influx of new immigrants often referred to as "State Negroes"[47]; the true concern of black freedmen was a loss of status and income to new arrivals, but the issue was manifested in their assessment of newly arrived black citizens as poor, more subservient, "lazy," and backward in outlook.[48]

Yet another tension in the complex relationships of "races" in Oklahoma is revealed in the court battles in which American Indians and African Americans have attempted to prove "who is an Indian ... [and] who decides."[49] The Oklahoma Seminole stripped African Americans who were on the Trail of Tears of tribal membership in 2000, although this was subsequently reversed by the federal Interior Department. At stake was the division of $56 million in federal funds. The Seminole maintained that their ancestors were slaveholders, not intermingled with "escaped slaves [who] lived free as farmers, warriors and political leaders among the Indians."[50] The attempt to prove one's ancestors are slaveholders—and the terrible division among the Seminole "who were themselves exiles and runaways from other tribes"[51]—illustrate the ugly consequence of continued federal oversight and its historical legacy of division by "race"—and who once "was the property" of whom. Such divisiveness extended to the Osage themselves: the petition of "full-bloods" in 1926 to protest against "mixed-bloods" holding office or voting in tribal affairs is illustrative, and there was early resistance to intermarriage, although virtually all Osage today also have white or African American heritage.[52]

Ironically, emigrants from Oklahoma, like my Grandparents Otto and Julia Hess, also faced oppression during the Dust Bowl of the 1930s. Historians "have long puzzled over the amount of animosity that native white Californians leveled at the more than 350,000 migrants who entered the state during the 1930s ... they were threatened, ridiculed, exploited, shunned, and encouraged to return to their native states ... poor whites ... had transformed from model frontiersmen into unwanted others."[53] As Peter La Chapelle argues in *Proud to Be an Okie*,

> native Californians [concerned about job loss] were also inundated with stereotypical images and reminders that members of the migration from the southern plains were "white trash" and Tobacco Road–like misfits—economic and hereditary inferiors who engaged in uncontrolled reproduction, lacked a proper work ethic, and destabilized functional structures of political and social control ... for a time they confronted obstacles typically faced by racial and cultural minorities, including police harassment, vigilante attacks, discrimination in public relief, and legal and extralegal restriction on movement across borders.[54]

Thus not only were American Indians, including "half-breeds," slaves, and black freedmen subject to race-based discrimination; whites themselves who migrated to California were subjected to such discrimination, described in journalistic accounts as "white trash," "pauper labor," "misfits," "marginal people," and "irresponsible wandering hordes," and subjected to quasi-facist vigilante acts, discriminatory legislation, and police brutality.[55]

For Osage, slave, freedmen, and poor white migrants in the nineteenth and twentieth centuries, "racial" identity was shaped by the perceptions and actions of oppressor and those who were oppressed. The American Indian commentator who stated, "Most American history has been written as if history were a function of white culture in spite of the fact that well into the nineteenth century the Indians were one of the principal determinants of historical events,"[56] and the contradictions in Camelia Berry's statement that "explorers that returned [from trips beyond the Appalachian mountains] brought with them tales of deserts, towering mountains, endless prairies, belly-deep grass, magnificent rivers, millions of buffalo, and the ever prevalent "red man." ... Until this time the central section of our country was virtually undiscovered, uncharted and unused,"[57] illustrate the complexity in a dominant culture of reconciling a subconscious need to identify and align oneself with those "encountered," at the same moment the dominant culture is engaged in violence, oppression, and the assumption of privilege.

The Importance of Narrative

In this book's account of the history of the Osage and my ancestors, reciprocity of identity, or a sense of an embodied, social self structured by intersubjective interaction, is located in "practical contexts of everyday life," which often take the form of stories.[58] To the extent that a storyteller "re-creates his vision in words," according to the Kiowa (Oklahoma) author N. Scott Momaday, "he re-creates himself.... He declares in effect, 'Behold, I give you my vision in these terms, and in the process I give you myself.'"[59] The narrator of the tale relates factual information, but as well the essence of the narrator her- or himself. Hence the stories related in this text are not merely anecdotes, but the embodiment of self, relationship, and everyday life aligned.

Much of what the stories and recollections in this text relate involves the daily actions of work—the details of ranching, caring for the land, and female domestic labor. Why do so many of the letters and memories preserved in my family archive focus on work? In Jackson's view, "[w]ork produces and reproduces both selves and societies ... [human labor] is the means whereby human beings create and recreate the intersubjective experience that defines their primary sense of who they are." Settler, Osage, and "slave," women and men, understand each other within a preexisting social ground structured by labor, into which individuals are "always already" thrown, and which is grounded in day-to-day practice.[60] The ground of the social is re-created and transformed in the context of human labor, in everyday practice and action.[61] Against a backdrop of misinformation and conflict, the everyday interactions of settler, Osage, and African American were re-framed and occasionally stabilized in trade, leases, domestic arrangements, land contracts, and political decision making arrangements, as well as daily labor and social exchange, recounted and embodied in the correspondence and written histories preserved by my family.

This book emphasizes what Paul Stoller terms "embodied experience," an approach to the intersecting histories and experiences of Osage and settler that grants special importance to personal experiences and accounts of ordinary life, and to the appearance and experience of the land. Stoller suggests that it is "especially important to incorporate into ethnographic works the sensuous body—its smells, tastes, textures, and sensations.... In many societies these ... senses, all of which cry out for sensuous description, are central to the metaphoric organization of experience; they also trigger cultural memories."[62] It is not enough to present the information extracted from documents, although that too is important; it is equally critical to describe the materiality of memories. When the reminiscences of my great-cousin, Jack Berry, state,

> Billy McGinty, famous bronc buster and Rough Rider, showed me his hands one day back in the '40s. He held them out, pointing out that his fingers were permanently twisted at a 45 degree angle from hanging on to ropes. He said they were taught to sink their fingers into the rope when holding a horse or cow. Billy taught Jack how to make a rope hackamore with a huge fancy knot. [A crude illustration demonstrates underneath: "Normal hand." "Billy's hands."][63]

The reader is pulled into a world of labor, cattle, the smell and the feel of leather, the horses and ropes, the feel of the rider's hands; one is transported to the experience of the rider, and amused at the story as if present for the telling. Similarly, when my Great-Great-Grandfather W.E. Berry relates of his brother-in-law, "He never married. One time he spent a week setting a second place at his table. He dipped up two servings, poured two glasses of milk or two cups of coffee, to see if he wanted to get married. After a week he decided it wasn't worth it,"[64] it is almost as though we can see the table, the reflective man, the glasses of milk and cups of coffee. The story brings the past back to us with a pleasurable immediacy. Stories evoke appetites, generational relationships, the sound of the human voice:

> Grandpa [Hess, from Germany], bless his soul, was a good man; but the poor old guy ate slowly and by the time he was ready for his piece of pie, there would only be one piece left. Grandma couldn't cut all the pieces the same, so naturally we young 'uns, having eaten faster than grandpa, had our choice. When he was ready he made the remark, "That's the way you do, effrybody takes the biggest piece!"[65]

"We are embodied social beings before we are anything else,"[66] Jackson states. It is in that embodiment—experiencing it, where possible, for oneself—that we can construct deeper historical understandings, and narratives of our lives that are richly resonant, oriented to materiality and place, and healing in their connection of self with others. Jackson states that such accounts "bear witness to our search for some kind of provisional faith or wisdom that will make life bearable, rather than to our need for transcendence ... stories help us reconcile ourselves to the way things are." For individual and researcher, immersion into experience, and the connectedness with one's family, brings about an "ontological security."[67] "Human beings need to belong to and engage effectively in a world of others.... When this balance is irrevocably lost, and both self and other are reduced to the status of mutually alien objects, we may then speak of pathologies of loss."[68] When the Osage in Pawhuska buried their loved ones and inserted into their tombstones beloved photographs, encased in glass—as my Mother recalls, and as photographs in the Osage archives testify—it is a reminder that humans can belong to a community of others, without numbers or categories, even in death.[69]

> One can only be one's own person to the extent that one belongs to a wider context than the self—family, clan, circle of friends, workplace, or imagined community ... unless one actually retraces one's ancestors' journeys through the country to which one belongs, and unless one is able to sing the story that recounts this journey in its archetypical form, one's life is, in effect, cut off from the deeper matrix of being that sustains it.[70]

The process of "retrac[ing] one's ancestors' journeys" is both a literal and psychological one, and here the mechanism I am employ for undertaking a psychological journey is an examination of the stories, memories, records and photographs contained in the archive.

3

The Settler, the Trader and the Cowboy

Arlette Farge states in *The Allure of the Archives* that "[a]n archive presupposes an archivist, a hand that collects and classifies." The relationship between conventional forms of documentation and historical claims to objectivity has been challenged by "the claims of groups who have typically been disenfranchised by dominant regimes of truth"[1]; a number of theorists have recently "engage[d] with the limits and possibilities of the archive as a site of knowledge production, an arbiter of truth, and a mechanism for shaping the narratives of history."[2] The knowledge that archives contain is frequently discussed in scholarly literature as a mechanism of colonial power and control. Yet as Antoinette Burton maintains, "all archives come into being in and as history as a result of specific political, cultural, and socioeconomic pressures—pressures which leave traces and which render archives themselves artifacts of history."[3]

The personal archive retains both these specific ideological traces, but as well the quality of the unexpected, the disorderly and picturesque. Unlike the printed and published document, which is "intentionally produced for public viewing and meant to be understood by a wide audience … [they] seek to make an announcement and create a certain belief, to modify the state of things by advancing a particular narrative or commentary."[4] The personal archive constitutes an accumulation of achievements and anecdotes, sometimes assembled haphazardly, with gaps and conscious inflections.

What is unique in my family archive is not this element of self-consciousness, but rather its extensiveness and breadth, an extraordinary preservation of a single family history over centuries. The appearance within this archive, always at the margin, of cultures—the Osage, the Pawnee, the African American—challenging, or coinciding with, a dominant narrative, also sets this archive apart. The following chapters explore the ways submerged cultural interactions emerge in the archival letters, photographs, and documents preserved by my family, and as well art, architecture and sense of space or "place."

The Beginning of the Journey

The earliest archival records of the Berry ancestors mark their encounters with American Indians on the East Coast. Accounts prior to the Revolutionary War emphasize not the genocide inflicted by the white "race," but instead the brutality of the Iroquois: "[t]he people living along the headwaters of the James and Roanoke Rivers in this period endured multiple hardships. Attacks by wolves, mountain lions, Indians, smallpox, hunger, floods and storms were the lot of the frontier settlements."[5] Camelia Berry noted that "[t]he Iroquois were terrifying enemies, so terrifying that the governments of the North East Colonies passed laws decreeing their extermination."[6] Descriptions of the family's engagement—under the direction of George Washington—in the French and Indian War are particularly gruesome:

> Massed in neat rows, redcoated soldiers were cut down like rows of corn. The dead accumulated in writhing piles as each terrified soldier fired wildly into the woods and tried to take cover behind his companions ... over 800 dead and wounded were abandoned to the Indian scalping knives. John Sharp and Edward King [my ancestors] escaped, but John's brothers were among those poor souls left behind to the Indians. A young Dutch prisoner at Fort Dusquene described seeing the prisoners marched through to the Indian camps ... and his unsuccessful night long efforts to shut his ears to their anguished screams as they were tortured and then roasted alive.[7]

Although my ancestors forcibly and at times violently occupied land belonging to the Cherokee, armed conflict with the Cherokee is depicted as courageous:

> On one occasion the Cherokees raided an outlying plantation, killing the parents and kidnapping the three surviving children. John Duncan and the militia began an immediate pursuit of the raiders, tracked them through the wilderness, rescued the children and killed the culprits. On another occasion when he and his men fought a battle with the Indians, one Indian managed to escape and crawl into a deep cave.... Duncan took a single shot pistol in one hand, and a torch in the other and crawled sixty yards through the darkness to find and kill his wounded enemy.[8]

3. The Settler, the Trader and the Cowboy 41

During the years of the Revolutionary War, my ancestors Sarah and Francis Berry travelled west through the Cumberland Gap to Blue Grass country, where they were "exceptional marksmen and hunted for meat and sport."[9] When the British attacked in 1780 with a combined force of British, Canadian and Shawnee troops, the Berrys took refuge in fortified stations. Like John Sharp and Edward King, Francis was a Cavalry officer under George Washington[10]; during the Revolution, the Berrys survived an attack by the Shawnee in which they were forced to surrender, but according to (unverifiable) family accounts, "once the gates of the fort were opened, the savages rushed in hacking unarmed men to death, scalping the wounded, and even throwing ... [one woman's] baby into the fires ... [of the prisoners of war,] [s]mall children were tomahawked to death. Men were hideously tortured. Stragglers were immediately murdered."[11] Only fifty-nine of three thousand survived and were marched to Canada as prisoners of war.[12]

When the Revolutionary War was over, the Berrys walked home to Tennessee and Kentucky, where a family "estate" was founded. Sarah

"Farm on Meadow Creek, Kentucky, 1857," by Camelia Uzzell Berry, in her *Oklahoma Prairie Plowed Under: The Story of Berry Bros. in Indian Territory* (courtesy Catherine Berry Hess).

regained her son, who had been kept in Tennessee by her brother to "protect him from Indians."[13] Nancy Jane Berry describes life on the 2,000 acre tobacco estate in the nineteenth century as both pleasurable and labor-intensive:

> Sometimes Grandfather Berry would use flint to start a fire. All the sewing was done by hand with a candle for light or by the light of the fireplace. The sheep had to be sheared, the wool cleaned, carded, spun into thread, woven into cloth and then sewn. Materials were dyed with bark from different trees, walnut for brown sumac for red, and so on. Most of their food was grown or raised on the farm. Sugar was made from the sap and cooking it down to sugar.... Candles were made from tallow ... all their shoes [were made] from cow hides by hand ... the oldest boy didn't want [the children] to ride so he would hide the bridles. But that didn't stop them ... they would peel the bark from a slippery elm tree and make their own bridles. Grandmother always liked to ride horses and always rode on a sidesaddle.[14]

Despite this agreeable account, family records indicate that much of the labor was done by African American individuals who were enslaved, although some wills set enslaved individuals free. Of those taken prisoner by the British, the archive reports that "John Dunkin had ten or twelve likely negroes, and a fine personal property, in stock and furnishings, of which he was altogether plundered ... and reduced to poverty.... Of the lost property, only one slave woman was ever returned to them."[15] Roughly one hundred years later, a bill of sale given to Thomas Berry—a farmer, blacksmith and wagon-maker owning one thousand five hundred acres of land[16]—states, "For the consideration of five hundred dollars to be paid, or secured to be paid, I have this day [December 16, 1848] sold to Thomas N. Berry one negro girl, named Milly, about seventeen years old, who I warrant to be sound and healthy and a slave for life."[17] Another will, that of John Wesley Berry in 1857, is almost entirely concerned in its fourteen provisions with the "disposition of property" after his death in the form of enslaved individuals ("I will to [my wife] ... the farm on which I live and Dick and Lotty two of my Black...").[18]

In the shock of reading this account of human slavery, it is some relief to discover the will of Sarah Berry, who on July 30, 1830, declared as her last request that enslaved individuals "be not sold to strangers, but retained amongst the heirs," and the will of Lafayette Berry, who on May 13, 1834, stated as her last request that "Neil her black woman be freed."[19] Despite the comment that "Great-Grandfather Berry was always good to his slaves and they felt like a part of the family"[20]—and, indeed, from many accounts, it would seem the Berrys treated those whom they enslaved better than some—it is a shock to uncover this aspect of the archive.

Interaction with the Osage

The absence of enslaved individuals to work the Berry property in Kentucky after the Civil War, and the violence and chaos ensuing from the Civil War—"citizens were imprisoned without trial[, and] roving bands of soldiers stole and terrorized the countryside"[21]—are believed to be the motivation for the emigration of the Berrys to "Indian Territory." The Berrys fought on the side of the Union, not the Confederacy: as Nancy Jane Berry relates,

> During the war [the Berrys] had to hide their food because if an army went by they took everything they needed. So they dug a hole out in the woods and hid their meat, coffee and other food in a big box. They usually knew when the Rebels were coming as runners were sent from house to house warning the people. Often times boys were hidden as they would be taken to fight.[22]

Some of the family had homes in Confederate territory, and "to move north they travelled at night using a cowbell to simulate grazing cattle, in order to get through the Confederate lines."

The views of settlers, including my family, toward American Indians in Indian Territory were mixed. Although the United States Supreme Court in *Cherokee Nation v. Georgia* (1831) and *Worcester v. Georgia* (1832) (and later *United States v. Kagama* [1886]) arrived at the studied conclusion that Indians were actually people, and capable of engaging in treaty-making ("for purposes of conveying legal title to their lands,") it also determined that they were "not sovereign enough to manage their other affairs as fully independent political entities."[23] The Court would a century later affirm that Indian sovereignty was a mere "legal fiction" conveying no real legal entitlements.[24]

This contradictory position—what Ward Churchill terms a "blatantly opportunistic monstrosity"—laid the groundwork for federal assertion of full power over Indian affairs and a "trust responsibility" over their assets.[25] The Supreme Court's decision reflected the political views of the Justices, and influenced federal policies and perceptions of those who migrated onto American Indian land. During the early months of the journey to Kansas, Missouri, and the region that would later be known as Oklahoma, the presence of American Indians—whose lives had been disassembled in virtually every meaningful way—was perceived by white settlers as a threat. "Many white men saw Indians as only filthy beggars and alcoholics. Since these were the Indians that most white people saw, this gave the Westward Trekkers a very wrong impression of their adversaries further west."[26]

The resistance of American Indians to forced removal was perceived as unprovoked violence. Many American Indians, including the Pawnee (whose reservation directly adjoined Osage territory) were falsely attributed with the practice of human sacrifice.[27] Misperceptions of the Osage were profoundly influenced by the policies of federal officials, who urged settlers to occupy territory owned by the Osage. Officials like Sidney Clark, Chairman of the Committee on Indian Affairs, "became consumed by the idea that the southwest should not be dedicated to Indian possession ... [and] urged the opening of [all] Indian Territory to settlement by whites."[28] The Kansas Historical Society records an instance when two American Indian scouts (likely Osage) came to Ashland and, witnessing a white man shouting, "the Indians are coming," observed the excitement with amusement, remarking that "as far as they knew there wasn't an Indian missing from any of the reservations."[29]

Family stories relate perceptions of American Indians in the Osage region through both personal experience and hearsay. My Great-Great Uncle Isaac King ("King") Berry, for example, states that

> [i]n those days [1875] the Osages often had held parties out to get scalps for important funerals. I slept in the cabin on the Harry Coons homestead, at the west landing of the ferry, and on this particular night Joe Carrion, an Indian boy[,] was with me. Early in the evening we discovered an Osage hair party coming up the west landing from the river and we knew what it meant and prepared to fight. Joe slipped out of the little black window of the cabin and raced on foot to an Indian camp one mile up the river for help and it was none too soon when they returned[,] as the Osages were trying to break in the door and demanding hair for the solemn rites of a funeral when he got back with help.[30]

One account shares a child's fear of both American Indians and cowboys: "we children lived in deadly fear of being murdered with tomahawks. A scare is very real to the mind of a child, and they never forget. The cowboys would come to our door when we first came here and several years afterwards and if they intended coming in would pass their guns in first. If I happened to go to the door I would be terribly scared."[31] Another woman recalled, "[t]he Osages would only grunt and look so mean we were most frighent [sic] to death."[32] Conversely, into the twentieth century, the Osage maintained a healthy fear of whites: in 2013 Chrissie Childers, who presently lives in the home once occupied by my Grandmother and her children, shared the tale of her father, whose truck had broken down knocking on the door of a man named Red Eagle: "Daddy scared Mrs. Red Eagle to death with that."[33]

The Osage resisted the encroachment of the Cherokee and early settlers on their land, but many of the stories that intimidated whites were propaganda generated by ranchers who wanted the property for their own. "Few are living nowadays who recall that the last Indian scare ... was a hoax born of the last desperate stand of the cattlemen for free range, who hired press agents to build up the scare, and resulted in the government going to the expense of sending 4000 soldiers to patrol the Kansas border—soldiers whose only threat was mosquitoes ... [the scare was a] giant hoax, a nuisance to the settlers and of no use to themselves. "[34] The hoax was confirmed by the Berry family: "as regards to 'The Indian Scare,' it proved nothing more to us, as no Indians were seen although there was a general uprising in the Territory, and the soldiers had to be called.... We have always thought our 'scare' originated with the ranchmen who disliked to give the country over to the settlers ... while we remained there for two years longer, we had no more 'Indian Scares.'"[35] A letter found from the State of Kansas Office of the Adjutant General, written to Isaac "King" Berry after his inquiry whether protecting the settlers from "Indians" during this time earned wages, states that "there are no state funds due you for military service."[36]

African America

Unaccounted for in this set of parallel and at times overlapping histories is the experience of African Americans, both enslaved and free. Camelia Berry relates the story of "civilized tribes" owning slaves, and of an Indian Vigilance Committee employing tactics of intimidation and overt violence:

> When the slaves were freed after the war, they soon became destitute as were their former masters because of the plundering of crops and livestock by both armies during the war. It became a "regular frontier industry." The jobless, homeless negroes took to petty thievery to stay alive and some organized and dangerous gangs, with able leadership developed. Added to these were homeless blacks from Texas, looking for free land. Finally, cattle and pigs and horses were stolen in herds. White men also were stealing horses and cattle until the situation was so serious that the Indians formed a secret Vigilance Committee. Their meetings were held on the open prairie in the day time. They had mounted patrols and their "methods were simple but severe." ... Any blacks caught with a slaughtered animal or a stolen one were often executed on the spot. The Indian Vigilance Committees were also on the lookout for renegade whites. Villages of blacks or renegade whites were scared off by methods later used by the Klu Klux Klan. The reason for such secrecy was that, nationally, sympathy was for the black man, not the red.[37]

The Ku Klux Klan was active in the region of Pawhuska, Hominy and Pawnee, and although never mentioned in conversation, once enjoyed substantial community support. The book *Pawnee Pride*, sponsored by my uncle and "express[ing] the attitude of the people of Pawnee County," describes the Klan's activities in the mildest of terms: "The Ku Klux Klan, which underwent a resurgence throughout America in the 1920s, also supported an end to the excesses of outlawry in Pawnee County, especially the vice and violence associated with the oil boom era. Klan members often took it upon themselves to rid a community of bootleggers, prostitutes, gamblers, and other undesirables[.]"[38] The Klan's role in lynchings is notably omitted here.

The violence exercised by the Ku Klux Klan and the Indian Vigilance Committee illustrates the complexity of interactions prior to and after statehood, and the discernment necessary in examining preconceived or romantic views of how each marginalized group interacted with another in the context of a dominant culture.[39] The late nineteenth century was a critical period in "race" relations, and the region that would be Oklahoma "represented the only place where the three 'founding' cultures of American society co-existed in significant numbers"[40]; according to Murray Wickett, "whites discouraged in African Americans the very ideals and values they so ardently attempted to instill in Native Americans."[41] Hence Camelia Berry's view represents a white but not necessarily nuanced perspective of the assimilation/segregation duality into which American Indians and blacks were placed.

Unlike the Choctaw, Chickasaw, and Seminole, the Osage never "owned" enslaved individuals. Yet the Osage refused to allow blacks to intermarry with anyone living on their lands, and banned all black-skinned individuals from living on the reservation.[42] Even today the story of the swinging bridge connecting the Osage reservation to "Colored Town"— across which, it is said, some stole in secret to meet their romantic interests—is shared in subdued tones. Murray Wickett recounts the story of a white man who brought his African American wife with him onto the Osage reservation, and "the full blood Osage Indians took him out and whipped him and ran them both out of the country."[43] Some of the original Allottees were African American as well as Osage. While never slave-owners, the Osage had an acute sense of hierarchy: a federal inspector reported after visiting the reservation in 1885 that "[t]he full blood Osage Indians are a very aristocratic people in their way … they look upon work as degrading and to plow and hoe only fit occupations for poor white men who have to work,"[44] and frequently applied to the Commissioner of Indian Affairs for permission to hire white as well as African American labor.[45]

The freedmen of Oklahoma nonetheless exerted a powerful influence within the state. The African American businessman Edwin McCabe, a "handsome man of Indian complexion"[46] (reportedly both black and American Indian), wished to transform Oklahoma into a black state, and established the town of Langston as a base for this plan. The population, fueled by the establishment of black towns, rose to 137,000 by 1910.[47] Whites made it clear, however, that white dominance would persist, reportedly "foaming at the mouth" and predicting McCabe's assassination over the notion that African Americans could gain control in the state. The *New York Times* reported the comment of one white resident about McCabe: "I would not give five cents for his life ... dead niggers make excellent fertilizer and if the negroes try to Africanize Oklahoma they will find that we will enrich our soil with them."[48] Twenty years later, the Tulsa Race Riots, in which more than one thousand homes and businesses were destroyed, hundreds injured and killed, and 10,000 African Americans left homeless, made good the threat, laying bare the violence that invariably accompanied a resurgence in white supremacy.

The environment of Oklahoma at the turn of the century was thus one of violent opposition to the usurpation of power by either blacks or American Indians from the majority culture. Nor was such racism restricted to overt violence; racism permeated everyday interactions, in the forms of derogatory expressions, social expectations, and institutional restrictions.[49] We do not know the position of my Great-Grandfather George Madison Berry, who was a delegate to the forming of the Constitutional Convention, although his liberal beliefs with respect to the empowerment of women and other social issues were well known; but most of the founding fathers agreed with the president of the Convention, William Murray, that "blacks should remain porters, blackboots, barbers, and farmers."[50] It was a false notion, according to Murray, that "the negro can rise to the equal of a white man in the professions or become an equal citizen to grapple with public questions."[51] At the convening of the first Oklahoma legislature in 1907, representatives moved swiftly to pass provisions that strengthened Jim Crow provisions.[52]

Yet as the scholar Jimmie Franklin notes, African American individuals in Oklahoma retained their principles and attachment to the land. "The black church [in Oklahoma] proclaimed the redemptive power of love and the idea that humans fulfilled their moral responsibility by reflecting the love of God in their social relationships."[53] All life, their faith taught, "was interrelated and interdependent, and blacks believed that divine providence linked all people in a common destiny."[54] The interconnectedness that was a fundamental aspect of African American faith echoes Jackson's notion of intersubjectivity, and demonstrates a mutually reinforcing identity or social dialectic with the members of a racially complex society. Ralph Ellison, the powerful African American intellectual from Oklahoma, reiterated this notion that "races" are inextricably connected and constructive of self: "By ignoring such matters as the sharing of bloodlines and cultural traditions by groups of widely differing ethnic origins, and by overlooking the blending and metamorphosis of cultural forms which is so characteristic of our society, we misconceive our cultural identity."[55]

Despite the presence of oppression and violence, then, the sense of connection to others, and to the land itself, motivated African Americans to remain. "[M]any of the blacks best equipped to leave Oklahoma [due to oppression and violence] did not move. A significant reason for the willingness to remain in the state was the attachment to the idea of place."[56] Roscoe Dunjee, a black Oklahoman, supplies an illustration of this connection to place that strongly engages the senses:

> Fifty years in the hills and valleys that stretch [across Oklahoma]; fifty years of blood sweat and tears. All our tender recollections of a half century are wrapped up in the land where mother and father are buried.... As we look back down the Sooner Trail toward the black jacks, brush arbors, stubbed toes and the creek where we used to swim ... those were the golden days, imperishable in memory.[57]

The Trader

The realization of settlers and entrepreneurs that the "Indian Scare" had largely been generated by ranchers eager to keep them away, and that the Osage had been given access to funds in their tribal trust account, led to exchange on the part of settlers with Pawnee and Osage alike. Only a year before the Osage tribal trust was established (1878), prior to the "opening of the Strip" (formerly Cherokee land, opened for the Land Rush), Isaac King Berry, having "worked on the Chisholm Trail and wintered cattle in the Indian Territory, "become conversant with several Indian languages, secured a license to trade at the [Pawnee Indian] agency ... and conducted a store for two years,"[58] as well as a stock business which sold "three or four hundred head of horses to the gypsies."[59] The trading post, according to a newspaper article from the era, was the first established in the whole of the Indian Territory prior to the nineteenth century; a second was established in Shawnee in 1881.[60] The exchange of goods by Isaac King and his brothers Thomas Embassy and George Madison (my Great Grandfather), was extensive:

3. The Settler, the Trader and the Cowboy   49

The **BERRY BROTHERS**, established at the Pawnee Trading Post, were not dealing in furs and beads. They were dealing with cash customers. The Indians now leased their land for real money, which was new to them, and they went to the post for blankets, guns, ammunition, beads, calico out of which the women soon made dresses like the white ladies. Sister missionaries to the Kiowas taught them to make quilts to sell to the settlers. The Indian women soon tired of the dim soft colors and conventional designs and began to design their own which were dazzling and sold [well] ... in the new towns.[61]

A dim photograph of the second post from the archives shows a large log cabin with glass windows, a shingled roof, and woodstove chimney; outside, poised on horseback, are King, Tom, and Andrew Berry, the proprietors, as well as Thomas Embassy, Juliet Sophia, Georgia Gaunt, Mary Susan, and Andrew Berry, and three children, Grace, Oak, and Emby. The pride the three generations of the Berry family took in this flourishing enterprise is evident, and the value of the post to the entire community is indicated not only by the array of goods sold, but also by its service as a mail outlet, with mail delivered twice a week by stage coach from Kansas to Pawhuska.[62] As Camelia Berry stated, her own perspective on settler culture in evidence, "The Indians had a great deal of money (cash) from leasing their vast lands to the white cattlemen. There was little opportunity to spend their capital, and the trading posts offered the wonders of the white world to the Indians on the reservations."[63]

Despite the profound gulf between the Osage and my ancestors, the commercial base for connection had therefore been established. This connection emerges in family legend, in illustrations rendered by family members and decades later, and in journalistic accounts. Isaac King Berry, for example, was employed as a beef contractor who introduced herds of cattle onto reservations and "held them for pasture until the need for beef indicated another slaughtering"; my Great-Great-Grandfather, George Madison Berry, is widely reported as having became familiar with Pawnee hunting and cooking, and becoming fluent in the Pawnee language as well as "universal sign language."[64] William Thomas Berry is said to have written a mathematics book for American Indians. "Thomas N. [T.N.] Berry was invited to the Indian Councils around Perkins and was always ready to help them. Thomas Berry's son, Jack Berry, carries the same sense of responsibility toward the Indians and has been asked to conduct" the funeral for Two Gun, who "worked for Jack as a hand on the Berry ranch in the 1940's."[65]

The intimate association between Osage and ancestor, of course, has to be considered with perspective in mind: another account relates that the

[o]lder brothers would work the fields and cattle, and ... [the youngest, Robert Crittendon Berry] stay home to attend to the trading post, and haul freight. The Pawnee Indian tribe gave him the name "Skit-a-use-to-skit-Tow," which translated jokingly as "big cheater." He apparently tried to trade rough with the Indians, but his brothers maintained that they stole him blind.[66]

It is unclear precisely in what context, and in what tones, these teasing interactions took place. The story of those who were present, ancestor and American Indian, historical and embodied experience, however, feels true to life. The individual voices of both family and American Indian render the individuals discussed that much more resistant to the dangerous historical fallacy of homogenization and abstraction.

The Cowboy

A prominent figure in the narratives that populate the family archive is the cowboy. The term "cowboy" was used variously to describe young men and boys who herded cattle. In 1883, the Denver Republican defined a cowboy as "a man [who] works on a salary and rides after the herd."[67] Although some were perceived as illiterate and mannerless, even criminal, the cowboy generally garnered respect for courage and the protection of women: "Rough he may be, and it may be that he is not a master in ballroom etiquette, but no set of men have loftier reverence for women."[68] In 1887, another journalist stated that the cowboy "is in the main a loyal, long-enduring, hard-working fellow, grit to the backbone, and tough as whipcord; performing his arduous and often dangerous duties, and living his comfortless life, without a word of complaint about the many privations he has to undergo."[69]

It was frightening for many early settlers in the Indian Territory to encounter cowboys who rode to their door, as family narratives relate.

> At the time of our location the county was unorganized, and many range cattle roamed over the hills. There were also deer, antelope, grey wolves, mountain lions, wild cats, and last but by no means least, the "cow boy," of whom we stood at that time in great fear ... [one day] out of a ravine near the house rode nine cow boys with their Winchesters, six-shooters and cartridge belts. Oh! How my heart beat, for I thought our time had surely come.[70]

Stories told by homesteaders invariably found the cowboy "mannerly and courteous"—standing politely at the door of households, for example, reaching into dwellings when welcomed and passing guns in first—but their reputation followed them.[71]

3. *The Settler, the Trader and the Cowboy* 51

"There were wild horses to handle the wild cattle," Camelia Uzzell Berry, in her *Oklahoma Prairie Plowed Under: The Story of Berry Bros. in Indian Territory,"* page 39 (courtesy Catherine Berry Hess).

It is not surprising, then, that cowboys were recalled dramatically by descendants who told their stories.

> [T]hose willing to face danger from the Indians and the outlaws, while living in the open with tornadoes, floods, prairie fires, sleet, snow, ceaseless wind, hunger and exhaustion, [had access to] man's priceless possession, land, vast grasslands as far as the eye could see. You've never seen a "Western" movie that didn't have a bit of the **"BERRY BROTHERS"** story in it. They dressed in home spun and leather, and bits and pieces of Civil War uniforms. They carried Civil War revolvers and carbines. Since William Edward Berry had spent four years in the Union Army as a sergeant, he was very handy with both. All "frontier-types" were skillful with weapons. It was a necessity. The latecomers, the settlers[,] equated the cowboy with the outlaw because he wore guns. They were deathly afraid of the cowboy! A cowboy needed guns, to turn stampeding cattle, to kill snakes, wolves, and cougars, to kill his horse if he broke a leg or if his horse was dragging him with his foot caught in the stirrup, to call for help, as well as to defend himself and others from outlaws and enraged cattle. And remember until the 1890's, the Indians were not really pacified.[72]

What was described as "pacification" was actually the consequence of access to Osage-owned allotment funds that the federal government insisted on controlling and dispensing (however erratically), mineral rights, and the leasing of grassland, which supplied the Osage with the funds to participate in trade.

While the description of the cowboy shared by family members omitted the extreme suffering of the Osage, Pawnee, and other American Indians in the same region, the challenges and dangers faced by cowboys were in themselves real. Colt and Winchester guns, heavy and less accurate than later weapons, were difficult to aim on horseback; horses and longhorn cattle posed as much danger as the snapping wolves and mountain lions, threatening a kick, a stampede, a roping accident, even drowning after being thrown.[73] Oklahoma and family history are shaped by such stories: "between 1872 and 1874 Berry worked as a cattle drover herding longhorns north from Texas through Indian Territory ... roping and branding and cutting longhorns, a truly horrendous job."[74]

In *The Land Rush*, Dora Berry Goodson states that in Texas, "ownerless wild cattle, an immense range of free grass almost cleared [sic] of Indians and buffalo, and wild horses ... were waiting for men bold enough to go in and take them, men who could master the wild horses and wild cattle and hold part of the range in a wild country. The history of the West was made by 'that kind of man.'"[75] According to Goodson, William, T.N., and King Berry were such men, running a thousand head of cattle between the Cimarron and the Pawnee agency north to the railroad, and driving horses home to break them.[76] Before the Land Run of 1889, the Berry family established an immense ranching and trade enterprise of 60,000 acres from the efforts of these cowboys, leased from Cherokee and extending into "Unassigned Lands," and supporting roughly two thousand cattle.[77] Established in 1880, it operated under the "backward B+ brand," and was believed to be the first ranch in the eastern Pawnee region.[78] Stories in the archive from this period of family history describe "ranching, range wars, barbed wire, famous cowboys and drovers, land sharks, frauds, rustlers, water rights, blizzards and frozen stock and people, gamblers, saloon owners, [and] pioneer women"[79]; they evoke a powerful and quirky sense of personality: "John McGinty, brother of the legendary Billy [and one of T.N. Berry's cowboys], rode his horse into the drug store, was afraid he couldn't get back on, if he got off! He drank vanilla when he couldn't get anything else. Once his horse reared up and put his feet through the top of a nearby car."[80]

What constituted Dora Berry Goodson's description of "that kind of man" in this era, however, would appear to be a man with the ability to withstand extreme duress, handle difficult and dangerous situations, and "break" wild and extraordinarily large animals. Encountering and breaking animals thus was an extension of a constructed masculinity, and the greater the challenge, the more exalted the man:

> Men who saw the immense herds remembered them as one of the wonders of the west. Once, a company ... met a drove of mustangs so large that it took over an hour to pass them, although both rangers and mustangs were travelling at speed and going in opposite directions! As far as the eye could see, a dense mass of horses covered the level plain ... "the trampling of their hooves sounded like the roar of the surf on a rocky coast."[81]

That the Berry Brothers, who had now acquired a new Cross Bell brand, went through this experience with mustangs and cattle was seen as a demonstration of their hardness, determination and masculinity.[82] My Grandfather on my father's side worked on the Chisholm Trail, which drove cattle from south Texas where they were worth three dollars a head, to Chicago, where they were worth fifty; it was shorter, less settled, had more water and better grazing than other trails, but "[c]owboys had to face swollen rivers, stampedes, Indians demanding steers for the passage, cholera, prairie fires, hail and rustlers."[83] At its peak the Chisholm Trail witnessed 600,000 head of longhorn cattle; nearly fourteen million cattle would eventually be led by cowboys before the Trail's end in 1880.[84]

In family memory and ideology, then, "[t]he cowboys and cattlemen were mostly from the south[,] with the south's tradition of chivalry and honor above everything else. They were armed, light hearted, unstable, adventurous, sometimes murderous and vengeful if their honor had been questioned."[85] The romantic association between the honorable but volatile cowboy and the cattle brand was never lost for me: the Cross Bell brand, later shared by both Berrys and Mullendores, was always connected in my mind with The Place, and a branding iron sat on the fireplace mantel of our home for many years, below an exquisite painting of a cowboy riding fence painted by my father.

Yet even this memory is complicated by questions over the origins of the original Cross Bell cattle. According to family history, "[a] big herd of Old Mexico cattle carrying the original brand was driven across the Rio Grande and on up the "Texas Road" across Red River near Paris into Indian Country," and the brothers purchased the whole herd of Longhorns and the brand, dividing the cattle between the Berrys and the Mullendores.[86] Lingering questions remain in my mind about this process, and about whether any relatives crossed the Territory line early and were "Sooners." The fact that the land on which my family's cattle grazed was taken by the federal government from American Indians is similarly unsettling. Roger Lloyd has argued that a hero narrative was generated in literature of the era around those who entered and organized the wilderness;

the romanticization of frontiersmen came to justify escalating violence against nature, and those who sustainably inhabited it.[87] An ideology heroicizing the conqueror and cowboy fits comfortably within a cultural narrative of aggression and control, but does not relieve speculation over the celebratory tone of the archive.

4

Architecture: The Church of Immaculate Conception and the One-Room School

As I visited my Grandmother's house in Hominy, Oklahoma, for the first time in forty-five years, I was struck by an awareness of what had changed and what had been left unchanged, and a surreal sense of physical groundedness and belonging. There was the dining room, the wallpaper unchanged; there was the kitchen, where I watched my Grandmother bake biscuits so many years ago; there were the brick streets, the old trucks, the brick building that once was a corner grocery that kept a running tab for Grandma. The lovely occupant, Chrissie Childers, a past friend of my uncle, Everett Berry, Jr., and longtime resident of the town, could not recall anything that might relate to my understanding of the relationship between the Osage and my family. As I was about to leave, however, she said with a wave of her hand, "of course, there is the roundhouse."[1]

The Osage roundhouse in Hominy, Oklahoma, is the only original Osage ceremonial house left in existence, last rebuilt in 1919. Inside and nearby the octagonal structure, empty and full of dust, dances and religious ceremonies, powerful drumming and processions in full dress have taken place for more than one hundred years. The roundhouse, unmentioned in my family for five decades, was walking distance from my Grandmother's home. Its proximity suggests a cultural interconnectedness that lies dormant in space and in memory despite attempts to suppress it—a cultural groundedness that is "subliminal, habitual, repressed, [and] unexpressed, and ... that [silently] shapes and reshapes, stabilizes and destabilizes the visible surface forms."[2] This chapter will address the interconnectedness of cultures in examining the architecture of the Osage,

Osage roundhouse, Hominy, Oklahoma, 2014 (courtesy Pbonchai Tallman).

the government structures established to supervise them at the end of the nineteenth century, and the dwellings of my family in both Indian Territory and Oklahoma.

Osage Architecture

Although historians describe Osage traditional belief in terms of a duality or opposition of earth and sky, masculine and feminine, peace and war, the Osage *Wa-kon-da* ("God") "was a single unified force that manifested itself in various ways in all living, moving things [emphasis added]."[3] Moreover, Osage rituals related to aspects of nature were intended to be expressions of, or metaphors for, this single, all-encompassing power.[4] Thus, while Osage villages and longhouse dwellings, which some scholars describe located along an east-west axis, were considered to be "a symbolic reconstruction of the sun,"[5] the central focus of architecture was a harmonic unity of forces. Similarly, scholars who claim that dwellings were arranged in a concentric fashion, with the lodges of the War Chief and Peace Chief of the Osage[6] at the center together with their soldiers, note that it was the unity of the village that was the focus of architectural space.⁷ Carter Revard, the Osage scholar and poet, describes the clear ground before the lodges as a point of distribution of "food and supplies to those members of the tribe whose families had not been successful" in the hunt.⁸ Beyond serving as an arrangement for military defense and "care of the tribe's poor and less fortunate members," the concentric pattern represented in ceremony "a symbolic embodying of the great cosmic order of Earth and Sky and Water ... the Osage village, the Osage lodge, the Osage family and polity, all were meant to embody the cosmic and earthly order."⁹

The construction of early Osage structures is discussed in Garrick Bailey's fine scholarship.

> The most common type of Osage dwelling was a longhouse, or *wa-sha-tsi*. These were rectangular dwellings made from poles stuck into the ground, bent over, and tied together to form a domed frame ... covered with woven cattail mats, bark, hides, or some combination of these materials. They were usually about twenty feet wide, forty to fifty feet long, and fifteen to eighteen feet high and oriented along an east-west axis ... the longhouses of common people had two doors opening on the south side, one toward the east end and the other toward the west.¹⁰

As the *wirige* suggests, architecture for the Osage meant more than a simple dwelling. The house was a metaphor for the orientation of the cosmos, "an ordered system that was dynamic, ever changing, and logically integrated, with everything in it having meaning and purpose."¹¹ Moreover, the home stored objects of critical spiritual significance, including the sacred *wa-xo'-be*.

During a seasonal bison hunt, typically late May or early June, the Osage people occupied smaller structures. Osage hunting lodges were typically fifteen feet long, seven feet wide, and four feet tall; they were constructed by driving lodge poles in the ground, bending them over, and covering them with buffalo skins.¹² After the introduction of the horse by the armies of DeSoto and Coronado in the sixteenth century, buffalo were followed on horseback, and portable teepees—made of buffalo hides laced over rigid wooden poles approximately eighteen feet long—were adopted, and arranged in a circular shape, with each group of relatives together.¹³ Rollings describes the fluid location and structure of Osage villages and communities, as well as their adaptable architecture; a white official noted, "It is next to impossible to enumerate them correctly. I have made several attempts in vain. They are continually removing from one village to another."¹⁴ The amorphous nature of Osage community structures suggests that the complexity, flexibility, and accommodation of Osage architecture was to some degree a reflection of their worldview—a worldview of kinship structures and the accommodation of differing cultures that, as the *wirige* song suggests, ultimately contributed to their survival.

The decline in the practice of the traditional Osage religion brought about by the virtual extinction of the buffalo, and a drastic decrease in population due to disease and starvation, led to the collapse of traditional village structures. As Rollings makes clear, Osage religion was not erased by the conversion efforts of New England Protestants or Roman Catholics until the turn of the century; although Catholicism had some appeal due to the immediacy of Catholic sacraments—the sacred vestments, objects, repetitive prayers, and ceremonies—Osage participation in Catholicism represented more a reflection of their own religion's inclusive nature, or affinity with Catholic ritual, than conversion.[15] Instead, the decline in traditional belief was a function of drastic changes in the environment, accompanied by the Interior Department's prohibition on traditional religious practice.[16] A mourning dance was performed at Gray Horse in 1911, and turned out to be the last public performance of traditional religious ceremony[17]; several men were initiated into clan priesthoods as late as the 1930s, but the traditional Osage religion is fading away.

The Native American Church (referred to by some white scholars as Peyotism), however, had a profound impact after its introduction to the Osage after 1890. The introduction of the Ghost Dance, while ultimately short-lived, led to overall acceptance of the notion of a religious revival[18]; within ten to fifteen years of its introduction by Quanah Parker and other Apache, Comanche and Kiowa, "the vast majority of Osage full-bloods had converted" to the new religion.[19] The arrival of the Native American Church led to the development of new architectural structures associated with Osage spirituality. "Big Moon" or "Half Moon" Peyotism, fostered by a Caddo Medicine Man named *Ni-Shu-Kun-Tu* or John Wilson, early leader of the Ghost Dance movement in Oklahoma,

> involved the construction of an altar with "a sunken area for the fire ... surrounded by an apron approximately two feet wide. Most Osage altars are approximately eight feet wide and ten feet long. Hearts are drawn at the head of the altar, at the point where the Peyote Road intersects the Cross Roads, and on the small mound at the end of the altar.[20]

As Bailey notes, "In some cases, a wood-frame octagonal 'church house' was constructed over the altar, replacing the tepee as the place of worship and providing protection from the elements that might erode the altar."[21] The music associated with the Native American Church was the same as that recalled by my mother from her early childhood.[22]

By the 1920s, church houses reflected new Osage affluence. "Churches constructed during this period were generally larger, and a framed vesti-

Top: Osage engaged in Peyote (Native American Church) ceremony, with altar on ground, nineteenth century. *Bottom:* Native American Church (rebuilt), near roundhouse, in Hominy, Oklahoma (courtesy Pbonchai Tallman).

bule extending from the front of the basic octagonal structure was a common architectural feature. Osage Peyotists focused their wealth on expressions of religious devotion, including stained-glass windows, cut-glass chandeliers, and marble statuary [.]"[23] Within one generation, the mat- and canvas-covered longhouses vanished, "and families now lived in spacious modern homes, many of which could be classified as mansions."[24] Bailey indicates that the Native American church "contributed to the purchase of the large stained-glass windows in the Catholic church in Pawhuska, while the Quaker church in Hominy was paid for primarily by local leaders in the Peyote [Native American] Church."[25]

One of the focal points in the Osage community in Pawhuska was the Immaculate Conception Catholic Church, a Gothic-style brick structure built by the parish in 1910. Stained glass windows in the northern transept of the church, imported from Munich in 1919, illustrate the Jesuit Father John Shoemakers with a group of Osage attired in plain and beribboned blankets, some Osage men depicted with beaver skin caps and fringed leggings. Shoemakers is depicted as bringing to the Osage people the transcendent light of Christ.[26] According to one account, the two Osage girls who are not attentive, but gazing at the viewer, are portraits of two children Shoemaker knew and taught; the "girls died tragically young of smallpox, a disease [brought by whites] that was devastating to the Native American peoples."[27] Ironically, an Osage figure to the far left holds up a huge Peyote fan, larger than Shoemakers' head, and as large as the priest's upheld cross.

With the acquisition of mineral wealth, the dwellings of the Osage changed dramatically. At the turn of the century, the Osage "often had two homes: one on their allotment and one in town. The Osage Allotment Act set aside three 160-acre tracts as 'Indian villages.' The Pawhuska and Hominy villages were located on the edges of the towns of the same name. A third village was established at Gray Horse[.]"[28] According to Bailey, the focal point for these villages, located approximately two miles from town, was the structure of the round house.

> In 1894 there were four such houses ... one each in Pawhuska, Hominy, and Gray Horse, and another on Bird Creek, near the modern town of Barnsdall ... [they] consist[ed] of many-sided wooden structures with a conical roof and single entranceway ... roofs [were] covered with tree branches to provide shade. In 1917 and 1918, the round houses were rebuilt.... These new structures were much larger and had pitched wood-shingled roofs ... with two doors, one on the east side and one on the west.[29]

Round houses were used for a range of events: political meetings, winter dances, and other social events, as well as large dances, celebrations, and guest dwelling in an open area near the house.³⁰ In my Grandmother's hometown of Hominy, a Christmas pageant and feast were held there. Round houses in Pawhuska, Gray Horse, and Hominy were constructed prior to allotment.³¹ Today, only the roundhouse in Hominy, near my Grandmother's house, remains, alongside a newly constructed Native American church, the site of the second to be constructed in the Osage nation.

During the teens and into the boom years, the Osage constructed secondary homes—often small, wood-framed houses painted yellow—in villages.³² The smallest homes took the form of a wood-framed bungalows with large front porches; the largest were two-story brick homes "designed in the style of English country houses."³³ The Osage often built near the village home a unique Osage structure called a "summer house," a long rectangular building with screens rather than walls, "and a cookstove, used for storage, family feasts, guest structures, and games and other social events ... about thirty of these country residences also had their own Peyote Church house,"³⁴ as well as a roundhouse. While older families maintained simple, sparsely furnished homes, the homes of younger families often displayed luxurious furniture, including sewing machines, pianos, radios, phonographs, and crystal chandeliers.³⁵ By some accounts,

Gray Horse roundhouse with dancers and drum, printed by Vince Dillon, Fairfax, Oklahoma, circa 1912. Feather roaches and eagle feathers on dancers are visible.

Osage roundhouse with dance arbor in the background, Hominy, Oklahoma, 2014 (author's photograph).

this furniture was little used, and many individual residents preferred to sleep on the floor, use camp fires for cooking, and draw water manually rather than tapping mains.[36]

Another structure unique to the Osage was the arbor created for the *I'n-lon-shcka*. In the early years, the *I'n-lon-schka* was performed outside; the ceremony was later held in roundhouses, designed after early Quaker meeting houses, and still later, with an increase in the number of dancers, was again held outside.[37] In the 1940s rectangular arbors of wood with brush roofs were used,[38] and ceremonies were held in Pawhuska in the 1950s in the "Indian schoolhouse"; the Wakon Iron Hall, "named after the respected elder, businessman and philanthropist Wakon Iron," was used for meetings in the 1970s,[39] while dances throughout the Osage region were performed in metal sheds and open air enclosures "constructed from steel pipes and trusses and covered with a metal roof."[40] In 2014, the Pawhuska District began construction of a massive new open air "arbor" or auditorium for ceremony. Such a structure provides a powerful contrast to the early roundhouses and brush structures that were employed centuries ago.

Government Structures

Michel Foucault's observation that spatial and architectural organization has served as a mechanism for the regulatory gaze has by now become a commonplace of academic scholarship.[41] Scholars of anthropology and cultural studies suggest that power is exercised not only in written laws and acts of regulation, but also in less overt and more pervasive forms, including institutional mechanisms for observation and surveillance—among them architectural forms. The orientation of forts, Indian Agencies, and administrative offices of Pawhuska can, by this view, be seen as a means for surveillance and control of the Osage. The establishment of commercial institutions, jails, schools, and private property extended the panoptic effect, and served as visual evidence of social reconfiguration and control.

Among the first structures to be established in the first half of the nineteenth century in Indian Territory were forts of the American military. These forts were constructed with wooden logs approximately twelve feet long; outer walls, called palisades, were erected with sharpened logs, cannons, and visionary outposts. In each fort a single entry gate opened outward. Barracks and storehouses for food and supplies, as well as an armory for guns and magazine for gunpowder, were located inside.[42] As military forts, trading posts, and Indian Agencies began to appear, opportunities for construction, farming, teaching, and services increased, with the consequent growth of small towns and permanent living structures. The grounds of the Indian Agency in Pawnee, for example, were home to offices, shops, barns, cottages, and the tribal police barracks, as well as an Indian "training school" with dormitories, shops, warehouses, and barns. The Southern Baptist Church also maintained a chapel and parsonage on the ground, and employed a superintendent, principal, physician, nurse, several clerks, teachers, matrons, farmers, general mechanic, and carpenters, all of whom lived nearby.

In Pawhuska, the Osage nation's center,[43] the former residence of the Osage Indian Agent, a boarding school for Osage children (with separate wings for the boys' and girls' dormitories), and the residences of Indian subagents stood at the crest of the tallest hill on Grandview Avenue. Dominating the valley of Bird Creek, immediately below the hill, was the sandstone Council House, topped by a bell tower; another two-story building of sandstone, the doctor's office and house and the Pawhuska House Hotel stood nearby. Across the road, a third stone building which was successively the blacksmith's house, the chief clerk's house, and a boarding house was erected. Two long wooden buildings, once primitive stockades, were transformed into trade stores.[44] "Across from the stores, at the foot of the hill, was a little log-house which was the remnant of the original Agency buildings, and close by was the small building with barred windows, which was the jail, and known locally as the caboose."[45] At the base of the hill in Pawhuska was a large dusty area, the center of the Reservation, where people gathered to talk and traders "moved across the area with the business usually assumed by Americans who sell things."[46]

The illustrated map drawn by Osage author John Joseph Mathews in 1932 indicates geographical features and settlements which surrounded this central street and the Agent office and schools at the crest of the hill.[47] Such settlements as the "Camp of Black Dog," the "Camp for Freighters," a "Camp for Visiting Indians," and the "Mashankashe Lodge," as well as a hide house, general store, an old mill, government barn for the Agent's mules, government school garden, government peach orchard, old salt well, and government pasture and farm are illustrated surrounding the central core of the Council House and Agent's office and the structures on the hill. Outlying these settlements and structures, Mathews depicts ancient Indian mounds, Cedar Vale Hill and "Lovers Leap," Osage Woman Swamp, the Indian graves, a glade of persimmon trees, Bird Creek—with a road extending north to Gray Horse—and cowboys coralling longhorn steers.[48]

The most prominent features in Mathews' map, titled "Map of Osage Agency—(Pawhuska, Oklahoma),"[49] are illustrations of women cooking and drying beef, the chief with his armbands and feathered roach, horses, razorbacks, deer, and coyote, three distinct varieties of trees, the rocks and hills, and most prominently, a finely illustrated hatchet pipe, of European origin but adapted for the Osage. According to Bailey,

> An artifact such as this [the hatchet pipe] seldom made it west of the Mississippi River and, as such, was extremely coveted by the Osage ... [who] would have had a blacksmith cut out the ... powerful heart motif, which may represent the leaf of the redbud tree. Wood from the redbud tree is considered sacred, and the charcoal produced from it was used to paint the body of a warrior who was then transformed into an agent of destruction, symbolically as devastating as a prairie fire.[50]

The prominent position of the land, the Osage people, and the poignant illustration of the pipe placed on a grave suggest a richly inflected vision of the Osage people that belies the title of the map.

With the coming of the Oil Boom, the architecture of Pawhuska changed dramatically. Hordes of construction workers swarmed over the city, along with geologists, oilmen, tradespeople, attorneys, doctors, bankers, and other businesspeople; brick houses spread down into the valley

Nineteenth-century Osage Council House with bell tower, Pawhuska, Oklahoma, 2014 (author's photograph).

of Bird Creek, followed by paved roads, bridges, and hotels, with the ever-present pumpjack derrick adorning roads and fields.[51] For businesspeople and those eager to spend money, Pawhuska assumed the brilliant, expansive air of New York in miniature, complete with its own triangular skyscraper on the former site of the distribution of rations, brick streets,

Triangle "skyscraper," Pawhuska, Oklahoma, 2014 (courtesy Pbonchai Tallman).

automobiles and business exchange. A photograph of the town from the 1920's reveals brick buildings, waving flags and striped awnings, signs for bars, boarding rooms, and oil exchanges, crowded sidewalks, and a traffic jam of Model Ts.[52]

From the perspective of some Osage writers, however, notably John Joseph Mathews, the rush of commerce and construction brought about by the oil boom had a markedly different effect on the town.

> There were "Art" shops and "Parisian" shops and "Ye Shoppes" of various descriptions, and many drug stores. Most of the old traders had passed on and the old stores had to put on new fronts and assume that which was believed to be the metropolitan air ... buildings were lighted with glaring lights at night when the extravagantly paid workers came from the fields and danced to the wheezing phonographs, bought corn whiskey, heroin and women, and sometimes were knifed or shot as a consequence.[53]

Small towns such as Woloco, Carter Nine, Big Bertha, Little Chief, and Denoya (Whizbang) also sprang up around Osage territory with an insinuating dominance: "[t]all, wooden, creaky, noisome oil derricks dominated the landscape of rolling hills of blackjack oak groves and tallgrass prairie

... [the 1920s witnessed] a forest of oil rigs, from the foreground to the distant horizon."[54]

When prices for oil dropped in the late thirties, major cities in the region declined dramatically. In Fairfax, Wynona, Hominy, and Pawhuska, commercial buildings of brick and stone sat empty after the boom ended, "some windowless and burnt out as if in the wake of a retreating army. These empty buildings, memorials to failed ambitions, give the towns an air of violation."[55] Dennis McAuliffe's description of downtown Pawhuska in 1989 strikes a similar note: expecting to see the city about which he had read—"marble office buildings, smart Fifth-Avenue-looking shops, and magnificent custom-built cars rushing by,"[56] McAuliffe states,

> Buildings were abandoned, some falling down. Doors were boarded up. Windows were broken, some held together by yellowing tape. Peeling paint hung like spiderwebs. Roofs sagged.... Pawhuska looked like the face of a frail and frightful old woman, baring her teeth ... in defiance of death.[57]

Towns like Wynona are sadly abandoned today, and buildings sit, paint peeling, even in Hominy, the site of both the Osage roundhouse and the elaborate home of the Drummond family. As McAuliffe notes, however, Pawhuska has enjoyed a resurgence due to the efforts of the Osage, and the refurbishment of buildings by Ree Drummond in downtown Pawhuska.

The Family and the Place

One of the noteworthy qualities of my family archive—full of letters, articles, gene-

Mural of cowboy on brick building in downtown Hominy, Oklahoma, 2014 (courtesy Pbonchai Tallman).

alogies, photographs, and wills—is the prominent position of maps. There are maps of the counties of northeastern Oklahoma; maps of the two portions of the Berry Brothers' Ranch, with illustrations of Indian settlements (teepees, individuals warming themselves by the fire, and a rack of drying meat), as if to assure the reader that the region still retained the now romanticized opposition of cowboy and Indian; maps of Indian Territory, dated 1888; and maps of The Place. There are maps of the Cherokee Strip, detailing the Ponca Reservation and the region of the Cheyenne, Creek, Ponca, Otoe, and Arapaho, as well as the Chisholm Trail and the Cimarron River, illustrating the wider surroundings of the Berry Ranch before the Land Rush; an early map of designated counties in the region; and genealogies with small illustrated maps of cowboys and American Indians in stereotypical garb.

As previously discussed, this urge to categorize and impose order can be understood as the extension of a "colonizing gaze."[58] The mapping of landscape "was not just an aid to the establishment and monitoring of different sorts of property ... but a force in the creation of changing social configurations."[59] The Land Ordinance of 1787, with its graphic overlay of organized and orderly units of settlement, had already established the example of the comfort of quantification and land division; family archives document the desire to track the divisions of territory, county, property, and genealogy, reflecting pride in property ownership and waning Osage influence.

For homesteaders in Indian Territory, the earliest housing was the covered wagon, followed by simple wooden structures.

> On October 6, 1897, mother [Nora Berry and her family] moved to the claim father staked. We took lumber in the wagon and built us a very small house. We put straw on the floor and our bedding over the straw. We cooked with a dutch oven over a campfire. We had the bed of the covered wagon and we lived that way six weeks before father was able to build us a house. The boards of the house were straight up and down, it was built fourteen by twenty eight feet. Jim and I carried water from the river the six weeks we lived there.[60]

Such was the first impression of Oklahoma that some family members immediately left: "She was 14 or 15 when she came in a covered wagon to the edge of Oklahoma Indian Territory, went into it to some small 'town,' but it was so noisy, some shooting, shouting, drinking no doubt, they turned back across the Kansas border[.]"[61]

For those who remained, houses made of sod, extracted from the ground in two-and-a-half foot blocks cut by a sod-breaking plow,[62] and simple wooden structures were the primary architectural features. The government required that homes be at least ten by twelve feet in size, but such homes were overwhelmingly flimsy and dank; insects, mice, rats, and snakes could gain access to sod homes, and "[t]here was no keeping anything truly clean, for the dried earth of the walls and roof constantly shed bits and pieces of dust and dirt on to everything."[63] Of my Great-Great-Grandmother on my father's side, Wilma Aloysia McGoffin, a family member wrote, "Mom lived in a hole in a bank in Clay Center Kansas; she said one could walk right on the sod roof from the prairie side of the house."[64] In Dora Berry's memory, her home was "just a shack. It had a dirt floor and I just had room for a bed, a table, a stove and a coal oil lamp. I remember I papered it with newspapers."[65] Water from a buffalo wallow poured through one sod home in a flood that required buckets to remove[66]; the dugout was later used as a barn, and a granary used as sleeping quarters.[67]

As properties and cities became more established, particularly around forts and rail lines, commercial structures were built in more substantial fashion.[68] Camelia Berry describes T.N. Berry's home as a two room log house below the south Cimarron bluff with a solid walnut floor.

> He spent his days clearing trees and stumps out of his fields. He used a six ox team, including Dinger, one of the first registered bulls in Oklahoma. He also used a logging chain, each link being 4" × 6". We have a section of this chain on our back patio and I can barely lift 3 of the links off the ground. He used this chain all day long to clear the land![69]

The family archive describes the home built by Jackson ("Jack") Berry on the former property of Jennie Berry, claimed after the Land Rush. "In 1939 the improvements were: a stone house built in 1927 by his brother Thomas E. Berry and a negroe, Bob Brown, the original dug well, three shotgun houses, various granaries (some were old oil tanks), one stone barn, one big Quonset type hay barn, a blacksmith shop, some very fine hogs and mule teams[, two hundred Leghorn hens] and one hundred geese!"[70]

The architectural and spatial organizations of settler properties depended, of course, on the incomes of those inhabiting them. My Grandfather Otto Hess, on my father's side, was born in Arkansas, and homesteaded in extreme poverty; his wife, Julia, taught in one and two room county schools, and raised nine children in homes he built by hand. "Both Otto and Julia came from impoverished families that always had to struggle to survive from meager returns gained by farming. Words cannot adequately describe their achievement, starting with virtually nothing ... [working as a farmers' produce manager in Anadarko, a letter carrier, and a construction worker, as well as farmer,] Otto was an extremely hard-working man."[71] According to Julia Hess' sister Josie, "when we come to Oklahoma ... the weather was either too wet and ruined everything or it was too dry and didn't make anything… Oh, I guess we liked to starved."[72] In 1937, during the Great Depression, my Great-Grandparents made the journey during the Dust Bowl to California, becoming "Okies" in the classic sense.[73]

The stories of both families indicate a variety of commercial structures built to accommodate a range of professions. In the Berry family, the range of professions suggest a multiplicity of architectural structures that once existed, but now are gone. Members of the Berry family worked as Pawnee Agency traders, dealing in flour, sugar, and other supplies; brokers at the I.K. Berry & Co. Pawnee Meat Market in 1898; ferry operators in Pawnee; legal practitioners; mayors, treasurers, and bookkeepers; real estate and loan officers; owners of the Pawnee Mercantile Company, and of a wholesale produce, fruit, and grocery business; establishers of trading companies and banks in Stillwater, Agra, Ripley, Pawnee, Norman, and Guthrie (one of which is said to have begun in a dugout)[74]; owners of the Pawnee Ice, Fuel and Bottling Company, which sold ice and Jersey Cream Soda, and a Dr. Pepper bottling franchise; and owners of coal wagon businesses and grocery and hardware stores (including Berry & Baird, in a frame building of twenty-five by forty feet).[75] The Mullendores owned refining operations, service stations, and banks,[76] all of which required substantial structures in the business regions of Hominy, Pawnee, Cleveland, Cushing, and Stillwater, the area referred to by whites as "the Osage."[77] The Drummonds—whose historical family home stands two blocks from my Grandmother's home in Hominy, and who were friends of my Grandmother's—operated both their cattle ranch south of Hominy, and the Hominy Trading Company, the nation's largest dealer of Pendleton Blankets, popular among the Osage.

At the very heart of all activities, negotiations, and experiences of the immediate family for the last one hundred years was The Place, the ranch where my mother was born. The Place was located in close proximity to the Osage towns of Hominy and Pawhuska; indeed, the property itself engulfed that of an Osage landowner. A relative stated of my Grandmother and Grandfather Berry,

> [My Grandfather and Grandmother] bought the land in the Osage directly from the Indians… Our land almost surrounded a small farm owned by [the Osage owner]. She was not allowed by the agency to sell the land to Daddy and she probably wouldn't have anyway. She and Daddy loved the annual powwow [sic] over the lease. She sat in the back seat in her calico dress and blanket, chewing tobacco which she spit into a large tomato can.[78]

My Grandparents purchased The Place anticipating profits from the oil-rich land once Osage ownership of mineral rights expired. Prior to

4. Architecture

Historic home of the Drummond family, Hominy, Oklahoma, 2014 (courtesy Pbonchai Tallman).

1937, a large percentage of Osage land (425,000 acres) had been sold to whites. "The deeds conveying these lands contained two contradictory clauses which formed the basis for litigation resulting in an investigation by the House Committee on Indian Affairs."[79] Under one section of the Act of 1906, it could be argued that the mineral rights reverted to the Osage, as original allottees; white purchasers contended that the mineral rights belonged to them.[80] Ultimately, to the settlers' dismay, the Indian Mineral Leasing Act of 1938 granted the Osage continued control over mineral rights.[81] Negotiations at The Place, however, continued.[82] Outsiders would occasionally lease the Osage property within The Place, perhaps due to interference from the federal agency, but "[e]ventually Daddy [my Grandfather] bought the land."[83]

Entertained by hired hands around the ranch, feeding ranchers and hands alike at breakfast in the kitchen, tending hogs, being picked up on horseback by her brother, Everett Berry, Jr., at the one room schoolhouse— my mother's memories of The Place center on the modest structures that contained a vast existence and punctuated an even more vast landscape. Such was the sense of connectedness and belonging in these spaces that,

The author, near an oil well at The Place, near Hominy and Wynona, Oklahoma, 2014 (courtesy Pbonchai Tallman).

decades later, my uncle, Everett Berry, Jr., hired the Pawnee artist Brummett Echohawk to render a painting of the schoolhouse, with its wood-burning stove and chalkboard listing the names of "naughty boys," including Everett Berry. Placed on a Christmas card, the illustration accompanies Berry's words:

> 'Tis the Season to remember the dusty, muddy, or snowy trail to school; the airy relief stations 100 yards back of the school; the carrying of wood or coal to heat the school room; the teachers who inspired each student to be another George Washington... the pie and box suppers to raise money so each child could have a sack of nuts, candy and fruit; [and] the practice sessions and Christmas program[.][84]

Osage, Cherokee, Otoe, family—all attended school together, and my mother's memory of their interaction is a harmonious one. The impression of the schoolhouse is overwhelmingly positive, and related with a sense of the embodied memory discussed by Jackson—a deep, evocative, and grounding memory that brings memories of the structure to life.

Stories about my mother and father's experience, and the land and

Catherine Berry Hess in front of one-room schoolhouse, circa 1947 (courtesy Catherine Berry Hess).

spaces where they lived, merged for me as a child with a kind of inchoate longing and displacement. My identity was rooted in Pawnee, Pawhuska, and Hominy, in the structures, landscapes, and people they contain; yet I grew up far away. As a child I found, in the mother's old bedroom in Hominy, a speech she had written decades earlier scripting conversations at the Constitutional Convention; sitting on her high childhood bed, holding the brittle pages, I felt a sense of historical and political responsibility, a sense of duty in carrying her dreams and the family's history forward. The feeling of deep connection to that place of blackjack trees, curving red hills and interwoven memories of family and Osage would remain with me, albeit submerged, for fifty years. Dennis McAuliffe, who returned to his Osage family history after decades away, explains that the process of awakening to an aspect of one's identity that has been ignored or suppressed is painful:

> My life, and my mother's, are testament that you cannot ignore who you are, and that the shunned side of you will one day rise up to be recognized. The truth about oneself ... originates seemingly out of nothing, with which it crafts the material that makes it nearly indestructible; it proceeds to fill a space where, once, a void had been; the experience is excruciating.[85]

Catherine Berry Hess celebrating her third birthday at The Place, near Hominy and Wynona, Oklahoma, 1940. Blackjack trees and wind vane are visible in background (courtesy Catherine Berry Hess).

And yet, as fellow exile Roger Lloyd notes, this inevitable awakening has the component of redemption: "[A]s I looked around me at the low hills, the scrub oak trees, the sparse clutter of wooden houses, there came a sense of inevitability, of not having chosen the place but of having been chosen by it … there came, like a redemption, joyous escape to the ranch in Osage county, to the bright summer sky."[86]

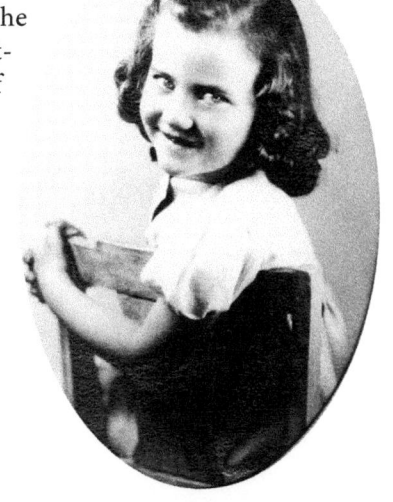

Catherine Berry Hess, age 5, studio portrait, Hominy, Oklahoma, 1942 (courtesy Catherine Berry Hess).

5

The "Invisible World": *Wa-Kon-Da*, Body Ornamentation and the Sacred Bundle

Osage art has always retained a tight connection with *Wa-kon-da* and with associated spiritual beliefs and practices.[1] The power of a zigzagging lightning flash of hematite, found placed on a bison skull in the region ten thousand years ago,[2] seems to persist, metaphorically, in what Robert Farris Thompson has described as "the flash of the spirit"[3]—the incredible persistence, resilience, adaptability, and grace of the Osage people, who, despite widespread suggestions to the contrary, continue to hold and practice traditional beliefs. This chapter will explore the central themes of this book—intersubjectivity, the daily materiality of experience, and the resonance of landscape—in the context of Osage art, specifically bodily ornamentation and representation. The chapter also focuses upon an exquisite and spiritually significant Osage object not involved in body ornamentation, but employed as one of the pivotal artistic and efficacious objects in the Osage spiritual realm.

Osage Ornamentation of the Body

Symbolic and spiritual design has existed in the region of Indian Territory/Oklahoma for thousands of years.[4] Scholars such as Garrick Bailey have explored the vast breadth of Osage art in the last several hundred years—feather fans, rattles, ribbon blankets, cloth leggings, breechcloths and skirts, headdresses, staffs, quirts, breastplates, pipes, hair ornaments, mirror boards, jewelry, cradleboards, bowls, calumets, shields, horse regalia, parfleches, drums, belts, wedding coats, dancing sticks, garters, whistles, peyote boxes and associated regalia. A narrow focus on ornamentation of the body (dismissively termed by some scholars "material culture"), including textiles and attire, can serve as a focal point/foothold in understanding the enormous breadth of art historical and theological analysis in the rich realm of Osage culture. According to some scholars, the deportment and ornamentation of the body is significant in establishing both the colonization and the free agency of the individual, and is therefore particularly worthy of analysis: as Victor Turner states, the human body is "the symbolic stage upon which the drama of socialization is enacted."[5]

In the absence of written descriptions of the body by Osage individuals, historians rely upon descriptions by Europeans and European Americans. That the individual bodies of the Osage were assessed and critiqued as a site for Euro-American colonization is evidenced by the assessment of a white traveller in 1811, who described Osage men as "objects rather disgusting; generally of a filthy greasy appearance, the greater part with old dirty buffalo robes thrown over their shoulders; some with ... brawny limbs exposed, and no covering but a piece of cloth girded around their loins. The women ... still more filthy than the men."[6] This description contrasts dramatically with the positive assessments of many European missionaries and travelers who noted their fine appearance, and the Osage practice of daily washing and perfuming with columbine seed, horse mint, and calamus root reported by Mathews.[7]

Detailed and informed descriptions of the Osage—some of which were assembled from a review of the possibly fictionalized *Memoirs of a Captivity*, and the observations of an interpreter for the Osage tribe[8]— were published in French editions of *Six Indiens Rouge de la Tribu Des Grands Osages*, or "Six Red Indians from the Tribe of the Great Osage," in 1827. According to the text, printed to accompany the exhibition of the six Osage who traveled to France, "[t]he skin of these Indians is coppery-red. The chiefs paint their chins and eyes bright vermilion and their cheeks and ears according to taste; they mark their faces with a specific sign to express mourning, peace, war, vengeance, or marriage. Their ears are split and decorated with strings of pearls, an operation performed on infants eight days after they are born. Both the men and women have white and even teeth."[9] Writer Washington Irving described the Osage in 1832 as "stately fellows" and "the finest looking Indians I have seen in the West... They have fine Roman countenances, and broad deep chests... like so many noble bronze figures."[10]

Some of the earliest images known of the Osage are those produced in conjunction with the 1827 exhibition and tour. The two earliest are images of *Ke-He-Kah Shinkah* (Little Chief) and *Mo'on-Sho'n A-ki-da Tonkah* (Big Soldier) from 1804 to 1805, produced by Charles Balthazar Julien Fevret de Saint Memin by means of a device known as the physiognotrace.[11] As the scholarship of William Least Heat-Moon and James K. Wallace reveals, the physiognotrace allowed for a "precise outline of a human profile, which then would be filled in with details and tone to create portraits that can excel in accuracy compared to other methods of rendition for that time."[12] The portraits show the confident and distinctive

Osage Chief *Shon-Ton-Ca-Be* (Black Dog) with bear medicine necklace, pierced ears, otter sash and hatchet, 1874 (Research Division of Oklahoma Historical Society).

profiles of the Osage men, their heads shaved but for a tiny strip allowing the attachment of a roach, and ears with multiple piercings and dangling shells or beads. Portraits of the six Osage by Guillaume-Francois Colson, Luther Brand and Louis-Leopold Boilly from approximately 1827 show women in high-waisted, striped dresses, with their hair parted down the middle and pulled back, wearing necklaces and multiple earrings; the men, heads shaved and with hair roaches, cloth headbands, multiple necklaces, earrings and armbands, are bare-chested and wear loincloths, drapes of fabric, and red facial paint around the eyes and chin.[13]

An 1834 watercolor by George Catlin produced of Chief Pawhuska depicts a tall and thickly muscled man with a wrapping around his waist, his hair in a distinctive braided roach, long earrings and armbands, carrying an enormous bow and quiver case.[14] A Catlin watercolor of Clermont, one of the more powerful chiefs of the Osage, reveals more elaborate attire: fringed leggings with multicolored strands, red and blue beaded moccasins, a flowing deerskin robe, red feather roach, elaborate earrings and necklaces—including what appears to be a Western medal on a blue ribbon—and a "gunstock" club fashioned in the shape of the butt end of a rifle, with a steel blade inserted into the stock, decorated with brass tacks and blue feathers.[15] That Clermont was a prominent leader is evidenced by the richness and variety of his attire, and what appears to be a relaxed and even deliberately adopted posture for the image.[16]

A French observer, Victor Tixier, reinforced many of these representations in 1844.

> The [Osage] men are tall and perfectly proportioned... [with] all the physical qualities which denote skill and strength combined with graceful movements. Their limbs are slender, lean, and wiry, without much display of muscles; their chests are expansive, their waists narrow, their necks short, their shoulders high and broad, their arms rather long, their legs lean and slender.... Their heads are ... flat. Such is the kind of beauty they are anxious to show, and, in order to obtain it, they press the heads of newly-born children against the boards which serve them as cradles[.][17]

Tixier continues with a minute description of Osage appearance, noting that "their calm, dignified faces ... [are] soldierly and serious," and that men shaved their heads except for two strands on the top that grow in a long tuft, between them two braids—what he describes as a "war headdress."[18] Documents from the 1827 exhibition and tour state that "[m]en are naked to the waist, the lower part of the body covered by a wool blanket they never take off even after their death when they are buried in this drapery. Men and women wear necklaces of shells, with a rather large shell suspended in the center. But the chief, in place of a shell, wears a silver medallion, with two bracelets of the same metal on his forearms, his head banded with multicolored silk … [their] faces [are adorned] with four colors: red, blue-green, white, and black. Their dress consists of a wool blanket draped over their shoulders in the manner of the ancient Romans; they cover their legs with large leather leggings fastened to a belt to which is also attached a strip of red cloth that hangs between their legs."[19]

The hairstyles of Osage women and children were rich signifiers—like so many other aspects of body ornamentation and art—of social standing and spiritual belief. According to the historian Willard Rollings, "[u]nmarried women wore their long hair braided and either brought it together in two rolls on each side of the head or wore it in one long braid decorated with beads, silver rings, and brightly colored ribbons. Married women simply gathered their long hair together behind the head and tied it with a leather or cloth tie."[20] The part down the middle of a woman's hair was dyed red to represent "the dawn road of Grandfather the Sun."[21] According to the *Histoire de la Tribu Des Osages*, Osage women, like men, wore "necklaces, ear pendants, medallions on the breast bone, and arm bands."[22]

Osage children wore their hair in styles affiliated with specific kinships or clans, including "shaving portions of the head and leaving tufts, notched ridges, or circles that had symbolic meanings for the clans."[23] With European colonization, and the introduction of boarding schools, children's hair was forcibly cut, and the middle of the scalp was no longer colored red, actions which had great symbolic significance. As Bill Nichols has argued, "corporeal management" such as this operated "to take over effective control of the body, to safeguard it, to regulate its activity, to oversee its movement"; for both dominant and marginalized societies, the body became "the battle site of contending values and their representation."[24]

As Catlin and Tixier attest, Osage men wore breech clouts (Tixier: "loin cloths") made of deer, elk, or buffalo hide. Later, Osage men wore trade textiles "in scarlet or blue, held by a belt adorned with beads, where they keep their knives in sheaths of painted skin, their pipe holders, tobacco pouches, bags for red paint, [and] mirrors.… Leggings and moccasins made of deerskin cover their legs and feet."[25] Women wore high moccasins and buckskin leggings, often dyed red or blue, and distinctive deerskin wrapcloths; "[o]ver the leggings women wore leather or cloth skirts or long buckskin shirts or tunics."[26] In later years buckskin was replaced by skirts made of blue or scarlet cloth: "[w]hen women cannot obtain material to make a tunic, they cover their breasts with a piece of calico, chintz, or sheeting, and, like men, wear a loin cloth to cover themselves from the hips to the back of the knees. They also have ... [robes] of buffalo or bison skin. When they are able to obtain scarlet cloth in order to make themselves a kind of pantaloons they decorate with brightly colored ribbons and sew with special stitches[.]"[27]

The extraordinary ornamentation worn or carried by the Osage is known to us by the few objects left behind, now dispersed in museums and private collections. The roach, or headdress, still worn in the *I'n-lon-shcka*, startles with a brilliant turkey feather dyed scarlet, and the underside of a white-tailed deer's tail, with exquisite colored beadwork. An eagle wing fan used by Chief *Wah-she-hah* (Star That Travels) employs "dyed red plumes ... from the underside of the golden eagle's tail ... the handle is wrapped with otter fur that is split and consecrated with paint. The wind produced by the motion of the fan re-creates the sacred breath of Wakonta."[28] The startling beauty of such objects as an early twentieth century ribbon blanket, made in black with scarlet and blue ribbons affixed, gold and white patterns representing arrows between the ribbons, and golden horses standing out against the black,[29] a twentieth century blanket in black with silk ribbon in blue, red, and green with brilliant pink silk applique hands, and a wedding coat with exquisite ribbon applique in brilliant red and blue—its style derived from U.S. military coats given to Osage men, but *too small and* adapted by women[30]—show that the distinctive and tactile attire of the Osage, characterized by vivid contrasts in color and texture, persisted through removals and enormous cultural change.

Virtually all of the symbols associated with Osage dress had spiritual significance or concrete meaning. The horse blanket, for example, used golden horses to indicate prosperity and in certain cases the literal surnames of families; "such blankets were placed on horses to be given away in gestures of gratitude and good faith."[31] The silken hands signify the support of others during the dancing of an *I'n-lon-shcka*, or, on the shirt of a man, signify severed hands, representing the conquering of enemies and therefore the high status of the man.[32] Most interesting are the tattoos once worn by Osage women, covering much of the women's bodies. These markings were more abstract than the overt symbolism of the horse or hand, and their spiritual significance deeper: the entirety of the body was a prayer for long life, and the majority of the tattoos represented the sun, stars, and elements of the sky. "The designs running from her shoulders down her arms to her wrists symbolized the 'paths of animals,' the 'path of life.' The design on the back of her hand was associated with the spider, symbolizing the earth or the snare of life."[33] My own, startling encounter with a tarantula the moment I stepped on the Tallgrass Prairie affirms the

Osage girl wearing ribbon blanket with silken hands, circa 1920–30 (National Museum of the American Indian, Smithsonian Institution, N27177).

Osage story about the spider's omnipresence. According to oral history, each Osage clan [gens] searched for a symbol of life.

> [E]ach wanted a strong, beautiful, graceful and courageous symbol, but there was one gens who was tardy in selecting a symbol.... The spider said, 'Why not take me as the symbol for your gens?'... [the leader] asked the spider, 'Why do

you think you would make a good life symbol for a gens of the great Osages?' And the spider answered, 'Where I am, I build my house and where I build my house, all things come to it.'³⁴

One of the most beautiful and striking aspects of Osage body ornamentation was the use of body paint. Tixier observed that

> The redskins [sic] seldom go out without painting themselves; the colors they use are, first, vermillion, then verdigris, and then yellow, which they buy from the trader; lacking these, they use ochre, chalk, or even mud. When their faces are covered with mud, it is a sign they are fasting or in morning. The Osage always paint red that part of their head around their hair, the eye-sockets, and their ears; these are the national colors, the war-time paint. The other colors, indifferently put on the other part of their bodies, depend upon their individual fancy.³⁵

The painting that he observed was created from "clay deposits of iron oxides (red), aluminum oxides (yellow), and copper oxides (blue and green), including vegetable dyes ... the four sacred colors were red, yellow, blue, and dark (usually black or navy)."³⁶ Ceremonies for initiation, birth, burial, war, and other significant events incorporated different patterns and colors. A series of blue and red lines on the forehead and cheeks, painted by the wives of Osage priests over the course of seven days, for example, assisted a war party in achieving victory.³⁷ The most fearsome visage, noted earlier by Custer, was a face painted black: according to Francis La Flesche, "[t]he act of putting black on the face is equivalent to the warrior taking a vow to show no mercy to his enemy."³⁸

The arrival of white settlers to the region had a profound effect on body ornamentation and attire. Beginning in the 1870s, boarding schools forced American Indian children to change their appearance in an effort to assimilate and homogenize them. One narrative from the 1920s describes a young woman returning home to the reservation "from an eastern boarding school [wearing] fashionable, 'civilized' attire: girdle, brassiere, bloomers, slip, blouse, skirt, jacket, gloves, and hat with a veil." When she found that the clothes were hot and unsuitable for housework, she "returned to the blanket," in the derogatory white phrase, borrowing cotton dresses to wear, much to the chagrin of the visiting white missionaries.³⁹ With the arrival of material prosperity, the Osage wore the fashionable attire of prosperous white society, which became their own, intermingled with traditional dress: satin dresses with black silk stockings and patent-leather heels, for example, or cotton dresses with blankets. A white observer disparagingly noted,

> One would think *une tres jolie* demoiselle of the Paris boulevards had inadvertently strayed into this little reservation town. The resemblance to type is amaz-

ing. There is the same glossy black hair, the same alluring dark eyes, the same white, colorless skin. The gown is Parisian, the hat is Parisian, the high heels are trippingly French [italics added].[40]

Ironically, while white administrators discouraged the Osage from wearing traditional clothing, adapting white attire after the Oil Boom was dismissed by them as artificial and mannered.

For Osage men of this generation the transition away from traditional attire was gradual. A family member maintains, "men wore large cowboy hats over their braids, often blankets also."[41] Yet she states, "[I] married in 1951 and I remember seeing only one Osage with braids and a blanket after that."[42] My mother recalls, "it [the transition from traditional to contemporary attire] all happened so fast."[43] In the eyes of Camelia Berry,

> Indians today are pretty inconspicuous. They have Americanized names, dress like everybody else, and without feathers and beads at a pow-wow it's difficult to recognize an Indian when you see one. But when the BERRY brothers were ranching in Indian Territory, Indians looked and dressed like Indians. They wore tribal costumes and combinations of Indian and white man's clothes.[44]

The sense that "Indians" should "look and dress like Indians" permeated not only the consciousness of certain individuals in Oklahoma, but also the American consciousness as a whole. This perception extended to the belief and federal policy maintaining that, unlike any other marginalized people, the American Indian had to prove "how Indian they were."

Settler Ornamentation and Body

The research of Linda Peavy and Ursula Smith indicates that rigid gender constructions applied to white women's clothing in the nineteenth century, as in centuries past. The Biblical passage that maintained "woman shall not wear that which pertaineth unto a man" (*Deuteronomy* 22:5) reinforced expectations that women wear long dresses and aprons—even hoop skirts—during travel and labor, while men wore more appropriate clothing, typically "heavy boots, stout trousers, woolen shirts, waterproof jackets and coats, strong leather gloves and broad-brimmed hats[.]"[45] Expectations of appropriate attire and body ornamentation among white women in Oklahoma varied according to class. One of my favorite photographs is that of a woman dressed in shirt and jacket and blooming pants tucked into work boots—and even, seemingly, a tie—flipping flapjacks with two hands and a confident smile[46]; such attire, unusual even for those in poverty, would never be seen on a woman from a prosperous background.

Photographs of my family at the turn of the century reveal an emphasis upon flounced dresses and hair bows for young girls, and even a dress with feathered collar and cuffs for boys who were toddlers, such as Fred Andrew Berry. Most surviving photographs from the turn of the century are studio portraits, and therefore atypical of daily life; a portrait of Addie Berry, for example, shows a woman poised in neck to floor dress, revealing nothing but her beautiful face and hands, her shirt buttoned tightly from neck to waist atop a flowing skirt. Her husband Andrew wears a three piece suit with pin striped pants and cravat; the tiny baby Mollie is dressed in a flounced, flowing garment. An extraordinary studio photograph of my Grandmother as a child shows her with three previous generations, each woman dressed "properly" and buttoned up to the neck.

By the turn of the century photographs of white settlers in Oklahoma, taken by family members or itinerant photographers, depict subjects casually. William Edward Berry's family, photographed in 1918, shows five girls seated on the ground on a quilt dressed in white with enormous hair ribbons; elderly men are dressed in suits, and one young man is dressed in suspenders. The outdoor portrait conveys a sense of the subjects' life: a large screened porch, farming implements, and a long row of trees is visible in the background. A casual photograph of my Grandmother at The Place reveals much different attire than in the previous century: her young face is crowned with upswept hair, she wears a loose sailor dress and button shoes, and in the background the land stretches behind her. A photograph of my Great-Grandfather shows him in a cowboy hat, suspenders and boots, deliberately feeding the chickens; and a young photograph of my Grandfather, Everett Berry, Sr., reveals a handsome young man in cap and tie, sleeves rolled up, carrying an enormous box with typical confidence. Both studio portraits and casual photographs of my mother as a child show her exquisitely dressed, although she is wearing cowboy boots; in one photograph taken at The Place with her brother, Everett Jr., she wears a beautiful dress handmade by my Grandmother Louella Berry out of paper.

A striking photograph of my ancestor Nancy Jane Berry Laughlin, from the turn of the century, reveals a seemingly odd appropriation of traditional dress and post–Revolutionary War attire. Proud of her membership in the Daughters of the American Revolution, Laughlin is dressed in the full regalia of a member: an awkwardly fitting powdered white wig and enormous gathered dress with flounced sleeves, a small cape with flounced streamers, pearls and a large broach pinned at the chest.[47] Like the Osage who integrated aspects of dress from ancestors as well as white military men and settlers, however, such attire illustrates both a pride in

Left: A young Everett Berry, Sr., working at a grocery store (courtesy Catherine Berry Hess). *Right:* Catherine Berry Hess with her brother, Everett Berry, Jr., at The Place, wearing dress made out of paper by her mother (courtesy Catherine Berry Hess).

ancestry and participation in contemporary life. For settler women particularly, ornamentation of the body signified and indicated femininity, class rank, ancestry, age and even marital status.

Industrialization and Marketing

By the early twentieth century, the advent of industrialization and mass marketing profoundly influenced both the attire and body ornamentation of white settlers, and the ideology behind cultural appropriation. Romanticized and/or homogenized descriptions of American Indian attire appear in the work of authors such as Zane Gray, in films by director John Ford, and in magazines, catalogues and advertisements.[48] A conflation of industrialization, advertising, and the intersection of cultures, for example, appears in a 1915 catalogue for Pendleton blankets directed at affluent white women.[49] Pendleton blankets were widely employed at that time, sold by the Drummonds in Hominy, and popular among the Osage: at the contemporary *I'n-lon-shcka* and other ceremonies, piles of brilliantly colored Pendleton blankets are given as an acknowledgement of service and achievement. In a 1915 catalogue, an illustration of a white woman surrounded by all of the comforts of home, including a Pendleton blanket on her couch, shows her wearing a shirt buttoned to the neck, reading a book, and, ironically, seated beneath a copy of the iconic symbol of Western civilization, the Victory of Samothrace. The Pendleton advertisement announces, "One of the Comforts of Home/Showing Decorative Uses of Pendleton Indian Robes."[50]

In contrast to this vision of European modesty, prurience and "civilization," (again, ironically represented by the half-naked "Victory,") the Pendleton advertisements employed illustrations of American Indian women depicted in the absence of backdrop or context. One illustration contains a colorized photograph of an American Indian woman wrapped in Pendleton robes, posed against a blank backdrop, appearing self-conscious and disconcerted; she is stripped almost to the waist with her breastfeeding child under the words "Pendleton Indian Robes: Pure Fleece Wool."[51] Another image of a woman seemingly posing as Native American shows her scantily dressed, with a Pendleton blanket slipping away from her breasts, as she holds one arm wantonly above her head, accompanied by the words, "Sacajawea: 'The Bird Woman.'"[52]

Although American Indian women would never appear in public in such attitudes, it seems critical to the construction of white femininity that women appear delicately seated, dressed from head to toe, engaged in intellectual activity, and surrounded by an environment of soft chairs, rugs, curtains, and a table with bases and flowers, while American Indian women by contrast made to appear partially naked, eroticized, and posed against blank backdrops—the blankness perhaps signifying the absence of intellectual pursuit or moral "restraint," the lack of a refined sense of the aesthetic, the absence of property—in sum, the absence of "civilization."[53] Ironically, however, the more American Indian people were "controlled" and integrated into the white economic system, the more a white population sought to emulate and incorporate aspects of American Indian life—in Pendleton blankets but also decorative motifs more broadly, in "squaw dresses" which represented "idealized femininity and American-ness because of their Native American origins,"[54] and in advertising for a range of commercial products.

The Sacred Bundle

In contrast to the elaborate nature of most body ornamentation, a virtually forgotten object stands as the central medicine object once employed by the Osage people. Abandoned by the Osage a century ago,[55] to the eye a mere bundle of textile and detritus, the *wa-xo-be* or sacred (hawk) bundle is perhaps the most captivating of the ceremonial objects the Osage once employed, in part due to the rich symbolic life, now past, to which it alludes. Unlike brilliantly dyed feathers, blankets, beaded clothing, blankets, and shields, the hawk *wa-xo-be* are pedestrian in appearance, although they once were the most potent of all sacred objects; Lloyd observes, "these are now drab objects, stiff, dark and dry, from which all sanctity has long since flown. They are like dusty relics in a cathedral vault; say, the shin bone of some forgotten saint."[56]

There is a great deal, however, that can be contained and revealed in such a relic. Is the power of such objects truly gone? What of their sacred nature persists? The vast majority of the Osage turned to the Native American Church at the turn of the century, a faith which demanded "total abandonment of traditional Osage religious beliefs and practices"[57]; most of the sacred objects of the original belief system were destroyed, and elders refused to discuss the faith, even with their children.[58] Yet, much as a sense of "aura" is perceived in art objects of Western origin, so too the energy and intention invested in Osage objects, including *wa-xo-be*, can be perceived as embodying spirit and the sacred, regardless of beliefs that have faded or been imposed. Prior to the arrival of Quanah Parker, virtually every aspect of material culture was invested with sacred intent: "[e]verything that existed in the universe was an expression of an all-controlling invisible force, called Wakonta; therefore everything was sacred."[59]

Suzanne Blier's scholarship on *bochio*, small, wrapped sculptures employed by individuals in Dahomey (present-day Benin) as empower-

Wrapped hawk *wa-xo-be*. Inside is a hawk head stuffed with human hair and associated sacred objects (courtesy National Anthropological Archives/Smithsonian Institution).

ment objects and "mechanisms" of psychotherapeutic practice, suggests that what appears dark, drab and even "strange and destabilizing" can be of pivotal importance to a people's culture and art.[60] The hawk *wa-xo-be*, like the *bochio* and other sacred art objects, is difficult to access and, as Blier states of the *bochio*, "clearly not an object of sublime beauty ... in their variated massing on the surface they emanate qualities of tension, anxiety and danger."[61] Yet Western perceptions of these sacred bundles neither determine their status as works of art, nor do these perceptions affect their importance, power/efficacy, and resonance for the Osage.

Traditionally, the Osage believed that the universe consisted of two inseparable realms: "[o]ne realm was the visible world, the world of the living, in which all things took a physical form, breathed and moved. The other realm was the invisible world, which was the spiritual world of W-ako-nda."[62] The two divisions of the cosmos—the sky and the earth, *Tzi-sho* and *Hunka*—were symbolized in clans, nine associated with the sky and fifteen with the earth; each clan was divided into sub-clans that possessed distinct names and symbolic totems.[63] Ceremonies that "solicited the approval and support of Wa-kon-da" accompanied important events, and included "the recitation of specific clan *wi-gi-e* [lengthy ritual prayers] and the ritual manipulation of sacred symbolic objects," including those contained in the sacred bundle.

In a text heralded by Sylvester Tinker, the former Chief of the Osage Nation, the hawk *wa-xo-be* is described in the context of these extended ceremonies. According to this text, the hawk served as a symbol of the tribe, selected by a council of seers (the "Little Old Men") because the bird was seen as courageous, swift, silent and clean, symbolizing "the courage and combative nature of the warrior"[64]; the bundle was seen as a shrine to depict the courage of warriors. Tobacco played a role in ceremonies involving the hawk *wa-xo-be*, smoked with the *wi-gi-e* that accompanied sacred gatherings.[65]

> The contents of the wa-xo-be varied according to clan and totem, but all contained a stuffed hawkskin symbolizing thunder, war, night, and courage. The hawkskin, along with other ceremonial symbols such as scalps, miniature pipes, or other such paraphernalia, were enclosed in a deerskin pouch, then placed in a woven rush pouch, and finally put, tightly wrapped, within another pouch of woven buffalo hair.... Osage wa-xo-be contained the religious artifacts of a hunting people: miniature weapons, pipes, scalps, and other hunting symbols. Despite the agricultural elements of some Osage rituals, surviving bundles contain no agricultural goods [whatsoever].[66]

The central hawkskin was stuffed with human hair. Among the various objects that might accompany it were "a dark human scalp, an eagle's claw and what looked like a scrap of dessicated skin[.]"⁶⁷ The stuffed hawk itself "was sewn in leather with the throat painted red and the rest of the body green and blue. It wore a collar made from a stag's tail, and to the lower part of the bird some pieces of human scalp were attached."⁶⁸

The *wa-xo-be* was manipulated in an intricate variety of ways according to the occasion. The hawk *wa-xo-be* was central in the decision to go to war: after a leader fasted and prayed for seven days, the *wa-xo-be* was dropped upon the ground; if it fell facing the west, the decision to go to war was confirmed.⁶⁹ After return from a war, the *wa-xo-be* was "unwrapped and placed on the ground."⁷⁰ Osage warriors who had demonstrated bravery dropped sticks on the hawk and recited their achievements, and if "[u]ncontested, they became o-don, valued sources of pride and status."⁷¹ Accounts of these objects differ, however. Bailey describes the *wa-xo-be*, handled by a "Great Bundle Priest," as containing "a cormorant skin, a pelican skin, eight tattooing instruments, ten to twelve scalp locks, seven weasel skins, and half a mussel shell, among other items."⁷²

The mention of the "Great Bundle Priest" in this context is noteworthy, as the function of the priest, or Medicine Man, is little discussed in accounts of the Osage. Texts from the nineteenth century offer few insights other than mention of the role of Medicine Men (derogatorily referred to as "jugglers") in addressing serious illnesses, serving as consultants in public affairs, predicting the outcome of war, and presiding over ceremony.⁷³ According to Lloyd, prior to the late nineteenth century, each Osage village had *ga-hi-ge*, or leaders, from the Sky and Earth peoples, who were separate from the paramount chief: "[u]nlike the clan priests who acted for the whole tribe and had ultimate authority in all spiritual matters and decisions of war and peace, the ga-hi-ge dealt only with the affairs of daily life ... they were believed to have special powers to heal the sick," and also had the authority of adjudicators and enforcers of legal sanction, and leaders of the hunt.⁷⁴

Francis La Flesche was one of the few historians with the insight and linguistic ability to record initiation and public rituals among the twenty-four clan priesthoods which existed among the Osage—each with its own seven degrees of ritual knowledge, and three tribal priesthoods—but by the time of his arrival, much of the knowledge of the Medicine Men had been irretrievably lost.⁷⁵ La Flesche's research, masterfully organized and published by Bailey, provides a sense of the organization of the priests, who "met almost every morning, sometimes officially but more often in an informal way,"⁷⁶ and their supervision of elaborate and extensive rituals that touched all aspects of Osage life. The "Little Old Men" were custodians of the *wa-xo-be*, which included peace pipes, great bundles, medicine bundles, and the hawk bundles here described. La Flesche's record of these objects is tantalizing: each object, arrangement, color, design, placement, color, knot, and fold represent aspects of the Osage cosmogony, all corresponding to songs and rituals enacted for practical and efficacious purposes. The art, dress, motions, arrangements of persons and objects, musical address, and recitations accompanying the appearance of the *wa-xo-be* hint at the dazzlingly complex relationship among material objects, religious practices, and Osage cosmogony.[77]

Many details about the hawk *wa-xo-be* remain unknown. We do not know the complete range of components they once held, the significance of some of the items included, the prayers used when the sacred bundles were assembled and disassembled. The Pawnee, who live nearby, have a similar tradition of sacred bundles, each for various clans, hung in a place of honor opposite the entrance to their homes constructed of earth[78]; very little is known, however, about the wider use of these sacred bundles, in particular those employed by Medicine Men, who were responsible for healings, psychological and spiritual interventions, and social guidance. None of the medicine bundles were in existence in the early twentieth century, and the Osage at that time could recall seeing only one.[79] As Blier indicates of the *bochio*, "these forms remain in many respects unknowable, resistant to interpretation ... the works themselves are not meant ever to be 'understood' in a standard sense, but instead remain enigmatic and obscure[,]"[80] to a large degree because their powerful and even dangerous content was even during their use known only by select priests or Medicine Men.[81]

By the 1910s the centuries-old Osage religion had virtually disappeared. "The clan and tribal sacred bundles were sold, buried, [burned,] or otherwise disposed of."[82] Garrick Bailey argues that with the passing of Osage religion, "all the ceremonies, rituals, and other activities that had been associated with it were also gone.... The production and use of other traditional ritual items—war standards, rattles, sacred mat cases, and buffalo-hair bags—disappeared," along with practices such as face and body painting and tattoos.[83] Belief systems shifted to the Native American Church, Catholicism, and other Christian religions, and, as previously mentioned, traditional architectural structures were abandoned.

What is tantalizing in the old descriptions of Osage belief, however, are the allowances made for phenomena for which even the clan priests had no explanation. As Bailey indicates, some Osage men and women believed they had the ability to foretell the future, change themselves into animals, and use supernatural power to harm others; some Osage believed in miniature people, ghosts, prophets, and other forces not accommodated within the traditional belief structure.

> The Osage religion did not consist of a single, unified, integrated set of beliefs and practices relative to the supernatural ... world, [which] was infinitely complex.... To the Osage priests, these inexplicable supernatural phenomena could exist without threatening their authority and at times could even prove beneficial to the people.[84]

Such an expansive perspective suggests that the adoption of Christianity among the present-day Osage may not preclude a continued undercurrent of meaning in the fragments of song which survive in the *I'n-lon-schka*, and in convictions—both those which are articulated, and those solely embedded in practice—which survive.

6

Turning the Century: The Land Run and the "Civilization" of the Osage

"Who is this white man to say how this money should be paid? We do not want rations. We are not dogs that we should be treated like dogs.... You tell your people that Osages are tired of this thing; tell them Osages will not be fed like dogs. Tell them that Osages are not many but they know how to die."—*John Joseph Mathews, "Wah'kon-tah"*[1]

In 1893, after prohibiting the Cherokee from leasing their land for cattle grazing, the federal government purchased the value-depleted land and opened it for a massive land "Run" or "Rush." This chapter relates the stories of those who made the Land Run, and the experiences of the Osage who survived the oppressive consequences of President Grant's "Peace Policy." These stories capture, in a way no other words could, embodied experience; they convey, in Paul Stoller's terms, the "pungent odors of social life ... [and] the sensuous shapes and colors that fill windows of consciousness."[2] To these extensive and evocative narratives I add the experiences of my Great-Great-Grandfather George Madison Berry. Berry's life—his involvement in trade, banking, and other commercial enterprises with the Pawnee and Osage, and his close involvement in the political formation of the state—constitutes a bridge between markedly different human perspectives at the turn of the century.

The Land Run

In 1835, in the "Trail of Tears," the federal government removed the Cherokee from their homes east of the Mississippi, but guaranteed them "a perpetual outlet to the west lying between the northern border of the Creek Nation and the southern border of what became Kansas[.]" In 1890, after an unsuccessful effort to negotiate grazing leases with the Cherokee Outlet in Pawnee County, near the Osage, the federal government prohibited the introduction of additional cattle into the Outlet and called for the removal of all cattle by a future date, making the land worthless to the Cherokee. In 1893, the Cherokee therefore sold the land to the government for far less than was offered prior to the prohibition of leases.

A condition of the subsequent Land Run was that ranchers who were in the region previous to the run were precluded from filing for homesteads, a provision that had, for the Berry Brothers and the Cherokee who leased to them alike, devastating consequences. A number of claims were made by "Sooners" familiar with the land who entered the Territory prior to the official "opening," although those who previously leased land from the Cherokee were excluded. The Cherokee themselves were informed in an 1891 decision that, contrary to the explicit language of six treaties in the previous century, the land was not theirs and they were entitled only to walk across it.[3] As Camelia Berry noted, her embrace of gender constructions in the era evident, "it must have been an incredible shock to all cattlemen[,] especially since they seemed to be the only ones not allowed to participate. It's hard to imagine the helpless fury of dynamic, tough, capable men, as they saw all they'd struggled for slipping away."[4]

After the loss of the Berry Brothers Ranch, partially located in the newly acquired Cherokee "Outlet," the Berrys participated in the Land

Oklahoma land run, April 22, 1889.

6. Turning the Century

Run. William Berry, Thomas and his sister Jennie, and Isaac "King" Berry rushed across the line in an attempt to regain their land. Stories of the run are worth citing at length, as they render the adventures of the young men who registered in vivid and immediate terms:

> We got the news in the Kansas City Star and the following morning the "Opening" was the chief topic of discussion around the breakfast table. I had just turned twenty-one and the thought of making the run took possession of my thoughts[,] for I was confident that adventure and fortune awaited me in this great stretch of unclaimed frontier ... [the] morning after our arrival, those of us who were going to make the run were issued a number, which we pinned on our coats. It took us two days to register and it was a hot wearisome task standing in line hour after hour in all the excitement and confusion ... it was next to impossible to manage the milling mob. The unbridled hysteria of the uproarious throng was uncontrollable and there was considerable gambling for such a scene presented a playground for the unscrupulous artists of the "shell game," galloping dominoes, and "bottom of the deck dealing."... [T]he morning of the 16th, [a] seething mass of 30,000 persons boiled like a huge caldron in the dust-choked, sun-beaten air. The excitement and tension were terrific. Two hundred feet back from the border the great line was formed. Men and women from every walk in life—in buggies, buckboards, wagons, on horse back, and men on foot fretfully waited for high noon and the signal to dash over the border to new lands and new hopes. At the stroke of twelve o'clock noon, a hundred United States carbines cracked sharply in the hot dry air, and all the pent up exultation was released from 30,000 dry, dust-clogged throats in a chorus of spine-tingling yells as the great seething mass dashed over the border like a huge cloud of wind-whipped smoke.[5]

This experience was replicated for many Berry family members who failed individually to stake a claim, but found other members who had and joined them, a solidarity characteristic of the family:

> Where my cousin was, with the chuck wagon, no one knew, and we were hungry and tired with no prospects of food or a place to rest save on our saddle blankets under the stars. The following morning was spent locating the chuck wagon and breakfast. After getting together we all felt better and set to work showing signs of proving up on the claim my brother had stuck. We felled several trees and cut logs for the foundation of the cabin. The shack, and that was all it was, when completed, was 12 × 14 feet and served us as a home for one and a half years. Our only companion while living on the claim was our English bulldog, Mike, who shared in our ups and downs and did his best to look after our safety.[6]

Mullendore describes the work that followed staking a claim.

> After the shack was completed, it had to be furnished. The furnishings were meager, to say the least. There was a small sheet iron camp stove that we set up on top of a big, strong goods box. The goods box served as a cupboard, pantry, and general storage closet. At the opposite end of the small room, we

built an oat bin and on top of this we made a bed. A straw ticking, and not too thick at that, had to serve us without benefit of springs. When this work was finished there came the heavy task of breaking the sod, building a barn for our horses, and all the other general farm work that we wanted completed before cold weather set in. The fall weather was mild and very dry. We took some time off occasionally, to visit around through the community and attended hearings in connection with disputes on claims. Spring finally came and the crops were planted, but drought continued; it seemed as though it just couldn't rain. Our crops withered and failed. We didn't raise a thing, which was very discouraging for we were only youngsters away from home and battling a wilderness.[7]

As a consequence of the Land Run, the entirety of the old Berry Brothers Ranch was lost. For many years, the homesteads, struggling to thrive, were the only evidence of what had once been a powerful settler presence of my family in the state; a few large tracts, including that purchased by my Grandfather Everett Berry near Wynona and Hominy, remained. Mullendore's testimony suggests that initial efforts at homesteading were devastatingly difficult, confirming suspicion about the arability of the land. The hours standing in line, the milling and increasingly agitated mob, the mass of dust-covered horses, the yelling at the crack of the carbines, the frantic race followed by exhaustion, disappointment, recuperation, and then the hard labor and recounting of everyday life—each detail makes the race and settlement seem a violent takeover of American Indian land, but also an effort of the settlers to survive.

"Peace Policy," Surveillance and Re-Education

At the same moment that claims by the Berrys and other homesteaders struggled and homes were established, the Osage endured a terrible period of oppression and starvation. As discussed in Chapter 1, the federal agenda of categorization, homogenization, and spatial planning had a specific objective: to eliminate American Indian nations as culturally distinct entities. When the Osage arrived in the region that would be Oklahoma, President Grant's "Peace Policy" established a rigid agenda of surveillance, discipline and cultural re-education, much like the rigid agenda of the Land Ordinance of 1785: "The communal ownership of land, the customs of hospitality, the dancing and feasting, all of these encouraged idleness and retarded advancement to civilized status and must be suppressed.... [The federal] policy had as its object not just control of the Indians by confining them to reservations, but turning the reservations into schools[.]"[8]

Osage who declined to "subscribe to the American orthodoxies of

Young Osage warriors, "Members of the Beaver Band," circa 1890–1906, with hair roaches, armbands, and other adornments (numbers written or original photograph; Research Division of Oklahoma Historical Society).

property and propriety," including the orderly structuring of land for agriculture and Western education, were subjected to the reduction of rations and other penalties, although the money for rations they sought was, in fact, merely the interest from their own "protected" money. The challenge to the Osage of alcohol is suggested by arrests for taking intoxicating liquor into "Indian country," an offense called "Introducing."[9] Alcohol, sold by "vagabond white people," "gamblers or whiskey peddlers," had a devastating impact on the Osage prior to the introduction of the Native American Church, whose adherents did not drink.[10] Missionaries—first Catholic, then Protestant, then Jesuit and Quaker—supported federal officials in attempting to displace traditional spiritual practices of the Osage, already weakened through a collapse in population, the loss of sacred property, and the killing of buffalo that sustained ceremony and spiritual leadership.

The purpose of federal policy related to American Indians was in large measure to break down the American Indians' culture and political structures. In Lloyd's phrase, the Indian was to be "crushed and reconstructed."[11] Courts of Indian Offenses were established to enforce federal regulations banning "dancing, traditional religion, gift giving, and other customs."[12] The Supreme Court held in *Lone Wolf v. Hitchcock* and *Cherokee Nation v. Georgia* that such regulations could not be challenged: ("[t]ribes, as domestic dependent nations, lacked standing to sue in federal court on their own behalf").[13] Prior to 1871, Congress entered treaties with American Indians as foreign, quasi-sovereign entities. After virtually all of the Indians' land was taken, the Supreme Court "dramatically expanded congressional authority over Indians, empowering it to pursue the central goals of the era: the dissolution of tribal governments, the involuntary assimilation of Native Americans into the dominant culture, and the allotment and acquisition of communally owned land."[14]

"Reconstructing" the Osage included forcing Osage children to attend boarding school in Pawhuska. If they did not attend, the entire family was denied food.[15] Students were beaten if they did not wear regulation attire, or if they spoke their own language; many tried to flee, and were brought back forcibly. A tiny set of handcuffs used for this purpose was recently discovered in Kansas.[16] Such shocking intervention in indigenous affairs was made lawful by the Major Crimes Act of 1885, which deeply inserted federal authority and legal norms into American Indian society.[17] The Supreme Court affirmed the legality of this intervention in *United States v. Kagama*, holding that Congress had an "incontrovertible right" to exercise authority over Indians, exactly because the government had destroyed them: "[t]he power of the General Government over these remnants of a race once powerful, now weak and diminished in numbers, is necessary to their protection, as well as to the safety of those among whom they dwell."[18] The policy of forcible education, astonishingly, was not officially renounced until the Indian Child Welfare Act of 1978.[19]

Two Catholic educational institutions were established for Osage children in 1887: St. Louis School for Girls at Pawhuska, and St. John's

School for Boys at Gray Horse. Other children attended the Osage Manual Labor School in St. Paul, Kansas, the Haskell Institute in Lawrence, Kansas, the Carlisle Indian School in Pennsylvania, and the Hampton Institute in Virginia.[20] Mathews relates,

> children [were] taught chiefly manual labor skills, forced to wear uncomfortable "citizen's clothes," [and] beaten if they spoke their own languages.... For Osage children, used to the warm family embrace and simple conditions of their life, it must have been a horror.... The Osage police brought [those who tried to run away] back tied to the police wagon, their arms bound behind their backs. On reaching the school some of the children would break away and run. The police on their horses chased the escaping children, lassoed them and dragged them up the dusty hill to the school building."[21]

In Mathews' fictionalized version of forcible education, the Indian Agent "always felt a pang when he saw those brown faces at the windows of the buildings at Carlisle and Haskell, and he realized that for some of them this was the greatest tragedy of their lives.... He wouldn't let himself think of these austere buildings as prisons[,] though they actually imprisoned

Osage girls at boarding school, in neck to ankle school uniforms, 1879. Photographer: John N. Choate of Carlisle, Pennsylvania (courtesy National Anthropological Archives, Smithsonian Institution).

Osage girls and young women at boarding school in school uniforms (courtesy National Anthropological Archives, Smithsonian Institution).

many sensitive spirits, and spiritual imprisonment was more tragic to the Indian than physical suffering."[22] Predictably, the white settlers' perspective differed: the *Arkansas City Traveler* reported in 1877 that the one hundred and fourteen students at the Osage Indian School were "pleasant, obedient and attentive, readily adapting themselves to the customs of and learning the language of whites."[23]

Despite this forcible acculturation, the Osage continued to turn every occasion for gathering rations or otherwise adhering to protocol into opportunities for communal sharing and ceremony. When the Osage began to receive cash annuities instead of rations, for example, the distribution was turned into a ceremony: as names were called by the Osage Crier, *Ho-Lah-Gany*, or Splendid Voice, individual families solemnly collected their rations. Osage author Joseph Mathews recalls this process with loving attention:

> With their horses and dogs they set up camp along the Bird Creek bottom or on the agency hill. Sometimes they remained for several weeks. Racks of jerked meat stood outside their hump-backed lodges. There would be feasting, smoking and talk. Drum-beats sounded from the camps and there would be dancing. There would be horse races, with prizes of ponies and fine blankets, the Osage punters urging on their favorites by waving their blankets and emitting war whoops and animal calls.... The men were silent in their buckskin leggings and moccasins, wrapped to the eyes in colored blankets, eagle feather fans slowly wafting the air from their faces. Under the roached heads, the beaver bandeaux, the slowly spinning scalp feather, observant eyes would examine the trader's goods ... long conversations would take place with the telling of tales accompanied by eloquent hand movements. At the end of a recital well told the audience would make the low sounds signifying appreciation.[24]

As in Mullendore's description of the Land Rush, Mathews' vision of the Osage gathering is so vivid that one can almost smell the sweating, moving animals and drifting smoke, feel the leather leggings, brilliant blankets, feather fans, soft fur hats and prickly, black and red roach feathers, and hear the sharp shouts and low-pitched murmuring, as well as the relentless pounding of drumming and the piercing yells that accompanied the gathering.

From the perspective of many Osage, the Land Rush brought interlopers and undesirables. While their land was not directly in danger with the opening of the Cherokee Strip in 1893, some settlers attempted to encroach upon Osage country, and some Osage witnessed the crush of arrivals with dismay:

> Covered wagons and buggies with dirty faced children peer[ed] out from the curtains, and weary, hard-faced women loll[ed] in the seat beside evil-eyed, bearded men. There were wagons with cows and mules led behind and chicken coops tied to the side; all descriptions of vehicles, some on three wheels and a pole dragging in the dust for the fourth[.][25]

A sympathetic Osage Bureau of Indian Affairs agent, Laban Miles, stated, "The presence of numerous vagabond white people on the reservation is a detriment to the welfare of the Indian. Many of them prove to be gamblers or whiskey-peddlers, who succeed in evading the officers until an opportunity offers itself for them to steal a horse or rob an Indian[.]"[26]

With the Organic Enabling Act of 1890, the federal government made the Osage Reservation a part of the Oklahoma Territory; in 1906, it was made a semiautonomous district. After Oklahoma became a state in 1907, the Reservation was designated Osage County, and Pawhuska was designated the county seat. With the solidification of each tribe's status, some tribes were able to come together in active resistance to white opportunism: in 1912 two members of tribes in the region—Redbird Smith (Cherokee) and Chitto Harjo (Creek)—established the Four Mothers Society, "a community-centered political and religious movement in northeastern Oklahoma that resisted allotment, preserved sacred practices, and reasserted indigenous notions of peoplehood."[27]

George Madison Berry

In bridging these markedly different human perspectives and experiences at the turn of the century in Osage land/Indian Territory—in attempting to move holistically from one vision of history to another, that is, to construct a sense of simultaneous experience—this section discusses the experience of my Great-Great-Grandfather, George Madison Berry. Berry was a rancher, banker, and politician, one of the original framers of the Oklahoma constitution; he stands as an archetype, although he was a profound original. Although no historical record exists of how Berry's friendship with the Osage and Pawnee was reciprocated, an unattributed publication reports that, at the same time, "[t]hrough his wide acquaintance with the Indians of the early territorial days Berry is looked upon today as one of the few remaining men who can speak authoritatively and from first-hand experience of many old Indian customs."[28]

An account from the American Historical Society states that after helping with the Pawnee Indian Agency in 1879, Berry "was also in the service of the United States Government engaged to teach the Indians how to break the prairie sod and raise crops."[29]

> By repute, Berry is the "daddy" of banking business in Pawnee County. Stories are told of his first banking ventures. He and his brothers loaned money to the Indians when funds ran low just before an allotment was paid by the government. When the Indians were paid, the two men spread a blanket near the cashier's window and designated by sign language just how much each Indian owed them. At one time, 1800 silver dollars were thrown into the blanket. The money proved to be a burden when it had to be transported to a bank in Arkansas City in a grain sack.[30]

In an unnamed newspaper article, George Madison Berry is attributed with writing a short history of American Indian cuisine. According to Berry, for example, "[i]n planting the corn the red man 'farmed' with the shoulder blade of a buffalo tightly fastened to a stick like a hoe handle"; grain scraped from the husk and roasted was stored in "a cistern-shaped cavity some eight feet deep dug in the bank of a stream … grass was placed on the bottom of the pit and raw hides stretched over the sides," and covered with shells.[31] Berry also observed Pawnee ponies dragging poles with rawhide hammocks, in which children accompanying hunting parties could ride.[32]

My Great-Great-Grandfather George Berry took a special interest in the affairs of the local Osage and Pawnee. Whether apochryphal or observed, the previously mentioned accounts suggest a close association or relationship between Berry and the local American Indian population, along with his many other business and political adventures. While Berry certainly had financial reasons to develop a close relationship with the Pawnee and Osage, one senses more in the many accounts of his interactions with American Indians in eastern Oklahoma. An oft-repeated family anecdote captures Berry's relationship with the Pawnee and Osage people:

> George M. Berry spoke the Indian languages and was well acquainted with the Indians and their customs … fancy clothes weren't a priority. People living in dugouts and log cabins don't worry about the press of their pants or the shape of their lapels. As these men grew older, they didn't get any fancier. One day when George was an old man, president of the bank, active in ranching and in state politics, with the biggest, most beautiful house in town, he went into the local Ice Cream Emporium in his town of Pawnee. As he was eating his ice cream, he heard a group of Indian school girls laughing and giggling over his funny clothes. They never dreamed he understood what they were saying. As he left, he stopped by their table and in their language, gently reprimanded them for their lack of respect for age and for their assumption that appearance is everything, and walked out leaving the girls satisfyingly embarrassed and amazed.[33]

Another version, which sounds more like the family, has Berry telling the girls in their own language what pretty girls they were, and how nicely dressed.[34]

Evidence for the relationship between George Madison and the American Indian peoples whose reservations overlapped Osage County is one-sided. We cannot know for sure how such interactions were received, or to what degree my Great-Great-Grandfather participated in the dynamic between the cultures as the century turned; there is no record of Berry intervening in the treatment of Native Americans, or advocating for their inclusion. Yet the constant overlapping of his story with American

Indian experiences suggests a unique interest, perhaps even rapport, and in maintaining a commercial relationship and respectful posture toward the Pawnee and Osage, his engagement was modeled for the family. My Uncle Everett, Jr., George Madison Berry's grandson, worked assiduously to keep American Indian culture in the forefront of community awareness—serving on the Board of Directors for the Gilcrease Museum, and attempting to organize a museum for the Pawnee—as a prominent figure in Pawnee until his death in 1998.

Although the Berry Brothers Ranch was lost at the conclusion of the Land Run, my Great-Grandfather George Madison Berry easily made the transition from trader to rancher to banker. Berry had oil holdings in Pawnee County, and after moving his family to Cushing, Berry became the Mayor of Pawnee for two terms, a member of the City Council, for many years a treasurer of the school board, and ultimately principal stockholder for the bank, in addition to being a father to his nine children.[35] The story is told of how he contracted to buy property for the First National Bank of Pawnee; when it was discovered that the lot he had purchased overlapped additional property, Berry threw in a saddle pony to purchase the two lots.[36]

During statehood Berry was state committeeman from Pawnee County, a delegate to a number of state conventions, and secretary of the county election board.[37] He ran the ranch my family termed "the Place," and was overwhelmingly elected to be a delegate to the Oklahoma Constitutional Convention.[38] A newspaper article from 1906 stated that his Democratic platform

> should be read by every voter in the county. It is a clear and ringing exposition of what the democratic candidate ... stands for. It is positive and aggressive, and truly in the interest of the people, and George M. Berry stands on it with both feet, and pledges to make every effort to carry it into effect. And every one who knows George M. Berry knows he will do it.[39]

George's brother Isaac was correct in offering to help with the election, but predicting that he would "have a walk off with it[.]"[40] As one constituent stated, "Accept my heartiest congratulations for the splendid victory you have won. It was a grand triumph for the principles of right, and assures a Constitution which will perpetuate for many years Democratic control, and jealously safeguard the rights of the common people."[41] Berry was an advocate of women's suffrage, and it may have been this issue an attorney in Ohio praised him for:

> The early returns ... warrant me in congratulating your state committee for the splendid work you did in the late campaign. Your five congressmen and your seven electoral votes in the next presidential election made this a national

issue with the states and federal government, and your economic questions in the constitution interest thousands of laboring men and investigators that you have not realized, and will be a great boon for your new state.⁴²

Berry did not achieve every political objective. "It is understood that the Woman's Suffrage lobbyists are disappointed because George M. Berry, of Pawnee, did not get a prominent place on the suffrage committee. He was the only delegate to the convention who was elected on a woman's suffrage platform."⁴³

Other issues were contested as well: "Delegate Berry, of Pawnee, might make himself everlastingly solid by getting Audrey township from Noble and the two northeastern townships ... attached to Pawnee. That would square up the southwest corner of this county just about as it ought to be."⁴⁴ In addition, Berry's "liberal" tendencies were sometimes criticized: "G.M. Berry, our delegate in the constitutional convention, is home for the holidays, and the chances are that Pawnee county will be against the adoption of the constitution unless a conservative and more desirable document is presented than is at the present time even hoped for."⁴⁵

George Madison Berry, from Camelia Uzzell Berry's *Oklahoma Prairie Plowed Under: The Story of Berry Bros. in Indian Territory* (courtesy Catherine Berry Hess).

A letter from one constituent suggests the array of competing demands faced by Berry in negotiating issues in committee.

> Dear Sir: Having the utmost confidence in your firmness and your desire to fairly represent your people and that you would gladly give your voice to the furtherance of their wishes, I beg the privilege of saying that I believe I come as near knowing what the people of Pawnee Co. want along one line as any one in the county and that is ... statewide *Prohibition* of the *liquor* profit. And if this convention will give us this you will have an army of grateful fathers and mothers who will stand by you.... We know the convention is looking after our money interests but friend[,] there is something dearer to us than money ... with vice-debauchery—and crime legalized, guilded, patronized—so much that should go for the comforts of the family is washed down the gutters—along with our boys and girls. Oh friend! If you ever expect to befriend a longing anxious people—do it now"[spelling corrected].⁴⁶

While Berry did not agree with the Governor of the State in every issue, Berry's achievements were widely recognized, as his biographies and eulogies later attest. The Cushing Daily Citizen described him as "a hale and hearty fellow"[47]; one account shared that "it is evidence of his popularity and ability, as well as the value of his public service, that he has never been defeated for any office for which he has been a candidate.... In public life, as well as business and private affairs, he has a large circle of friends and men place implicit trust in his integrity as well as abilities."[48] Berry was known for loaning money to local residents when he knew there was little chance of repayment, particularly during the Depression.[49] His appeal is illustrated by my mother's recollection: Will Rogers came to have coffee with George Madison Berry, but although all of the children hung on the bannister to hear Rogers' stories, my Great-Great-Grandfather talked the entire time.[50]

As with so many other family members, Berry loved above all things his ranch, which bordered on the property of Pawnee Bill, and the activities that accompanied tending the land. Berry regarded his nine years on the ranch in the pre–Rush years as the most interesting of his life.[51] Among his favorite stories was hiring a cattle hand "who had no sense of direction and so was of little use"; Berry finally gave him a job as ranch cook. "During leisure moments the erstwhile cook wrote poetry of a sort. Among his poems was one later published as a song and familiar to residents of the southwest as the classic 'O Bury Me Not on the Lone Prairie.' Another ranch hand whom Berry characterized as 'too lazy to work and no good as a hand'"[52] would later become the well-known writer O. Henry. The *Cushing Daily Citizen*, which along with other newspapers reported many of the activities of George Madison Berry, Erd and E.C. Mullendore, tells the story of how "his heart's desire in recent years has been a good riding horse"[53]: Berry visited his nephew and namesake, George Laughlin, and admired a fine saddle horse. When Berry asked the price of the horse, his nephew stated that it was "the present I've always meant to give you"; Berry "was so delighted that he was only prevented from riding it back to Pawnee by his wife's refusal to drive the car."[54]

George Madison Berry's desk, which he used at the Constitutional Convention, made its way to my Uncle Everett Berry's home office, and many nights as a child I crept in to sit at the desk and gaze at the framed portrait of the Oklahoma Constitutional Convention. Surrounding the desk were objects of American Indian origin, including objects from the Osage; dominating the room was a mural painted by my father of the state of Oklahoma, complete with careful renderings of Native Americans. I dreamed then of making significant contributions and carrying forward the Berry family legacy; I listened closely to the stories, even though the threads did not then cohere in my mind. The involvement of my family in commerce, politics, and the founding of the state seemed to merge in my mind with Osage and Pawnee history. The stories became for me a landscape of memory and identity[55]; and in their immediacy and color, in being received and not read, they invoked for me "a time when direct experience constituted a [larger] form of truth, when wisdom and knowledge had not parted company, and stories were the commonest way of communicating and sharing the trials of life."[56]

7

"Even poor varieties may be made sweet": Women's Labor and Constructions of White Femininity

PEACH PIE

1 cup cream, ½ cup sugar, 2 teaspoons flour. Peaches enough to cover pie tin when cut in halves. Line pie tin, put in halves with cup side up. Mix flour and sugar and sprinkle over peaches. Pour cream over and bake in slow oven until fruit is tender.—Mrs. A.G. Drummond, The First Presbyterian Church of Hominy's Cook Book[1]

In recipes handed down by the women in my family, and in those printed and disseminated in regional women's associations and churches—including the recipe for peach pie donated by Mrs. A.G. Drummond, ancestor of "Pioneer Woman" Ree Drumond—close attention to the details of ceaseless production and strong creative pride is evident. For women in Oklahoma, labor was relentless; yet it reflected both gender standing and fierce moral principles. My Grandmother Louella Fairchild Berry's cookbook, *The First Presbyterian Church of Hominy's Cook Book*, printed in 1927 and given to me by my mother, suggests these high objectives:

> Within the corners of this book will be found the answer to that perplexing question confounding every housewife—what to serve for the coming meal. No recipes were accepted from professional cooks, all of them are the favorite recipes of normal housewives ... may our Guild, imbued with the spirit of helpfulness, continue to strive for that which is philanthropic, democratic, and that which tends to higher and moral conditions.[2]

As my Grandmother's cookbook suggests, the labor of women extended beyond outstanding production in the kitchen, and into the realms of car-

7. "Even poor varieties may be made sweet"

Louella Fairchild Berry sitting on her mother's lap, with her great-grandmother (center) and grandmother (courtesy Catherine Berry Hess).

ing for the sick and "preserving" a husband ("Even poor varieties may be made sweet, tender, and good by garnishing with patience, well sweetened with smiles and flavored with kisses to taste. Then wrap them in a mantle of charity, keep warm with a steady fire of domestic devotion, and serve with peaches and cream. When thus prepared they will keep forever").[3] This chapter will examine the labor expected of women, the impact of industrialization on the construction of gender, and the perceptions and experiences of women who were not in the dominant culture.

Linda Williams Reese has argued that work roles at the turn of the century in Oklahoma served to "break down a rigidly patriarchal family structure" and "reshape gender ideologies into new configurations based on mutual respect."[4] Reese maintains that American Indian and African American women, as well as white women, in Oklahoma found a measure of unity in striving toward middle class stature—a status which indicated not merely economic security but as well "ideas about basic education, cleanliness, moral behavior, respectability, cultural accommodation, and social uplift," and the supposedly "natural characteristics of women: purity, piety, submissiveness, and domesticity."[5]

The labor undertaken on a daily basis by women in my family, however, and correspondence that suggests an expectation of female modesty and delicacy that only increased with the emergence of industrialization, reveal a uniquely dichotomous culture, shaped by the challenge of homesteading and the social construction of gender. Camilla Berry notes that women's existence, at least in the years of the settler, was shaped by the dominant authority of men.[6] At the same moment, women often worked outside the company of men, had extensive social authority in arenas not legally recognized, and faced monumental challenges related to physical labor.

Female Labor

CHOCOLATE PIE
(Mrs. E.A. Acott)

½ cup chocolate	2 egg yolks
1 cup sugar	butter size of egg
1 cup hot water	meringue
1 tbsp. corn starch or flour	

ORANGE PIE
(Mrs. Luckett)

1 cup orange juice	2 egg yolks
grated rind of 1 orange	½ cup sugar
1 cup boiling water	1 large tbsp. sugar

1 heaping tablespoon corn starch dissolved in 2 tablespoons water. Cook in double boiler until thick. Cover with whites of 2 eggs, well beaten. Add 2 tablespoons sugar. Brown in oven.[7]

In my family, as in other Oklahoma families, women's lives were characterized by the juxtaposition of societal expectations of delicate "femininity," psychological strength, and hard labor. Massive quantities of food production were a backdrop to all other tasks expected of women, in addition to labor they contributed to ranches and homesteads. A letter from a family ancestor, Bertha Mackay, written in 1915, attests to this effort:

> Tell Georgia that I will be by and answer her letter in a few days I have been so busy I have canned 95 cans of peaches we have so many this year I have put up nearly 200 can of fruit beside my jelly's I had the fruit and I just keep putting up first one thing and then another.[8]

In addition to this staggering labor, the Berry women also made food to sell on the reservations: "Nancy Jane ... baked cakes and cookies and the children sold them to the Indians."[9]

My childhood memories evoke the readiness my Grandmother had to cook anything, anytime, for anyone, a readiness that represented an extension of the humility, generosity, and effort that was the hallmark of a respectable woman in Hominy. My Grandmother—who lived two short blocks away from the historical Drummond home in Hominy—served glazed ham, beef, biscuits with homemade jam, beans snapped by hand, orange salad, fruitcake, fruitcake cookies, jam cake, and oatmeal cake made with an icing of coconut and pecans; she thought nothing of killing chickens by grasping their necks and spinning them, plucking the chickens, boiling frog legs, slaughtering hogs, and any number of arduous activities for food production. This ceaseless labor on the part of women and even children, breathless in its recitation, is echoed in an early letter to Juliet Sophia Berry in 1848:

> Perhaps you would like to know what I am working at. I have a good deal of cooking to do & I put in all the time I can spare cutting carpet rags. Jannie and Dora [her daughters] tack them. I want to make two carpets by spring. I must tell you how smart my baby is. She can wash the dishes & keep the house as nice and quick as any thing[.][10]

In addition to the details of food production, the family archive relates the vast array of tasks expected of women in the nineteenth and twentieth centuries. Nancy Jane Berry, for example, tended her garden and livestock, cared for her children, kept house, churned butter by shaking it in a half-gallon mason jar, handled men who came to the door for work during the Depression years, and took responsibility for religious education, advising her son to "stay away from bad women from whom I could get diseases, and to leave liquor alone."[11] Nancy Jane relates stories of riding side-saddle down the streets of Cushing during Pioneer Days; by her account, she gave birth by herself and put out the laundry on the same day.[12] The matriarch of the family, Juliet Sophia, is known by the story told about her migration from Kentucky to Oklahoma: Camelia Berry relates how Juliet insisted on fording the first wagon across each river ahead of her children and their wagons, "figur[ing] she was expendable."[13] Many of the Berry women initially lived alone with their children in Kentucky, Kansas, Missouri and Texas until their homestead was established, leaving them to take care of entire farms, homes, and households alone.

Accounts from the family archive describe cooking, sewing, and taking care of the ill by girls as young as eleven.[14] Women were expected to clean sod homes or tar paper shanties, and gather sagebrush, hay or buffalo dung for kindling. (A grandson of Jane Berry stated, "She told about going out on the grass prairie and gathering buffalo chips for fuel. I thought the use of them would have been odorous and repugnant. I was wrong."[15]) The presence of fierce weather was a constant: Camilla Berry tells the story of how the refined Addie Henry Berry stored her best china in the storm cellar to protect it from tornadoes. "Unbeknownst to her

"Grandma always took the first wagon across. She figured she was expendable," by Camelia Uzzell Berry, from her *Oklahoma Prairie Plowed Under: The Story of Berry Bros. in Indian Territory* (courtesy Catherine Berry Hess).

someone decided to house pigs in the cellar. The pigs had a wonderful time rutting up the cellar and destroying all of her fine china[.]"[16] Another woman recounts the effect of an "embryo cyclone" that blew the tent down and sent men and women scattering: "We were treated as usual to a negligee spectacle."[17]

One aspect of caring for family members was making clothing, candles, and cloth, raising sheep and carding and spinning wool to make socks and sweaters.[18] The grandson of Nancy Jane Berry describes her making "tapers from old newspaper ... which she kept in a coffee can in her room."[19] Making soap was

> a laborious and odiferous process that involved pouring water through fireplace ashes to make lye, which was then mixed with leftover household grease, brought to a boil, and stirred constantly until the moment when the soap "came" and could be dipped in a barrel or can ... those women who had no wells either hauled water from springs or streams or used what they'd caught in rain barrels[.][20]

Often female homesteaders had to join in traditional "male" labor, such as digging storm cellars and wells, plowing fields, building houses, erecting fences, and slaughtering livestock, as well as harnessing horses and plowing fields. Jennie Cannon, the daughter of Dora Berry, describes her father and mother both "rising at four o'clock and working until late hours with mules and machinery of the early day."[21]

Among the duties of the female homesteader was the creation of bedding, including spinning, weaving, and quiltmaking. Creating quilts was an extension of the essential skills of the seamstress, and a necessary one; but quilts also carried unique significance as heirloom, demonstration of feminine skill, and even personal and social statement. The double Irish Chain quilt made by Juliet Sophia King Berry in approximately 1870 is but one example. This quilt, given as a wedding gift to William Berry and Mattie Brown in Kentucky in that year, survived migration to Oklahoma, tornados, and all that came after, and was last exhibited in Stillwater in 1987.[22] A letter from Dora Berry Goodson states that it went through a tornado, as well as a rough wagon crossing and moves through Kentucky, Missouri, Kansas, and Oklahoma: "I wanted you to have something from your grandmother ... this is old—will soon be 100 years—time goes fast."[23]

The labor expected of men at the turn of the century was also staggering. In addition to being traders, bankers, attorneys, cattlemen, oil entrepreneurs, real estate operators (including owners of a general store, a harness, wagon, and carriage business, and a cotton brokerage, among other businesses), and politicians, my male ancestors were wagon makers, blacksmiths, shoemakers, fieldhands, hunters, and nonprofessional veterinarians, and later cattlemen, longhorn and horse drivers, builders of homes, farmers, and members of the military; they were deeply involved in the church, the American Legion, city councils, and civic organizations. Yet the secondary status of women, the legal strictures upon them, and the expectation of stoicism and hard labor, combined with the expectation of emotional caretaking and a finished, modest, and feminine appearance, indicate a unique and gendered burden.

Occasionally homesteading women in Oklahoma were able to escape the occupational confines of gender. Harriet Berry, wife of the Berry Brothers traders, was also known for being "a doctor and nurse to every family for miles around."[24] Sharp-shooting stars of Wild West shows such as Annie Oakley and May Lillie, "Champion Girl Horseback Shot of the West," were able to retain their qualification as "feminine" while excelling at traditionally masculine skills. Lucille Mulhall, who did not tour professionally but was well known, "learned to ride, rope, and shoot on her family's 80,000 acre ranch in Oklahoma Territory ... weighed only ninety pounds, yet could 'break a bronco, lasso and brand a steer and shoot a coyote at 500 yards.'" As if to assure readers that she conformed to gender expectations, a journalist from the *New York World* noted that Mulhall could "play Chopin, quote Browning, construe Virgil, and make mayonnaise dressing ... [although] a little ashamed of these latter accomplishments, which are a concession to the civilized prejudices of her mother."[25]

Women and Illness

A critical aspect of female culture at the turn of the century in Oklahoma was serving as caretaker for the dying. It was not uncommon to have huge families: Nancy Clark and John Wesley Berry had thirteen children in the mid-nineteenth century. Yet six of them died, five as babies. The strength required to handle this depth of loss is hard to fathom.[26] A poignant letter to Martha Brown Berry from her son-in-law, a schoolteacher, states, "I take pleasure in sending you this picture of dear little 'Bessie.'... The school children crowded around my desk today and they all wanted to know whose picture this was and they wanted to know all about her when I told them she was dead."[27]

In the early days of homesteading, any number of dangers threatened the family beyond the round of diseases. One young girl recalls a rattlesnake biting a neighboring rancher, and her husband washing his mouth with salt and sucking out the poison; "the leg swelled terribly but her life was saved. We [the women] wrapped her leg in coal oil after as much of the poison had been sucked out as could be."[28] The frequent illness of children and family are documented repeatedly in family correspondence: a letter from Martha Brown Berry in 1881 states, "I am sorry that Gracie & then Baio has the hooping cough this winter & think it generally goes hard with anyone in winter. Our children had it last winter.... Jannie & Dora has had the mumps this winter I think it vary strange that Tommie did not take them to [*sic*] We are all well but Tom he was taken sick Thursday and is not well yet tho he is better."[29] George Berry writes to his wife of his doctor, with dark humor, "I feel like this one looking for something bad and I am afraid they will find it."[30]

The personal losses are thus presented in family archives matter-of-factly, but the pain experienced by women who cared for the ill is evident. My mother alludes casually to the intense suffering others experienced (and she herself must have) when stricken with polio; a woman who lost her baby in childhood, a relative said, would "cry and cry for no apparent reason."[31] My Great-Grandmother Berry, writing to my Great Uncle Roy Berry about the death of his sister Jennie Berry, relates,

> I hope never again to see such suffering.... *Everything* that even could do, was done to save her ... [a friend] wanted us not to let the children [my mother's cousins, Charles and George] see her, and I advocated doing so.... [I asked the children] if they would like to see her. Charlie took one and I the other and lifted them up, and talked to them about how pretty she was, and how she had another father who wanted to have her come to *His* house awhile, and bye & bye they might come, too. We held them and talked to them quite a bit. Then I told them to tell her good bye and sleep good[.][32]

A similarly devastating story that reveals the role of women in managing, and communicating about, illness and loss is shared by my Great-Grandmother, Eliza Claunch, in writing to her daughter Julia about my Great-Grandfather Hess' death:

> A man got in his car and left and was not out of sight when Dad breathed his last. He was on his knees in the shed and fell backwards. Charles ran to the house for me. As soon as I saw him I knew he was dying. I called to him several times. If he tried to answer I didn't know it. I had got in the shed and was holding his head up. He never struggled a single time. His breathing seemed easy. I knew by the calm peaceful look on his face that he was not in pain. His eyes were open when I first got to him but he closed them, closed his mouth, folded his hands and was gone. Julia, I wish you could see him then, even after death, it would not be so hard for you to give him up. He had such a peaceful restful look. Just like he knew he was laying every burden down and was perfectly at rest. Death gave him a majesty I can't describe.[33]

Illness was rampant among the Osage and Pawnee, and settlers sometimes died from the diseases caught by the Osage: Camelia Berry speculates that Tom Berry contracted tuberculosis living at the Pawnee agency among them, leaving behind a wife and five children to fend for themselves.[34]

Appreciation for women's strength in handling these losses, although expected and seen as natural, did not go unacknowledged. One family member stated that "my mother was indeed a pioneer woman, the bravest little soul that ever lived, no task was too great for her, but she left for her children to carry on the work she had begun[,] which they have very faithfully done."[35] Indeed, the literature attests to a less equivocal admiration for matriarchs of the family in some respects than exists today. There is no doubt, however, that the expectation both of brute labor and of feminine modesty and delicacy was a "peculiar institution" for many women of the era, although the latter was modified by social class. Prior to industrialization, the legal and social restrictions placed upon women and their "feminine frailty" contrasted markedly with the work that wore on them. In the earliest days of my family's settlement in America, the expectation of specifically gendered behavior was evident: in one account of eighteenth century life, said to have been "kept alive" by women in the family, Elizabeth Sharp, an ancestor of the Berrys, found herself and her horse being stalked by a mountain lion. When the beast charged her she threw her bonnet at it. The cat was so startled it allowed her to escape. When it came at her again she threw her shawl to frighten it off. It was undoubtedly something of an exaggeration when her family reported they were all very shocked to see such a proper Christian woman coming home only half dressed.³⁶

According to the family archive, after capture by the British in 1780, a female ancestor, Ellen Sharp Duncan, "wrote a nasty note to the British military commander informing him that they were ladies of quality who were accustomed to having servants … and if he really was the gentleman that he claimed to be, he 'would either provide them with the servants to which their position entitled them … or at least allow their men free to help with the heavy work.'"³⁷ Both strength and conformity with societal expectations of feminine behavior is illustrated in such early stories:

> it was the women's skill at fine sewing and lace making that provided for the families during their captivity. British officers paid them very handsomely for the beautiful shirts they created. While at the store buying supplies … [Elizabeth Markham, a Berry ancestor] observed a classic encounter between the Captain's Lady and a British officer's wife. The woman approached the impoverished P.O.W. offering, "I am looking for a good washer woman." Ellen Sharp Duncan coolly replied, "So am I. Do let me know if you find one.³⁸ When the British authorities suggested that the American women should work in the Officer's mess, Mrs. Duncan turned them down coldly. We are accustomed to having servants, sir[,] NOT being servants.³⁹

It is also recorded that a Berry ancestor—Elizabeth Duncan Laughlin—used her employment with the British to help the men, who were about to be impressed into the British navy, escape. When they were themselves ultimately freed, George Washington paid their way home.⁴⁰ A century later, Juliet Sophia Berry, the same woman who forged streams ahead of her male relations, is said to have been informed by her son, "If you can face the [Indian] Nations after what I've just told you, you're surely the woman I always thought you were." In Camelia Berry's account, Julia answered, 'If I can help Georgia a little before my strength gives out, I'd think it worth while.'" Julia Berry was only fifty-two.⁴¹

Advertising and Industrialization

Industrialization and advertising at the turn of the century drastically altered the construction of what constituted white, "feminine" behavior in Hominy and surrounding towns, including Pawhuska. As Linda Williams Reese states in her scholarship on women in Oklahoma at the turn of the century, "[a]n ideology of domesticity emerged ... among urban, middle-class white women that permeated national thought. This ideology centered on the supposed natural characteristics of women: purity, piety, submissiveness, and domesticity.... Faced with new demands and experiences, [settler women held] to familiar ideals and worked toward the day when they might resurrect them again."[42]

The emerging effect of advertising and industry on the conflicting ideals of white femininity—hard labor/humility, beauty/delicacy—is evident in my Grandmother's dress, in her weekly visits to the beauty shop where the small town women shared their stories, and in the products that increasingly made their way into the home. In my Grandmother's cookbook, the value placed upon economy and charity is wed with an emphasis upon physical attractiveness: one advertisement admonishes sternly, "Help Those Who Help Themselves," while another, an advertisement for the Hominy Beauty Shoppe, where my Grandmother spent so many hours, suggests that "Regular visits to this Beauty Shop/will make you as attractive to/your husband and family/As the food prepared from the recipes/in this cook book."[43]

The merging of the ideals of feminine grace and charity with those of hard labor and industrial advancement is evident in the *First Presbyterian Church of Hominy's Cook Book* advertisement for the Hominy Cotton, Oil and Ice Company. Even products that seem inevitable are rendered through the new field of advertising as a revelation, with women engaged in "certified home management":

> **Experience Speaks**
> and in no uncertain voice, says:—
> **"I Am for Ice"**
> Quite voluntarily a well-known gentle-woman of our community recently expressed her opinion as to what, from her long experience, constituted the best method for assuring adequate and dependable refrigeration in the home.— Her unqualified decision in favor of ICE is based on many years of certified home management, during which she constantly concerned herself not only with the appointments of her drawing room but with the needs of her culinary department as well. Time and again this social leader has been besought to "try out" other methods of refrigeration but has remained and will remain loyal to ICE. This loyalty is not born of sentiment but comes from an intimate study and thorough understanding of the superiority of ice over these mechanical-chemical substitutes—as proved by its absolute safety, its dependability, its abundance in emergencies.[44]

Ice is characterized as the consequence of scientific study and the choice of the most genteel, even as a note of desperation sounds in an oncoming era of refrigeration.

It is hard to envision the combination of intense physical labor and gentility—placed in juxtaposition to the imagined lack of gentility of others—that was expected of homesteading women, and those who came after. As the Presbyterian Church's cookbook suggests, a combination of intense labor, frugality and conformity with standards of femininity promoted by advertising and industry was expected. Virginia Harrison describes her Grandmother, who kept a modest household, in approximately 1915: she "had a gas stove to cook on, but she used card board matches, strips of cardboard to light other burners from one that was going. She was very saving."[45] Yet the enticements of commercial items and advertising, and the desire to appear feminine, conflicted with and occasionally overrode these concerns. The family tells the story of Mary Susan Berry, "considered the prettiest of the daughters," who "could still toss her head like a Kentucky belle even with her gross overweight. She claimed the Lord had sent her fat as a penance for her vanity while young." Her granddaughter Gayle noted disapprovingly, "she could only cook in quantities."[46]

A description of Edwina Berry in a publication titled "The Voice of Oklahoma Women" emphasizes the combination of labor, stoicism, and femininity expected of the ideal woman.

> As Mrs. James Berry, an official hostess of the State, Edwina is perfect. Accomplished in the womanly art of needle work and homemaking. She is brilliant in her conversation, while being a pal to her husband and to her children. If the undimmed merriment of her brown eyes has never known the wash of tears over lack of necessities for loved ones, that fact has never dulled her sympathy or retarded her program of helpfulness to the less fortunate.[47]

My mother tells the story of how she was expected to conform to all the dictates of femininity, even as she rode her horse to her one room school, where she shared an outhouse "unpainted, the holes not even sanded, with a Sears catalogue."[48] Women always wore dresses (although my Grandmother borrowed pants to ride horses and examine the fences), and were expected not to swear, drink, or smoke; at some social gatherings, women were expected to sit separately from men. In the city, women attended beauty shops, wore elegant clothing, and adhered fast to the stark distinction that divided women into two rigid categories: "ladies" and "whores."[49] A distinction existed, of course, between women of different classes, and between those who lived in the country and city; the harsh dichotomy persisted nonetheless. My mother, free spirit that she was, however, had her moments of defiance (but maintained her figure, finishing school manners and noteworthy cooking skills, nonetheless).

The expectations for women of all classes in rural areas—intensive labor and delicacy, constant production and fragility or modesty—seem irreconcilable. Yet before the advent of mass advertising and the changes brought about by industrialization, and the even greater expectations related to women's appearance, to come, it would seem that these expectations were largely accepted with a sense of inevitability. Coupled with the extreme disparity between the socioeconomic authority of white men and women, and the absence of legal or economic recourse in domestic arrangements, the expectation that white women maintain an air of dependence, docility and femininity rigidified an already challenging subculture.

Osage Women

From the perspective of white settlers, authors, and filmmakers, as well as early anthropological accounts, the American Indian woman, like the white woman, was docile and subordinate to the authority of men. Yet as Annette Jaimes and Theresa Halsey document, "it is [in fact American Indian] women who have formed the very core of indigenous resistance to genocide and colonization since the first moment of conflict between Indians and invaders."[50] The efforts of female warriors in battle are documented by Jaimes and Halsey, including that of *Cousaponakeesa*, Mary Matthews Musgrove Bosomworth, "who led her people in a successful campaign against the British at Savannah during the 1750s.... Female fighters were never uncommon once the necessity of real warfare was imposed by Euroamericans."[51] Lakota women maintained at least four warrior societies; warriors among other tribes included the Cherokee *Da'nawa-gasta*, or "Sharp War," head of a women's military society; the Creek society, "Beloved Women"; the Piegan "Strong-Hearted Woman," a permanent warrior society; Buffalo Calf Road (who distinguished herself at both the Battle of the Rosebud in 1876 and during the 1878 "Cheyenne Breakout); and other comparable figures and societies.[52]

The tradition of female warriors and war societies "serves to debunk the tidy (if grossly misleading and male/female, warlike/peaceful dichotomies)" deployed by some historians to characterize American Indian women.[53] Their role in making a range of decisions about socioeconomic life, included (depending upon the nation) the right to decide the fate of captives, the right to choose which males would serve on Tribal Councils, the right to choose whom and whether to marry, and the right to wage war.[54] Most American Indian nations were matrilineal: because "men joined women's families, not the other way around ... [and] men were usually expected to relocate to join the women they married,"[55] the position of American Indian women was radically different than that of women in white culture. American Indian women owned all or most of their property, were entitled to keep their homes and children if there were marital problems, and held crucial leadership positions in spiritual life, including becoming Medicine Women in some belief systems.[56] As Winona LaDuke states, "Traditionally, American Indian women were never subordinate to men."[57]

Osage women were granted the honor of sustaining and protecting children, particularly young girls, and were given the spiritual and physical responsibility for agriculture.[58] Although women did not "play[] a significant role in Osage government and politics,"[59] the powerful role they played in protecting and sustaining culture is suggested by the disapproving voices of federal agents seeking to eliminate traditional culture: in 1902, Agent O.A. Mitscher found Osage women "a persuasive and negative influence" in "the manner of correcting uncivilized customs," and reported, "[t]he women of the tribe are the bane of progress.... If it were not for the ... female it would be ... only a short time when civilized manners and methods would prevail."[60]

According to Jaimes and Halsey, "[t]he reduction of the status held by women within indigenous nations was a first priority for European colonizers eager to weaken and destabilize target societies."[61] Replacing traditional roles, in which "Native American women ... had power as agriculturalists, potters, food preparers, and leather workers," with a trade economy "shifted the power to the men, the hunters who obtained furs, the basic commodity of trade."[62] In both religious and civic efforts to "civilize" Indians, positions of power, including spiritual leadership, were reduced. Polygamy among the Osage was a particular target, even though, ironically, the arrangement was a consequence of decades of European invasion: "[men] married the widows of the increasing numbers of comrades killed in battle."[63] Not a single treaty or agreement between the federal government and American Indians involved women as negotiators, or addressed any issues related to women.[64]

Although Native American women who conformed to white standards, such as those indoctrinated in the Cherokee Female Seminary established in Tahlequah in 1851, were seen as personifying "ideals such as honor, beauty, intelligence, wealth, and refinement," serving as "living models of assimilation,"[65] most American Indian women—notably, the Kiowa, "seen only as insignificant dependents of a warrior society"—experienced diminished respect and political authority. The division between the Tahlequah Cherokee and the Kiowa—a "racial" distinction scholar

7. "Even poor varieties may be made sweet"   121

Nancy Parezo describes as a dichotomy between "princess" and "squaw"[66]—was used by white Americans broadly to justify the denegration and sexual and physical abuse of all American Indians, male and female alike.[67]

By the 1880s "squaw" became associated with anomie and dysfunctional behaviors (drunkenness, idleness, begging, dirtiness and sloth) and was indicative

Mrs. Arthur Bonnicastle in traditional dress. Photograph by H.T. Love Studio, Pawhuska, Oklahoma (Research Division of Oklahoma Historical Society).

of hopeless poverty. As a marginal person, a squaw lived on the edges of border towns or as a homeless person in urban areas. Settlers conceptualized these squaws, often labeled prostitutes, as ugly, with faces scarred by smallpox or venereal diseases. An 1858 newspaper editorial called such women "a most vile nuisance, calling loudly for abatement." To be a squaw meant that a woman was not fit to be a member of civilized society.

In contemporary terms, the word "squaw" became synonymous with the grotesque English term, "cunt."[68]

The profoundly negative view held by white authorities of American Indian women was reflected in the separate materials and assignments given to boarding schools for boys and girls. Merial A. Dorchester, a special agent in the Indian School Service, charged

> [t]hat Indian girls were not accorded "an equal, chance with boys out of school hours, and in some places the girls are neglected even in the school room." ... She also complained that girls were usually restricted to a high-fenced pen, while the boys ranged all over the school grounds. This was true at the Osage reservation boarding school.[69]

The St. John's and St. Louis' boarding schools complied with the agent's 1884 request of education based upon gender: Osage girls were to "be instructed carefully and thoroughly in all branches of housekeeping ... including ... cooking and dairy work," while boys "receive[] instruction in stock raising, carpentering, cobbling, and shoemaking."[70]

Ironically, given a history of suppression of Osage women by whites, the Osage Tribal Council repeatedly turned aside efforts to extend the right to vote to women. The Allotment Act of 1906 passed by Congress provided for the election of a principal chief of the Osage, an assistant chief and eight members of a tribal council as the governing body of the Osage Tribe; none of the members were women, and in 1908, the Council defined qualified Osage voters as "only male members whose names appear on the rolls of the Osage Tribe approved by the Secretary of the Interior[.]"[71] In 1922, 1935, and 1936 efforts to include Osage women were rejected; the Osage Council did not extend the right to vote to women until 1941, and an Osage woman would not be elected to the Council until 1978.[72] Thus the authority enjoyed by Osage women in many aspects of traditional life would not translate into the political realm reorganized by whites for at least a century.

It is noteworthy, however, that in 2012, the first council of the Osage village in Pawhuska was elected consisting solely of women—Paula Stabler, Paula Farid, Renee Harris, Asa Cunningham, and Jodel Heath.[73] That all members of the Board in Pawhuska—the center of the Osage Nation, and the site of the largest *I'n-lon-shcka*—are now women, and the now-frequent candidacy of women for both Chief and Assistant Chief speaks to vastly enhanced political power of Osage women, and the great respect afforded them in public life today.[74]

Sandy Maker, left, and Paula Farid, Osage, dressed for *Playground of the Native Son*, 2012. Farid is a member of the Five Woman Council (courtesy Paula Farid).

African American Women

In the context of the dichotomous expectations of white women in Oklahoma, the "othering" of Osage women experienced throughout the colonization process, and the violence and terror experienced by African American men subjected to the White Supremacist movement, African American women faced extraordinary pressures and expectations. Land Runs led many black families to move north to Oklahoma to escape Jim Crow Legislation, joining freed slaves; "hundreds came, by train to Guthrie and by foot or wagon to Langston, ill-prepared for the circumstances."[75] Anticipating town infrastructure, many black families were forced to live in tents and makeshift buildings; women entered racially mixed towns to secure domestic work. Labor in the field, in addition to childrearing and care for the home, was undertaken by black women,[76] who also faced violence at the hands of white men, and occasional disrespect by black men.[77]

The poverty faced by new arrivals, on top of the antipathy of freedmen with tribal citizenship, the hostility of some American Indian nations, the institutionalized prejudice of the white establishment, and even the distorted perceptions of some black men, created a brutal and precarious environment for women in Oklahoma based upon "race." A demographic study conducted in 1930 revealed that black women in Oklahoma "had a stillbirth, maternal death, and infant death rate that was nearly three times higher than that of any other racial group in the state."[78] According to a study undertaken by Mabel Bridgewater, and reported by the scholar Linda Reese, the majority of women incarcerated for insanity came from rural and impoverished districts, and 83 percent listed their primary occupation as "housewife." Bridgewater's conclusion from the data was that "[t]he principal cause of female insanity in Oklahoma is overwork and deprivation."[79]

African American women, beyond all of these obstacles, also had to face the perverse dichotomy endured by white and Osage women—black newspaper editors in predominantly black towns, for example, "printed directives admonishing women to be frugal and hardworking," but also "gentle, yielding, and generous in their relationships with their husbands."[80] At the same moment that African Americans were struggling for respect, a cessation in violence, and equality before the law, some black men expressed a preference for the lighter skin and straight hair characteristic of white culture, as well as a submissive and docile demeanor. Despite these obstacles, African American women managed—perhaps better even than their white or American Indian counterparts—to engage in entrepreneurship. Black communities in general applauded the efforts of women at managing small businesses, including millinery, refreshments, hair styling products and straightening services, and boarding houses, as well as their employment in other areas.[81]

In reflecting upon the historical experiences of women at the turn of the century—settlers, American Indians, and African American women alike—I am struck by the clarity, immediacy, and embodied experience which specific stories evoke. The recollections of Camelia Berry about the labor of Harriet Berry, for example, make the dichotomous expectations of heavy labor and pride in feminine achievement come to life:

> Harriet described the cooking and the women in the kitchen that helped her feed the thrashers and the haying crews.... Harriet was famous for her biscuits. [The local] Home Economics Department came out to get her to show them how she did it. She showed them her bin or bowl of flour. She measured a cup of sour heavy cream, a pinch of salt, a pinch of soda, poured it into a pit in the flour bin until there was a sticky dryish ball which she patted out, cut and put into the oven. They came out three inches high, fluffy and fantastic. So they measured her pinches, tools, notes, etc. I don't know whether they ever made biscuits like hers or not.[82]

In the description of Harriet's food production, one can almost smell and taste the biscuits and feel the flour dusting the bin. Envisioning this relentless effort brings back memories of my Grandmother Louella Fairchild Berry, the wife of George Madison's Great-Grandson, Everett Berry, Jr., baking biscuits in her kitchen, exquisitely turned out, the sun streaming through the window, the ranch hands sitting at the kitchen table with their legs stretched out, as I observed it all from the flour-dusted floor.

What is it that, distilled from the conflicting pressures of labor, beautification, self-control, humility, and even superiority, that evokes for me the vision of my Grandmother's kitchen, her standing perfectly coiffed in her dress, the smell of baking biscuits while the ranch hands waited? What makes the memory so pivotal in my mind? Perhaps it is a romantic attraction to the rancher and the cowboy, or the sense of completeness of extended family together; perhaps it is the integration of work, both male and female, the integration of two sets of working worlds, the perfection of the community working together. Undoubtedly it had to do with the complete realization of an ideal, a moment of each "culture" of the working day at peace, interacting, and cooperating, and the embodied memory—feel, taste, smell—of the workaday moment. As Jackson states, "[n]ot only does work provide the livelihood of persons, it creates modes of sociality and sustains a vital sense of what it means to coexist and cooperate with others ... interaction with others, and groundedness in daily praxis, is the very baseline of the sense of being."[83]

BISCUITS

Anybody can make good biscuit dough by following the principles which govern its production. 1st—A very soft dough. 2nd—Very light handling. 3rd—A hot oven. The hands should come in contact with the dough as little as possible. The milk should be cold.[84]

BAKING POWDER BISCUITS FOR TWO
(Grace Bishop)

2 cups flour	2 tablespoon lard
1 teaspoon salt	1 cup cold milk
4 level teaspoon baking powder	

Sift flour, salt, baking powder three times. Rub in shortening with fingers or fork. Add milk gradually. Turn out on well floured board. Roll lightly till ½" thick. Cut and bake 12 or 15 minutes.[85]

8

Family and Osage Extravagence and the Oil Boom

In 1939 a reporter visited the ranch of E.C. Mullendore, cousin to George Madison Berry, and observed the sumptuous interior of his home, describing the fine details in furniture and decoration matching in ostentation the scope of the land and livestock the ranch sustained.

> Step up the stone walk, cross the long front porch, and you find yourself in a huge front room, a treasure spot of Western luxury. The high walls are paneled in knotty pine to the high beamed ceiling, and the shiny hardwood floor has black walnut pegs instead of nails. Crackling flames in the large rock fireplace cast a soft glow across the mounted cowhides and Indian woven rugs.... Mrs. Mullendore's bedroom [by contrast] is definitely very feminine and very modern. The color scheme of chartreuse and rose is carried out in the thick carpet and the drapes.... Just a step away is the sleeping porch with nine beds. Each has a matching spread with one letter to spell out "Cross Bell."[1]

For the Osage the twenties was also a time of outsized luxury: as one journalist breathlessly reported,

> Sometimes the glitter came from diamonds studded in the Osage women's patent-leather slippers, which showed the flash of silk stockings at the ankle. When a limo broke down, or just got a flat tire, the Osages would not bother with repairs—they simply bought another automobile.... They—their chauffeurs, rather—parked their cars outside the Osage's mansions, filled with the finest in furniture, paintings, sculpture, china, and other luxury items[.][2]

This chapter examines how extraordinary wealth arrived to the Osage, the Berrys, and the Mullendores, how their staggering affluence was perceived and represented, and the tragic consequences of wealth for both family and Osage.

The Oil Boom and the Osage

In 1906, a year prior to the admission of Oklahoma as a state, the federal Interior Department made a census of the Osage nation, and listed 2,229 individuals entitled to equal shares, or "head rights," in Osage land and the mineral rights it contained.[3] "The Osage tribe continued to hold its land in common after individual allotments of acreage had been made" to other American Indian nations.[4] "Any profits from [grazing or mineral] leases must be paid into a common fund for equal distribution among originally assigned "headrights" of all members of the tribe ... the only inequalities of wealth among the Osages came about slowly through death and inheritance."[5]

In the early 1920s, every Osage who was enrolled earned more than $100,000, and those who inherited "headrights" earned much more.[6] When translated into today's dollars, every Osage earned approximately $1 million a year between 1925 and 1932.[7] Between 1907 and 1929, the Osage received $233,000,000 in royalties and bonuses.[8] The companies from whom this flow was leased benefited richly as well: "[m]any of the oil barons who sat under Pawhuska's 'Million Dollar Elm'"—Skelly, Marland, Getty, Phillips, Wrightsman—"where quarterly auctions for the tracts were held, made their first millions from Osage oil."[9] So successful was the auctioneer, Colonel Ellsworth Walters—on April 20, 1916, an auction lasted until midnight, and garnered bonus payments for the tribe of $2,100,000—that the Osage presented Walters with a diamond ring.[10] Later auctions were held in the Osage Tribal Museum itself, in a special auditorium built for that purpose.

Historians of the time perceived this situation as inappropriate and shameful. "The folly was that of children turned loose with a free hand in candy and toy shops."[11] Sensationalized accounts of Osage extravagance emphasized the excesses of Osage expenditures, both legitimate and imagined:

> There were more Pierce-Arrows—the Rolls-Royces of their day—on the Osage lands in Oklahoma than anywhere else in the country. The limousines often bore—etched in solid gold on the side panels—the initials of their owners, giant Osages, larger than life itself, sitting in the leather back seats while their chaffeurs navigated the pits and bumps of the dusty dirt roads. The Indians wrapped themselves regally in brightly colored blankets and sparkled majestically, head to toe, from the vivid array of beads that dotted their long, shiny black hair, their necks, wrists, dresses, broadcloth trousers, handbags and moccasins....
> [Their mansions were elaborate,] but often [had] no occupants. Many Osages preferred sleeping outside, on their lawns[.][12]

Oil gusher in Oklahoma (Research Division of Oklahoma Historical Society).

Osage women in ribbon blankets with Model Ts and large, contemporary homes in the left distance (© Dickinson Research Center, National Cowboy & Western Heritage Museum, Oklahoma City, Oklahoma).

The Osage made trips to expensive vacation sites after the oil boom brought them affluence, just as the same boom led my Grandmother and Grandfather Berry to take an expensive excursion to Mexico. The Osage reportedly purchased, at prices vastly inflated by white salespeople, expensive belongings that were never used, or that clashed with their traditional lifestyle: grand pianos, for example, were said to rot outside in the rain, and women purchased "diamonds, jewelry, fine rugs and tapestry."[13]

The observations of journalists who witnessed the "Million Dollar Elm" auctions and their aftermath, embellished and overwrought, suggest a misunderstanding of spiritual priorities and sense of place, and bordered on the absurd.

> [The Osage] would take his blankets down to the living room and sleep on the hard floor before the fireplace, where the wraiths of his ancestors ... danced out of the smoke to tell him the white man's lodge and the white man's black magic of the flowing ground-deeps [oil wells] were only the dreams of a fever.[14]

The misunderstanding of the Osage relationship to the land—the emphasis of federal officials and journalists on mineral and grazing rights,

8. Family and Osage Extravagence and the Oil Boom

From left, unidentified Mexican tour guide, Roy Berry, "Bob" Berry, Everett Berry, Sr., and Louella Fairchild Berry (courtesy Catherine Berry Hess).

rather than a spiritual and communal connection—as well as the initial spending among the Osage people, generated the racist perception that American Indians as a class were primitive in reason and required paternalistic—and lucrative—supervision. To justify Congressional hearings on the distribution of Osage allotments—money that belonged to the Osage from the sale of Kansas land, but was "held in trust"—the federal government and the media invoked "a stereotype of Indians ... [as] lacking in common sense."[15] Apparently, little had changed in the preceding one hundred years: Tixier said in 1839 that "[I]f they happen to have money, they cannot keep it, they spend it like children.... The savages have no idea of the relative value of money."[16]

As Harmon argues, "remarkable Indian financial gains triggered public discussion of economic ethics, and the discourse plainly owed its distinctiveness to the moneymakers' Indian identity."[17] The spectacular wealth of the Osage was taken up uneasily within dominant "racial" narratives, and various structures of federal guardianship—such as placing those without "certificates of competency" under the supervision of the Secretary of the Interior, and legal quantums of "race"—were employed to distinguish, re-install, and enforce ideals related to American prosperity among the dominant culture. Access to undreamed-of wealth was accompanied by the continuation of federal intervention, paternalism, and racism: as Harmon argues,

> [a]t their richest hour, hundreds of Osages [still] could not retain full control over their own money. Instead of buying them freedom from overbearing outsiders, copious oil revenue provided an excuse to institutionalize U.S. domination.... Lawmakers and administrators responded to a twentieth-century turnaround in Osage fortunes by adopting rules and practices that perpetuated the power imbalance and confirmed the Indians' infantile legal status.[18]

This sensibility is reinforced by the recollection of a relative:

> [m]any of the Indians would spend all their money as soon as it came and would then borrow from friends and neighbors. [An Osage woman] had a farm and lovely home near us and had owed Daddy money for quite some time and always had some excuse for not paying. One day Mother went to get the money ... [offering the woman] a long story about needing money for the children's Christmas. The neighbor lifted her skirt and there were pockets sewn all over her slip and each pocket was filled with dollar bills.[19]

The explosion in affluence among the Osage generated not only the opportunity for business, but also for fraud. Those Osage who did not receive "certificates of competency" from the federal government were subject to the utter humiliation of having white "guardians," many of whom defrauded their subject/clients.[20] White lawyers, oil lease brokers, speculators, judges, public officials, merchants, and loan sharks all took advantage of the Osages' spectacular wealth, encouraging unnecessary purchases, overcharging exorbitantly, and escaping prosecution for their theft and usury. Guardians for the financially "incompetent" alone managed to extract eight million dollars from the Osage; in 1925, the "Interior Department filed twenty-five suits against guardians for recovery of stolen Osage money," but none went to trial.[21] As Lloyd argues, the guardians' theft was but one part of a "widespread, if genteel and unspoken, conspiracy to separate the Osage from their wealth."[22] This conspiracy involved "the dishonest merchants, the elected county judges, the banks charging usurious rates of interest, the elected county judges, the unscrupulous businessmen, the shopkeepers selling vanilla extract [and alcohol] to alcoholics, the doctors prescribing addictive drugs"[23]—and those who murdered the Osage for their headrights.

The Office of the U.S. Indian Agent on Grandview Avenue in Pawhuska kept precise records of the money each Osage received, records that any merchant could see.[24] Like other records documenting the names of Allottees, their "racial quantums," allocated properties, and expeditures, such official archives were a blunt instrument of power that insured successful supervision and control. Making matters worse, those who stole, many with the assistance of the archive, had easy access to escape:

> Osage County and the surrounding territory contained very wild stretches of country, thickly wooded with timber.... This area, with its almost inaccessible canyons, afforded excellent concealment for the hideouts of the many notorious criminals who flocked to the territory[.][25]

Illustrations contained in the family archives suggest the element of the outlaw: a dramatic illustration of "Bella Starr, the bandit queen," depicts the beautiful Bella riding sidesaddle on a powerful mount, shooting "Sheriff Nicols" for some misconstruction of justice. Others, showing men with dark faces in long trenchcoats and hats pulled low over their faces, depict the James Brothers, Hanging Judge Parker, the Hole in the Wall Gang, and the Dalton gang, headed by Bob Dalton, notorious for horse theft, bootlegging, bribe-taking, even murder.

Most ominous in all of the manipulation, theft and paternalism characteristic of the Oil Boom era was the greatly increased rate of homicide. Although a relative states that,

> White people who married Osages were looked down upon because people suspected them of marrying for money. Many of the marriages were long lasting

and proved to be good. My best friends were half Osage. Their mother had died years before but they had a loving father and I cannot believe that he had not cared for his Indian wife.[26]

Osage wives and husbands were killed by poisoning or shooting; some white men even advertised for wives, stating that the richer the Osage woman found, the higher the fee. In one famous case, three Osage women were killed by dynamite.[27] Another common method of assassination, according to the Federal Bureau of Investigation, "was to get the Indian drunk, have a doctor examine him and pronounce him drunk, then kill him with a massive injection of morphine under his armpit. The doctor's certificate would read 'death from alcoholic poisoning.'"[28] Dennis McAuliffe documents that between one to three percent of the entire Osage Nation was killed before oil prices dropped: "[t]he 24 to 60 murders of Osages translate to a staggering rate of 1,500 to 3,000 per 100,000[.]"[29] His research revealed a document in the FBI Osage murder file that suggests a mountain of unsolved murder cases.[30] The number of (unwanted) "abortions" and "suicides" recorded by Osage Agency doctors during this time period was also shockingly high.[31] Forced sterilization, aggression by whites seeking headrights, and murder—the "reign of terror" among the Osage—came to an end as oil prices dwindled, but not before the population had been drastically reduced, and headrights scattered among many non-Osage.

After the Boom years of the 1920s, and during the Great Depression, most Osage had money from mineral rights—but not all. The few dollars they received "kept all Osages from participation in government relief and recovery programs."[32] After much effort on the part of Osage officials, the Osage were allowed to participate in the Indian Division of the Civilian Conservation Corps, which allowed young men between the ages of eighteen and thirty-five to work on public projects in Colorado, and on public parks such as the Osage Hills State Park in Oklahoma[33]; John Joseph Mathews persuaded the WPA to release funding for the creation of the Tribal Museum.[34]

But many of the Osage remained destitute; over a third of the land allotted in 1906 was gone.[35] The famous photograph by Dorothea Lange of a migrant worker with a child, symbol of the Depression and Dust Bowl, was an Oklahoma Cherokee, and there were many Osage like her.[36] "Perhaps the most interesting aspect of the wealthy Osage is how quickly it all changed," one family member states; an Osage neighbor's "grandchildren went to school with Katie [my mother], lived only one house away from Mother and Daddy when they moved to Hominy. They were lovely people … and money is a great leveler."[37]

The Mullendores and the Settler Boom

Ironically, in my mother's memory, the Oil Boom era was a time of calm within the community. Falling asleep at night, she heard the chunking and clicking of the oil wells, and the distant sound of Osage drumming.[38] The prosperity brought by Osage income, and white ranchers and businessmen who obtained oil leases, led to a welcome expansion of contract labor employment and the swift emergence of small towns. In the oil-boom town of Whizbang, whose white workers "whizzed all day and banged all night," sixty-nine derricks were visible from any strategic point in the city; in addition to the three main Osage towns, twenty-eight boomtowns grew up in the Osage countryside between 1906 and 1928. Thousands of white oil field workers lived in these small towns, while their employers leased 160 acre tracts from the Osage.

Many non-Osage profited and built upon prior claims, paying "cash bonuses per tract for the right to drill and then a royalty on each barrel extracted." Two oil companies paid a million dollars for a tract in 1922; "seventeen other tracts also topped the million-dollar bonus mark in the 1920s," and millions were made by oil barons who bid by the "Million Dollar Elm."[39] The Land Rush property bought by my ancestor Sarah Jane (Jennie) Berry, who married E. C. Mullendore, is illustrative. Sarah Berry and Mullendore's son Eugene married Kathleen Brown, the granddaughter of the chief of the Osage from 1918 to 1920, Chief *Shon-kah*, and built a financial empire.[40] As journalists would later point out, "[f]alling in love with a girl whose brother soon would have powerful political influence [George Madison Berry] was merely the first of several fortuitous events in Erd's life."[41] Erd Mullendore came a long way from the early days. A family story relates that Mullendore opposed the law against cutting wood on a claim on principle; refusing to pay the $25 fine,

> he knew they'd pick him up. So he told them (friends) that he "wanted out of here by Saturday evening." So some guys, about 200 or so, with guns showed up at the court house, and they turned Erd Mullendore loose! Nor did they come after him any more.[42]

Erd (E.C.) Mullendore was prosperous and charismatic, but enjoyed the ruse of dressing poorly—as so many of my family members did—despite his position as President of the Cleveland National Bank and interest holder in banks in Hominy, Pawnee, and Cushing. Mullendore managed companies (some with Thomas and George Madison Berry) that produced, refined, and marketed oil in Texas, Oklahoma, and Illinois, but maintained a characteristic outward humility[43]:

Portraits of Erd C. Mullendore and Jennie Berry Mullendore, from Camelia Uzzell Berry's *Oklahoma Prairie Plowed Under: The Story of Berry Bros. in Indian Territory* **(courtesy Catherine Berry Hess).**

He apparently roamed his land on horseback, or in his model T. Ford.... When people connected him to the oil business he always told them he was just a dirt farmer ... Mr. L.C. Mueller[,] who worked in E.C.'s bank ... says, "He looked just like a farmer. He'd come in here with his boots and big overalls on from working cattle and you'd never know he was a millionaire. He remembers E.C. ... [as] a real wheeler and dealer. You couldn't keep up with him.[44]

8. Family and Osage Extravagence and the Oil Boom 137

My mother tells the story of her father helping E.C. brand cattle: someone shouted, "look out!" and Grandfather Berry said, "who's that damn fool in the way?" A cow hit him and broke three of his ribs. "He was so embarrassed," Mama said.[45]

After getting married and beginning a family Jennie and Erd Mullendore built a modest frame house. In 1913 they built a home three quarters of a mile from the Osage Reservation.

> The new house had a brick two-story garage with servants quarters above. It also had a brick chicken house divided in two sections. The house had marble fireplaces, stained glass windows and one of the first central vacuum-cleaning systems. Jennie and Erd filled the house with beautiful "turn-of-the-century" furniture.[46]

The Mullendores also had "a colored maid, Sophrona, who was like one of the family for thirty-five years.... Sophrona stayed until Jennie died."[47]

By the mid-forties E.C. and Jennie's grandson Eugene (who "was dressed in specially made cowboy togs including boots as soon as he could walk, and was buying bulls ... at ten)[48] built an even more spectacular mansion on the Mullendores' 130,000 acres. In 1950 a journalist described the home: "the electric lights in old-fashioned coal oil lamp brackets rise from a replica of a big wagon wheel. Mullendore's own bedroom has furniture with his original design. The pine beds have the 'M' and Cross Bell brand worked into huge [patterns] which form the head and base."[49] Mullendore's dining room was decorated with a mural depicting a chuck wagon scene; on the exterior of the house was a Cross Bell brand outlined in electric lights,[50] and, my mother recalls, a swimming pool in the shape of the brand.[51] One Tulsa journalist reported that Mullendore had a private airplane, a ranch "as big as a medieval mansion," and a pinewood "dining room table as long as some town's air strips."[52]

The Mullendores also had "the state's largest herd of Hereford cattle, herds of buffalo, deer, longhorn cattle and cattalo—a cross of buffalo and cattle. It has some of the most expensive cattle money can buy and one of the largest quarter horse brood mares in the nation ... it was so far from the beaten path that grocery shopping was often done in Kansas City by family plane."[53] The vast Mullendore ranch was described as "a feudal barony where ranch hands still ride with rifle in saddle and trespassers often hear the whine of a warning shot if they cross into Mullendore land, even by mistake."[54] According to another source, "The cowboys say the dining room is so big they do not pass the serving plate. They just send a jeep for it."[55] My mother recalls E.C.'s Grandmother, Jennie Berry Mullendore, arriving in a chauffeur-driven limousine each Christmas with presents for the children; sipping pink champagne poured by E.C.'s wife,

Kathleen; gazing admiringly at her twenty-five carat diamond ring; and flying in the luxurious private plane which E.C. kindly flew to bring her home from my father's army base when her father died.[56] When I was born, Kathleen sent me a sterling silver cup and spoon with my initials: J.G.H.

The sad and dramatic conclusion of the Mullendore marriage—Mullendore's grandson, E.C., was murdered in his home, his Osage wife placed before a grand jury, the Mafia suspected of loans over overextended property, and the mortgage of the Osage allotment questioned—throws a shadow over the history of the magnificent ranch. Journalists sensationalized every aspect of the case, from how much E.C.'s wife spent on perfume and lingerie, to the expense of the buffalo and long-horned cattle he kept on the place to remember times gone by.[57] Yet the wife of E.C. continues to be recalled in Pawhuska as "just the nicest, nicest woman."[58] For both the Mullendores and the Osage, it would seem that tremendous wealth was acquired at a tremendous cost.

9

The "Empire of Vision": Exhibition, Photography and Pawnee Bill

In 1931, the Osage Chiefs Fred Lookout and Bacon Rind presented the president of Phillips Petroleum, Frank Phillips, with a horse, saddle, bridle, and blanket, an honorary membership in the nation, and the name *Hulah-Kihe-Kah*, or Eagle Chief. In accepting the gifts Phillips was gracious, and his friendship with the Osage apparently genuine. The Osage officially stated that they had awarded Phillips membership "[b]ecause of his great friendship with the Osage Indians and the part he has taken as a pioneer in developing their vast resources."[1] Phillips assembled a vast and exquisite collection of American Indian art, including the art of the Osage. Much of the Osage art displayed in his museum today was a gift from the Osage; it would not be preserved had it not been collected by Phillips, and maintained by the Phillips Foundation.

It is noteworthy, however, that Phillips Petroleum had paid the Osage more than $50,000,000 in royalties and oil leases. Also noteworthy is the letter he sent acknowledging congratulations on his membership.

> Most gracious of you to congratulate the Osages, through me, on my appointment as a white chief of their tribe. Senator Owen, whom you know is a Cherokee, called upon me this afternoon and we were thinking of having a conference with Will Rogers, who is also a Cherokee, and Vice-President Curtis, who is Kaw, with a view to starting a movement to take this country back. The white folks seem to be making such a mess of things that we think we Indians should have the nation rightfully restored to us, and see if we can't do a better job in running the country.[2]

Phillips concludes the letter to his friend, General R.L. Bullard, "Incidentally, we might need a white general to lead our forces."[3]

The complexity of Phillips' interaction with the Osage is revealed in photographs taken in the massive summer lodge near the Woolaroc museum on Phillips' estate, both of which are filled with rooms of American Indian and Western art. Chief Lookout and Bacon Rind appear with Phillips, who appears in an elaborately adorned shirt with fringe and an enormous war bonnet with eagle feathers, neither of which was traditional for an Osage warrior or chief; in a photo dated March 1931, Phillips poses with arms crossed in front of a buffalo robe inscribed with a petroleum rig, tanker, Model T, and biplane, a robe designed by Zach Miller of the 101 Ranch, a fellow white rancher who ran a Pawnee Bill–style extravaganza.[4] The assemblage of rhino, zebra, lion, reindeer, moose, buffalo, and other stuffed heads surrounding the hide, and the Western landscapes, leather-bound books, American Indian blankets, and assorted objects surrounding Phillips all suggest the range of interests represented in a collection generated by investment in oil wells in the Osage region. Phillips was not a "white chief," nor was he an Indian in a position to tell "the white folks" how to operate the country; he was, however, a man in a position

Frank Phillips (with full feather headdress) being inducted into the Osage nation at his summer lodge (Woolaroc), September 27, 1920 (courtesy Woolaroc Museum, Bartlesville, Oklahoma).

to extend enormous monetary profits to the Osage, who in turn presented him with objects brilliantly curated today.

The National Cowboy & Western Heritage Museum in Oklahoma City—formerly known as the Cowboy Hall of Fame, located, as the name of my father's column implies, on the crest of Persimmon Hill—manifests a similar ideological complexity in its assemblage of a range of American Indian and Western objects and art. The initial, overwhelming impact made by the museum lies in the enormous statue located directly across from the entrance, an eighteen-foot high plaster statue by James Fraser titled *End of the Trail*. Although known as "one of the most recognized symbols of the American West,"[5] and perceived by many as a memorial to the American Indian, it is also a monumental image of subjugation, and little acknowledgement is provided of how "the end of the trail" was reached. The genocide of so many peoples could be perceived almost as "an inevitable natural disaster[,] rather than the product of vicious programs and policies of business and government."[6]

Depicting an American Indian slumped on a spent horse, Fraser's subject's head is dropped, braids and spear falling forward in exhaustion. A critic of the sculpture noted that it strikes a nostalgic, regretful tone, and asks of sculptures like the Remingtons that dominate the Cowboy and Heritage Museum, "[w]hat exactly are they mourning? ... we see in Fraser's sculpture a white culture grieving for itself, for the loss of its own inner wildness of soul."[7] That the huge statue dominates the entrance gallery to the museum suggests that cowboy and Western culture once required—or, at the least, identified with the notion of—the romanticized obliteration of a people.

This chapter examines the ideological complexity behind photography, collections and exhibitions in the region of the Osage nation, and the ideological mechanisms that shaped the representation of both Osage and settler in photography, exhibition, and art.

Photography

Studio portraiture of white Americans in the nineteenth century was conducted on rare and serious occasions, and the relatively fine dress evident in such images is therefore unsurprising. A comparison with photographs of American Indians, however, is striking. Dominated by cultural clichés, they frequently reveal people from a range of cultures dressed in the attire of Plains Indians, simply because it was the expectation of a consuming white public. While the slowness of early photography con-

James Fraser's *End of the Trail*, at the National Cowboy & Western Heritage Museum (© Dickinson Research Center, National Cowboy & Western Heritage Museum, Oklahoma City, Oklahoma).

tributed to a lack of smiling faces in formal photographs, "the sternness seen in many Indian faces has been translated as stoicism, [although] [i]t could just as easily be a sign of annoyance with the pose[,]" or the standard seriousness of early photography.[8] Such images as a young Shirley Temple learning sign language from a Blackfeet Indian in full headdress (a film still from *Susannah of the Mounties* [1939]),[9] and a startling photograph in which a man named Long Wolf points a pistol at his wife and small child,[10] enact stereotypical expectations of difference and drama, and the photographs of Osage people are little different.[11] These distressing stereotypes were perpetuated in "[c]omic books, toys, games, television programs, movies, and county fairs" of the era.[12]

The "scientific" photographs of unadorned American Indians taken by physical anthropologists seeking to document genetic features, and to illustrate the effects of "pure" and "contaminated" Indian bloodlines, are equally heartbreaking and bizarre.[13] As Richard Hill notes, "[p]hysical anthropologists wanted to record facial types in an effort to develop a catalogue of measurements for each tribal group, much like a visual genetic database social scientists believed that racial determinants of intelligence were based upon the size of the skull and brain."[14] This goal—studying skull sizes and shapes—became "the leading rationalization for museums and universities to collect Indian remains[,]"[15] and presumably Native American art as well.

Yet despite this agenda of racist portrayal, photographs arranged by the Osage themselves, and informal photographs of Osage ceremonies and gatherings, reveal richness, variety, and the gradual appropriation of modernity, much like the photographs of the Allottees in the Tribal Museum. A photograph of the Council of the Osage—including White Horn, *Ne-Kah-Wah-She-Tun-Kah*, Governor Bigheart, W.T. Leahey, Charles Prudom, Joe Boulanger, Black Dog *Ola-ha-wal-la, A-she-gah, Tsa-mah-hah*, Julian Trumbly, Saucy Chief, and *Mo-sha-to-moi*—illustrates a range of proud Osage elders. The attire of the men in the photograph is striking: far from the stereotypical Plains attire imposed in studios and films for a white audience, the Osage are dressed in white shirts and Pendleton blankets, some with the otter turban headdress of a highly respected member of the tribe, and others with bowlers or cowboy hats. One member of the Council wears a Western suit.[16]

Photographs from the turn of the century also illustrate a striking mix of tradition and modernity. A photograph of Leo Miles and Charley Whip from approximately 1920, taken in front of a modern clapboard house, shows the men in full Osage attire, including a roach made from the long black hairs of a wild turkey or porcupine guard hair (Miles),[17] and an eagle fan made from the underside of a golden eagle's tail and handle of otter fur; between them stands their white housekeeper.[18] A photograph of an Osage wedding procession from the same time period reveals two Osage men in the clothing of the cowboy leading a carriage containing a bride and two elders dressed in red and blue wedding coats, adapted with ribbonwork and applique from U.S. military coats given to the Osage during their diplomatic visits to Washington, D.C. The women are wrapped in Pendleton blankets and adorned with enormous felt

Front row, from left, John Abbot (Osage), Lone Chief Matlock (Pawnee), Frank Phillips and Chief Red Eagle (Osage) at Phillips' Woolaroc ranch, near Pawhuska, Oklahoma, September 27, 1920. Others unidentified (courtesy Woolaroc Museum, Bartlesville, Oklahoma).

plumage atop felt top hats, with traditional jewelry and a ribbon blanket dressing the carriage horse.[19] Other photographs show traditionally dressed families and individuals in Western dress with touring cars, parked alongside traditional domed homes, arched with saplings and covered in brush.[20] A photograph of Frank Phillips with both Pawnee and Osage elders similarly reveals a mix of traditional and white/Western dress.

Exhibition and Art

As many historians and anthropologists attest, art history tends to be "contingent on a corpus of known works, however accidental their survival and however arbitrary ... the reasons they became prized[.]"[21] The criteria of the Osage on what constitutes an object of value have rarely been taken into account in the collection and exhibition of Osage art.

During the Victorian era, and particularly during the Arts and Crafts movement of the late nineteenth century, American Indian art became popular among white audiences; yet their understanding of what constitutes "art" was profoundly different from the considerations of the Osage.[22] The market for Indian art expanded precisely at the time of assimilation. Yet the commodity most desired by white collectors was a romanticized vision of authentic "Indianness"—"the Indian as noble savage, tragic warrior, or new-age mystic."[23] The trade, purchase, and receipt as gift of art by Western collectors can also be viewed in the context of coercion, violence, or misrepresentation, stripping communities of cultural reference points.[24] In each case, the selection of what was exhibited and characterized as art was enacted within a power system derived from the ability of institutions to classify, categorize, and hierarchically rank cultures.[25]

The history of the exhibition of American Indian art thus reflects a view of non-Western cultures as exotic or curious. The conception of anthropological knowledge as a system of "collecting, comparing, and classifying impressions" was revealed in perspectives on exhibition—perspectives that have been described as characteristic of the Western philosophical tradition in which "the Other, as the object of knowledge, must be separate, distinct, and preferably distant from the knower."[26] Thus, in the seventeenth through the nineteenth centuries, American Indian art—such as the *wa-xo-be* of the Osage—was exhibited in curiosity cabinets without specific attribution and interpreted by Europeans "as strange or grotesque."[27] American Indians themselves were exhibited as exotic items on display: Osage and other members of Missouri peoples, for example, were ordered in 1725 to be "exported" and displayed by the King of France at the Bois de Boulogne, "presented with coats and hats trimmed with gold lace and required to dance at the Theatre Italien. They were taken to balls and routs. The peaux rouges were immediately found to be exotic, sexy and thoroughly fashionable."[28]

During the nineteenth century, art created by American Indians was collected as part of an effort to demonstrate a lower stage of human evolution.

> Native-made objects came to be regarded as scientific specimens, "artifacts" that contained information about the stages of technological development.... Ethnological collectors assembled huge quantities of Native American material in museums newly built to receive them, as part of a large scholarly project designed to reconstruct the historical evolution of mankind.[29]

In the early twentieth century, European Modernists and American Abstract Expressionists looked to American Indian art for a sense of primal or intuitive creative essence. Although American Indian art was praised, the art was displayed and appropriated in the absence of the social context or intentions of the art, or input from the artists; the visceral appearance and perceived expressive quality of the art to white audiences was presented as admirable because it reflected a "primitive subconscious."

In the work of the Oklahoma "Kiowa Five"—all from my father's hometown of Anadarko—and the Southwest and Studio styles on the 1950s, a different expectation was imposed on Native American art. The perception of the art as "primitive," however, remained: a "modern, flat, decorative style" that illustrated images of traditional life. The uniform, two-dimensional format continued to be encouraged, and to fulfill white expectations of a "sedate predictability."[30] The work of Stephen Mopope, for example, my father's favorite artist, profoundly influenced the commercial artwork of the era.

One exception to this flat, decorative style was the work of Oscar Howe. After a painting of Howe's was rejected for the 1958 Philbrook Annual exhibition, he responded,

> Who ever said that my paintings are not in traditional Indian style has poor knowledge of Indian art indeed. There is much more to Indian art than pretty, stylized pictures.... Are we to be held back forever with one phase of Indian painting, with no right for individualism, dictated to as the Indian always has been, put on reservations and treated like a child, and only the white Man knows what is best for him? Now, even in art, "You little child do what we think is best for you, nothing different." Well, I am not going to stand for it.[31]

Similarly, when asked whether his work was "appropriate Indian art," the Mohawk artist Rick Glazer-Danay replied, "My work is always appropriate Indian art. My work is how I define myself as an Indian person in the twentieth century."[32]

Osage art from the preceding two hundred years has been dispersed in museums and private collections around the world, as well as stolen, traded or destroyed. To provide but one example, Gordon Lillie ("Pawnee Bill") established a tourist attraction in 1930 that led to the destruction of much art from Osage County. The "Old Town and Indian Trading Post" containing facsimiles of a trading post and the dwellings of the Cheyenne, Comanche, Kiowa, Seminole, Pawnee and Pottawatomie, featured a "model of the mysterious ancient cliff dwellings of the Southwest."[33] The Tewa House, as it was called, served as a museum of American Indian art and relics; in 1939 it burned to the ground, and all of the art it contained was destroyed.[34] Trade and acquisition by collectors has led to the Osage community's loss of objects of immense religious and historical significance. My relative George Laughlin "had a big collection of Indian costumes, beaded and multicolored, including ... headdresses, moccasins, tomahawks, beaded shirts, leather britches, peace pipes ... a whole room in Cushing was devoted to his Indian artifacts."[35] My Great Uncle Earl reputedly acquired the staff of Quanah Parker, the great leader of the Native American Church, and incredibly, traded Parker's staff, of immense religious and historical significance, for a Western landscape.

One of the largest collections of Osage art in Oklahoma is at the Gilcrease Museum in Tulsa, Oklahoma, where my Uncle Everett Berry, Jr., once sat on the board of directors. Gilcrease was one-eighth Creek, and his first wife was Osage[36]; he may, therefore, have had a personal sensitivity with respect to American Indian art. The Gilcrease Museum holds American Indian objects in a separate wing as art, although its 2003 catalogue discusses the objects as part of an "anthropology collection ... includ[ing] archaeological, historic, and contemporary objects produced by the indigenous populations of the Western Hemisphere."[37] That American Indian art was considered separate is indicated by a curator's statement that after 1955, "Gilcrease continued to collect fine art and manuscript materials although this activity was eclipsed by his growing interest in archaeology ... [and] anthropology."[38]

The collection of essays by Gilcrease curators published in 2009 describes this art as a "collection of anthropological artifacts,"[39] and no American Indian object is contained in the Chief Curator's discussion of the "Masterworks of a Master Collector."[40] The bright hallways displaying Remingtons, Russells, Sharps, and other master paintings depicting cowboys stands in marked contrast to the shadowed rooms displaying fragile Indian objects. The expectation in virtually all American museums and galleries that contemporary American Indian art conform to the work of artists like the Kiowa Five, who "synthesized their own historical and artistic traditions with a modern, flat, decorative style" suggests that "native peoples, grasping for cultural legitimacy and survival in the industrialized West, [are often forced to] accept the economic option of converting culture into commodity."[41]

The Gilcrease Museum, like the Phillips collection, however, is noteworthy for its preservation of extensive collections of art that might otherwise have been lost. Both Acee Blue Eagle and Woodrow "Woody" Crumbo, prominent artists in the 1950s, were close to Gilcrease; Blue Eagle, who was also Creek, told Gilcrease in correspondence that "You have been indeed a grand person to me outside of our business, and beyond that connection you have touched my heart with your personal feelings and soul ... you have a spiritual quality about you that is carried over to people of a creative talent!"[42] It is striking that the Osage Tribal Art Museum, located at the heart of the reservation in Pawhuska, contains so few objects, and has such minimal resources for display, when museums not controlled by the Osage hold many of their most sacred objects. While the Osage author Wiley Steve Thornton described his experience at the National Museum of the American Indian in New York as disheartening, however, stating, "[i]t is a strange place to work ... [the non–Indians] seemed to feel more for the objects in their care, however, than for the actual Native people. They certainly didn't understand that some of these things were still alive with a spirit in each one,"[43] the Osage willingly sold art and artifacts to museums such as the Gilcrease after the 1920s. Indeed, it is museums such as the Gilcrease that prevented sacred objects no longer wanted by the Osage from being discarded or destroyed.

Exposition and Extravaganza: Pawnee Bill

In the nineteenth century the interaction between the cowboy and the American Indian in Oklahoma was sensationalized. Films, extravaganzas, travelling shows, and associated ephemera demonstrated, as a bill for "Princess Wenona and Edith Tantlinger [of Millers Brothers and Arlington] 101 Ranch" claimed, "A Marvelous Exhibition ... [of the] Real Wild West."[44] Immediately adjacent to the property of my Great-Grandfather George Madison Berry, and a friend of my family, Gordon W. "Pawnee Bill" Lillie established "Pawnee Bill's Historical Wild West Indian Museum and Encampment Show" in the tradition of William F. "Buffalo Bill" Cody and James Butler "Wild Bill" Hickock, a show that toured Europe, Canada, and America, and became one of the largest expositions in the world.[45] Lillie's ranch, which attracted tens of thousands of visitors,[46] showcased the achievements of his wife May, "champion girl shot of the West and the most daring and graceful bronco rider in the world," Mexican vaqueros, and staged Indian American scenarios, as well as "a realistic Indian village, pony express act, and a stagecoach re-enactment."[47]

As a young man Lillie lived in a dugout, and "he opted to spend his time visiting nearby Indians, who often camped along the Ninnescah River."[48] An English-speaking Pawnee taught Lillie the Pawnee language, and Lillie "became obsessed with the dime novels that depicted "the lure of the Wild West" and tales of Indians.[49] Lillie moved to Kansas, where he killed "Trigger" Jim Braden in a gunfight; he was acquitted and moved to the Pawnee reservation, where, according to Glenn Shirley's research, he acquired a Pawnee name and became friends with *An-re-Kah-rard*, or Rush Roberts; Ruling His Son; and Left Hand, chief of the Kitkahahki.[50] Shirley claims that Lillie participated in the last buffalo hunt with the

9. The "Empire of Vision" 149

From left, standing: *Pa-So-Top-A*, unidentified, infant, Mary Lookout, Jean Standing Bear (obscured), Chief Fred Lookout, unidentified, Mrs. Julia Lookout, unidentified; seated: Col. Zach Miller of the 101 Ranch, Pawnee Bill (Gordon Lillie), Frank Phillips with Standing Bear's baby, Francis Revard, and Will Rogers, 1920 (Research Division of Oklahoma Historical Society).

Pawnee and a Pawnee war with the Comanche, and afterward became the interpreter and secretary for the Pawnee Agency, as well as a teacher (and apparently harsh disciplinarian) at the Agency Boarding School for the Pawnee.[51] He later worked as a cowboy, engaging in a series of jobs and violent incidents (gunfights), and ultimately joined Buffalo Bill Cody's Wild West Show.[52]

> By 1887 Lillie organized his own Wild West show, gathering "165 horses, mules, and broncos for 84 Pawnee, Comanche, Kiowa, Kaw, and Wichita Indians, 50 white and Mexican cowboys, and 30 trappers, hunters, and scouts who were to perform with the Pawnee Bill Wild West Show. Billed as the "Rifle Queen" and the "Princess of the Prairie," May [Lillie] was a star performer as she rode around the rink shooting targets out of the air from horseback. Buckskin Joe's Wild West acts, which included Annie Oakley, also were added to Lillie's entourage.[53]

Lillie's later show, Pawnee Bill's Historical Wild West, Indian Museum, and encampment, again starred "the famed guide, government interpreter and Oklahoma Hero, Major Gordon William Lillie (Pawnee Bill), and May

Lillie, champion shot girl of the West and the most daring and graceful bronco rider in the world."[54] Lillie's brother Albert, billed as "Oklahoma Al," king of the cowboys, and "Mexican vaqueros from Chihuahua, Mexico," were included in the show[55]; a circular of 1901 describes his show in Wisconsin as "Purely Educational, Genuinely Historical, Delightfully Amusing, A Good Inspiring Exhibition, consisting of Cow boys, Indians, Mexicans, Arabs, Cossacks, United States, English, German and French Cavalrymen. Roosevelt's Rough Riders and History of Light Artillery."[56]

To publicize the Wild West Show, color lithograph posters and heralds (printed folio sheets "lithographed on the outside with vivid illustrations and crammed with flowery and informative text") were distributed by advertising crews throughout the region in which the show would be held. An author of the time described these heralds as "extolling the amazing, prodigious, colossal, stupendous wonders of the forthcoming show."[57] The heralds show handsome images of "Major" Gordon W. Lille; images of Indians attacking prairie schooners and performing staged dances; and portraits of American Indians such as Geronimo and the Sioux performers Iron Shell and Crow Good Voice.

In Pawnee Bill's performances, "little attention was paid to cultural or historical accuracy."[58] In some cases re-enacted battles portrayed the American Indians as aggressors; even the Battle at Wounded Knee, in which three hundred of three hundred and fifty Sioux were slaughtered,[59] the dead left lying in a blizzard where they had fallen, was reenacted, depicting the Sioux as the aggressors.[60] All of the American Indians in the show, regardless of their nationality, were dressed in Western style black pants and shirts, generic breastplates, and enormous feather headdresses. The magnificently ornamented wagons, decorated in gold raised relief with tableaus of historical events, also show historically inaccurate images of the "discovery" of America, the slaughter of American soldiers, "Pocohantas Saving the Life of Captain John Smith," and other romantic and imaginary scenes. Ironically, Gordon Lillie claimed that his show was the only accurate portrayal of the West:

> Wild Western stories as a rule, bear but a slight resemblance to the actualities of life beyond the frontier, the realities of which are vastly more romantic, picturesque and extraordinary, than were ever dreamed of or painted by the untutored and inexperienced butches who have the hardihood to launch volumes of putative sketches of "life and those who enjoy it to the Wild West," upon the much polluted sea of literature.[61]

Pawnee Bill melded together performances of "famous light horse cavalrymen from the far off Russian Steppes, the desert born Bedouins and their fleet footed native steeds, Vaqueros from Old Mexico and … wonderful Bolus throwers from South America" as well as "Australian boomerang throwers, Japanese atheletes, and Hindu fakirs," in an exoticizing hodge-podge that claimed to be "the most complete, most entertaining, most instructive, most truthful, most moral, most humanitarian, and most exciting exhibition" of the "habits and customs of the red men."[62] Included in Pawnee Bill's exhibition, according to a herald from the early 1900s, were "braves of council smoking the peace pipe," "Indians of many tribes led by their palated and stately chiefs, headed by the only Indian brass band in the world," and "not the least attractive, stone-faced papooses that never cry."[63]

The phenomenon of spectacle was not limited to Pawnee Bill's exhibitions, or to the many local exhibitors who mounted minor extravaganzas. As early as 1827, four Osage men and two women, with the encouragement of the French entrepreneur and showman David Delaunay, traveled to France, Belgium, the Netherlands, Germany, Switzerland, and Italy.[64] The travellers—*Ke-He-Kah Shinkah* (Little Chief), *Wash-inka-Sabe* (Black Bird or Black Spirit), *Minkcha-tagonh* (Young Soldier), *Mo'n-Sho'n A-ki-da Tonkah* (Big Soldier), *Mi-Ho'n-Ga* (Sacred Sun), and *Gthe-Do'n-Wi'n* (Hawk Woman)—initially encountered vast crowds, rendered curious by the notion of the "noble savage" disseminated by Jean-Jacques Rousseau.[65] "[U]pon arrival of the New-England in Le Havre on July 27, the docks were crowded with gawkers, some of whom climbed onto spars and into the rigging of nearby ships to catch a glimpse of the strange and colorfully attired sauvages."[66] At times the Osage experienced utter humiliation, as when some young men in France "approached Sacred Sun and Hawk Woman, and, with borrowed Osage phrases, attempted to question them about amorous matters":

> In Verviers, Belgium, a casino proprietor demanded four of the Osages, including the two women, to sit on chairs atop a billiard table and be ogled like exhibits in a freak show. Sacred Sun and Hawk Woman lowered their heads and wept in forced humiliation. When Big Soldier fell ill in September of 1829 and his recovery was in doubt, there came an offer to buy his corpse for display in a "menagerie, stuffed like the late Hottentot Venus." ... In Paris, hustlers peddled images of the Indians painted on fans, stitched on work bags, cast into metal paperweights, and even baked into spiced-bread figures for hoi polloi to chomp on as they gaped at [the Osage].[67]

Ultimately, as the group travelled through Belgium, Holland, Germany, Switzerland, and Italy, interest in the exhibitions declined, as did their treatment: the Osage had to split into two groups and rely upon charity to find their way home, and two of the group died along the way.[68]

In a much later iteration of the journey of spectacle, again a journey of six Osage including Raymond W. Red Corn, Jr., shared their skills at the British Boy Scouts' World Jamboree of 1928. Red Corn reportedly danced a flamboyant dance characteristic of other tribes, instead of performing the traditional Osage Straight Dance, and won championship contests among the assembled Boy Scouts; the boys, camped at the Jamboree in teepees, were visited by Lord Baden Powell (both the founder of the Boy Scouts and an oppressive colonizer), Prince George (later known as King George VI), and the Prince of Wales. The dancers made fry bread and danced with their visitors. Later, a Royal Car was sent to bring the Osage performers to dine with the Royal Family at Buckingham Palace and Windsor Castle.[69]

The appetite of Europeans and white Americans for cultural exhibitions—which coincided in time with efforts at colonial domination—was seemingly inexhaustible. As Timothy Mitchell maintains, cultural exhibitions were representative of "a particularly European concern with rendering things up to be viewed.… The apparent certainty with which everything seems ordered and organized, calculated and unambiguous … its political decidedness … [constituted a] seemingly determined relationship between representations and 'reality.'"[70] As in the Land Ordinance of 1787, the architectural and spatial design of structures containing administrative offices to "manage" the Osage, and the detailed state, region, county, and property maps maintained by my ancestors, exhibitions rendered people and cultures subject to categorization and control, and fixed individuals in a historical and romanticized past.

Yet it is striking that the Osage, at the height of their prosperity, elected to disseminate representations of their culture that conformed to the expectations of a European audience. At a historical moment when the Osage enjoyed substantial material agency, representatives at the British World Jamboree—as well as individuals who performed in Pawnee Bill's show—willingly conformed to the appetites of an uninformed, and perhaps ineducable, audience. Such participation has been interpreted by some as acquiescence or internalized racism: Edwin Wade, for example, argues that the rise in the popularity of "ethnic" art represents "an interactive form of culture change, wherein native peoples, grasping for cultural legitimacy and survival in the industrialized West, accept the economic option of converting culture into commodity."[71] Such choices, however, may also be viewed as an assertion of agency, a willingness to engage in and experiment with cultural appropriation, or even a defiant posture or acknowledgement of audience ignorance. Clearly, the Osage had access to public performance of their own identities, and made decisions about what those performances would reveal.

10

"The View from Persimmon Hill": My Daddy, My Mama and Federal Policy in the 1950s

> If I close my eyes, I can see Dragonfly there beyond the hedge. I can see my young parents walking toward the creek in the late afternoon, a coppery light on the path. I can hear my grandmother's voice in the rooms of the house and in the cool corners of the arbor. And these are the sacred recollections of the mind and heart.—*N. Scott Momaday*[1]

In my favorite photograph of my father, taken in the mid-1950s, Daddy stands in front of a furniture store in his painter's work clothes, handsome, with the kind of smile only those eternally young and hopelessly in love might display. He is painting the window with an advertisement, as the professional artist that he was, illustrating a man on horseback carting away all of the furniture from the store. Yet here, at the hand of a highly trained and skilled artist, who deeply respected both the experience and wisdom of the American Indian as well as his own ancestry, emerges a caricature of "the" Indian, a comic rendering of features, clothing, attitude, and posture; here is no identifiable Osage, Pawnee, Otoe, Kansa, or Cheyenne. This single photograph of my handsome, gifted, and hardworking father illustrates the juxtaposition of a personal attitude and a social shorthand, a juxtaposition evident in social policies, literary representations, and commercial advertisements of the day.

This chapter will examine my father's later, great contribution to art and journalism—his illustration and representation of American Indian and settler culture in "The View from Persimmon Hill." His work exists

Ross Hess, painting display window of furniture store, circa 1960 (author's photograph).

against a backdrop of oppressive and annihilating federal policy and predatory or denigrating representations of American Indians, some endured for strategic purposes by American Indians, including the Osage. I examine this ongoing colonization, including the alignment of commercial interests with representations alluding to, or overtly representing, a homogeneous vision of American Indians in the 1950s. Against this confused and conflicted backdrop I position the Osage people's representation of themselves—both in the art of individuals and in the *I'n-lon-schka*.

Federal Policy in the 1950s

By the era of the 1950s, the violence against the Osage characteristic of the 1920s, and the poverty of the Great Depression, had ended. Federal policy addressing the sovereignty of American Indians, however, had a devastating impact on their quality of life, and on the legal and effective existence of specific nations. The General Allotment Act of 1877 required each "qualified," "mixed breed" Native American to accept citizenship in order to receive the deed to a parcel of land (the rest was seized by the federal government); in 1924, the Indian Citizenship Act declared all American Indians to be citizens of the United States.[2] As a consequence, resource negotiations could "be conducted between 'American citizens' rather than between representatives of separate nations, a context in which federal and corporate arguments 'for the greater good' could be predicted to prevail."[3]

In announcing the passage of the Indian Citizenship Act, President Calvin Coolidge appeared in front of the White House with four Osage men. Coolidge would later present an award thanking "the OSAGE TRIBE for their unswerving loyalty and patriotism, the splendid service rendered, the willing sacrifices made and the bravery of their sons in the military and naval service of the United States"[4]; noteworthy in its absence from American history is the fact that his Vice President in 1929, Charles Curtis, was an Osage, Kaw and Potawatami Indian, the first American Indian (and non–European American) to appear on a winning presidential ticket. Yet Curtis' early actions in the direction of assimilation would ultimately facilitate the destruction of some American Indian nations. The Curtis Act of 1898, of which Curtis was the original author, amended the Dawes Act to bring the Choctaw, Chickasaw, Muscogee, Cherokee, and Seminole within the purview of General Allotment, resulting in the loss of approximately 90 million acres of land formerly belonging to American Indians; it effectively abolished tribal courts and governments by transferring the authority over who qualified for tribal membership to the federal government, and facilitated the establishment of Indian boarding schools. Ironically, Curtis' own bill resulted in the Secretary of the Interior, Ethan A. Hitchcock, terminating his own Osage National Government, and replacing it with a Tribal Council consisting of individuals under the direct supervision of the BIA.[5]

In 1952, the Bureau of Indian Affairs submitted to Congress a list of the American Indian nations it had determined

> were "ready to undergo ... complete termination of all federal services" and "an end to the exercise of federal trust responsibility over their affairs." Promoted as a measure to "liberate American Indian tribes from federal domination," the concept of termination was really intended ultimately to do away with tribes [and their] reservations," at least those which had not been amenable to conversion into resource and profit generators for the U.S. economy.[6]

That the overriding concern of the Termination Act was financial is indicated by the fact that the Congressmen behind this measure—Arthur Watkins, Patrick McCarren, Hugh Butler, and Richard Neuberger—represented constituents whose interests disrupted tribal resources owned by American Indians in Utah, Nevada, Wisconsin, and Oregon.[7]

The first of the nations targeted under the Termination Act was the Osage, whose representatives testified in Congress to dissuade authorities from unilaterally dissolving their nation. The most compelling argument to the Congressional committee was that the nation was "self-sustaining and will pay all expenses for Federal supervision during the continuance of the mineral period."[8] An acid exchange between the representative of the Osage and a United States Senator regarding termination demonstrates that the focus of the government was on money, not empowerment:

> MR. HARRISON: Did I understand you to mean that the tribe is willing to pay all of the costs of the tribal operation? ... That means not only [the $300,000 to run the tribe, but also] ... the cost of supervision and review from the area and Washington office of the Bureau of Indian Affairs, the Office of Audit, and Inspection by the General Accounting Office, and the costs involved in reviewing Osage tribal budgets and the appropriation of tribal funds and also the cost of the liason staff and the cost of local hospitals and everything? I understand you to say the Osages are willing to pay all of those costs?
>
> SENATOR MONRONEY: I do not know about these intangible costs. They are part of the United States. Maybe the gentleman would like to have them pay the cost of the Internal Revenue Service, because they have to collect taxes from them and other things. But I do not believe that is the policy of Congress.[9]

Although the Termination Act of 1953 ultimately terminated—i.e., suspended federal services to and recognition of[10]—a total of 109 nations, the Osage were able to successfully resist termination due to the efforts of the Tribal Council.[11] The BIA did, however, successfully punish the Osage "by making them the only Indians of all the nation's 544 federally recognized tribes to need a 50 percent blood quantum to be eligible for BIA scholarships and jobs."[12]

The Osage were also able to escape the effects of Public Law 280, 1954, which increased the number of terminated nations, although it, like all other nations, experienced a reduction of sovereignty as a consequence of the law. In an extension of the "unilateral assertion of U.S. 'plenary power'" articulated in *United States v. Kagama* (1886), Public Law 280 subordinated the status of indigenous national governments to the federal government, effectively diminishing their sovereignty to a level roughly the same as counties.[13] The Relocation Act of 1956, which financed American Indian individuals and families to relocate to urban "job training centers," denied funds for training economic development on reservations; those who relocated were required to sign agreements that they would not return.[14] While few Osage took advantage of the program, the result was a diaspora of American Indians: by 1980 "more than half of the 1.6 million Indians in the U.S. ... [were] scattered to cities across the country."[15]

Accompanying these legislative acts were decisions by the United States Supreme Court that continued the gutting of the rights and sovereignty of American Indians. In *Tee-Hit-Ton v. United States* (1955), for example, the Court determined that a band of the Tlingit Nation, who had never been subject to conquest, could not establish title to the 350,000 acres of territory they had used and occupied since "time memorial."[16] The decision, as Ward Churchill and Glenn Morris state, "neatly finished the U.S. reversal of the 'Discovery Doctrine' concerning who conveys title to whom in North America, and effectively gutted whatever was left of aboriginal rights in U.S. jurisprudence."[17] It was decisions such as this that would give rise a decade later to the powerful resistance movement known as the American Indian Movement (AIM).[18]

Commercial Representations

Against this backdrop of the destruction of American Indian sovereignty, and the growing resistance to that suppression, existed a simultaneous expansion in their commercial depiction as a cartoonish, homogeneous "type." As a number of scholars and activists have noted, the American Indian emerged in advertising beginning with the cigar store Indian in the 1700s; "[i]n nearly every case, American Indian references tend[ed] to be an amalgram of lifestyles, practices, and artifacts of various indigenous groups ... collaps[ing] cultural histories into a sort of frozen and unchanging time before contact with Europeans."[19]

Perhaps the archetype of corporations which appropriated and/or exploited representations of the Osage were banks and companies in the oil industry. In the Osage Tribe's Centennial Celebration volume, commissioned and approved by the Osage Tribal Council, entities including Phillips 66 Petroleum, Skelly Oil, Bigheart Pipe Line and Crude Oil Corporation, the Sooner Pipe and Supply Corporation, the Ponca City Security Bank and Trust, the Ponca City Savings and Loan Association, the First State Bank of Fairfax, and the First National Bank and Trust Company all eagerly employed photographs and illustrations of the Osage in an attempt to wed their commercial interests with the Osage Nation.[20] The advertisement for Bigheart Pipe Line Corporation and its affiliate Bigheart Crude Oil Corporation, for example, is dominated by its corporate logos, huge hearts pierced by a pipeline and a crude oil tanker, respectively; the print below extolls the fact that Bigheart is fourth in Osage County and seventh in Oklahoma in crude oil purchases, as well as the fact that their corporate name was derived from Chief James Bigheart, for whom the town of Bigheart (now Barnsdall) was named. The somewhat distressing imagery of an oil tanker bursting through the center of a red heart is portrayed as a beneficial merging of cultural references.[21]

Even more complex and confused is the advertisement in the Osage Centennial for Sooner Pipe and Supply Corporation ("Sooner the Better.")[22] The very name of the corporation, "Sooner," is a reference to individuals who stole across the line during the Run to stake claims on what had previously been American Indian Territory; the name itself promotes the taking of land from those whom it claims to benefit. The sale of leases brought great material benefit to the Osage, explaining the advertisement copy ("Great things have happened, and will continue to happen, since the formal opening of our store on July 21, 1954, the 105th lease sale at the Osage Agency")[23]; certainly, however, the arrival of big oil forever eclipsed traditional ways of life. The featuring of two photographs of "*Pa'-ta zhi'-ga* [INFANTS]" in traditional cradleboards and blankets, positioned bizarrely on either side of a longbow and arrow, is hard to comprehend in this context, as is the matching blue of the aggressive corporate logo and the letters spelling the Osage word for "infant."[24]

Examples of the awkward juxtaposition of cultures and interests in Centennial advertisements are abundant. To cite but one further example, the advertisement for the First National Bank and Trust Company of Ponca City, and the Exchange Bank of Skiatook, Oklahoma, is dominated by a huge photograph of what appears to be a meeting of banking executives and Osage elders in a corporate room. The expressions on the faces of the Osage elders are best described as confident or stolid; the white executives, however, bear facial expressions that can only be described as disgusted, alarmed, or nauseated. The use of the photograph to advertise the banks is baffling; it can only be explained by the simplistic equation that "we were in the same room together; therefore, we have a commercial association." Tellingly, the most modest and therefore sophisticated of these advertisements are those for the local banks in Pawhuska,[25] institutions which undoubtedly had personal interaction with Osage elders and the Tribal Council.

Examples of overt racism in advertisements from the 1950s are abundant. Hertz Rental Car, American Express, Old Gold Cigarettes—all employed caricatures of a homogeneous "Indian" far less respectful and more degrading than advertisements of over a century previous. Coca-Cola and Levi Strauss featured nonspecified "Indians" to advertise their products, although it is hard to understand why the image of a warrior dancing around a fire in a generic, full feather Prairie war bonnet wearing Levi jeans had beneficial effects on product sales. Perhaps most invidious were advertisements employing the dichotomy of idealized Indian "princess" and "squaw." Although the image of the "princess" used to sell such products as Land O' Lakes butter appeared positive, it was always balanced by the negative image of the "squaw."

"The View from Persimmon Hill"

My father's weekly strip for the Sunday *Oklahoman*, titled "The View from Persimmon Hill," later titled "The Western Adventure," thus emerged in the context of ongoing colonization by the federal government—including the use of blood quantum standards for entitlements that effectively served as a "eugenics mechanism"[26]—and the prevalence of racist imagery in commercial advertisements. "The View from Persimmon Hill," and his subsequent column, "The Western Adventure," by contrast, beautifully documented and illustrated the equipment, labor, and challenging life of the cowboy. His illustrated discussions were introduced into the Cowboy Hall of Fame, and echoed the experiences of family history. His first illustrated article, published September 5, 1965, sets the tone for the series:

> Nothing in the history of the Nation has so completely captured the imagination as the saga of the winning of the West. You'll see the dreams ... ideas ... the tools ... and the dwellings ... the skills ... the work ... the outlaws and famous events ... the battles ... the places ... and personalities of the young west.[27]

Daddy's description of cowboys is extensive and complete with detailed illustrations of equipment, gear, and dress. His discussion of the saddle,

The COWBOY'S GEAR
PART I
SADDLES

THE FIRST SADDLE WAS JUST FOLDED PADDING TIED TO THE HORSE WITH A ROPE...

...FROM THIS CRUDE BEGINNING SADDLES WERE DEVELOPED TO SUIT A VARIETY OF NEEDS. ...WESTERN SADDLES WERE DEVELOPED FROM EARLY SPANISH WAR SADDLES. THEY WERE HEAVY AND WELL BUILT ...THEY *HAD TO BE!* THE STRAIN OF 1200 POUNDS OF ENRAGED STEER ON ONE END OF A ROPE, AND 1000 POUNDS OF STUBBORN HORSE ON THE OTHER REQUIRED A STURDY RIGGING!

A SADDLE WAS A COWBOY'S PRIZED POSSESSION, AND HE CHOSE ONE WITH GREAT CARE... AFTER ALL, HE SPENT MOST OF HIS LIFE IN ONE! HE WORKED ON IT, SLEPT ON IT, AND OFTEN IT WAS THE ONLY THING, EXCEPT THE CLOTHES ON HIS BACK, THAT HE OWNED. HE MIGHT PAY A YEARS WAGES FOR A SADDLE... MORE IF IT HAD MUCH DECORATION... MONEY WELL SPENT FOR A LIFETIME INVESTMENT!

SADDLE RIGGING

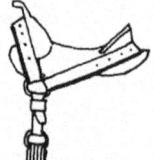  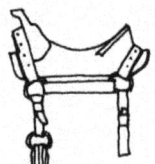 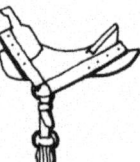

SPANISH RIG ··· CENTER FIRE RIG ··· DOUBLE RIG ··· 3/4 RIG

10. "The View from Persimmon Hill"

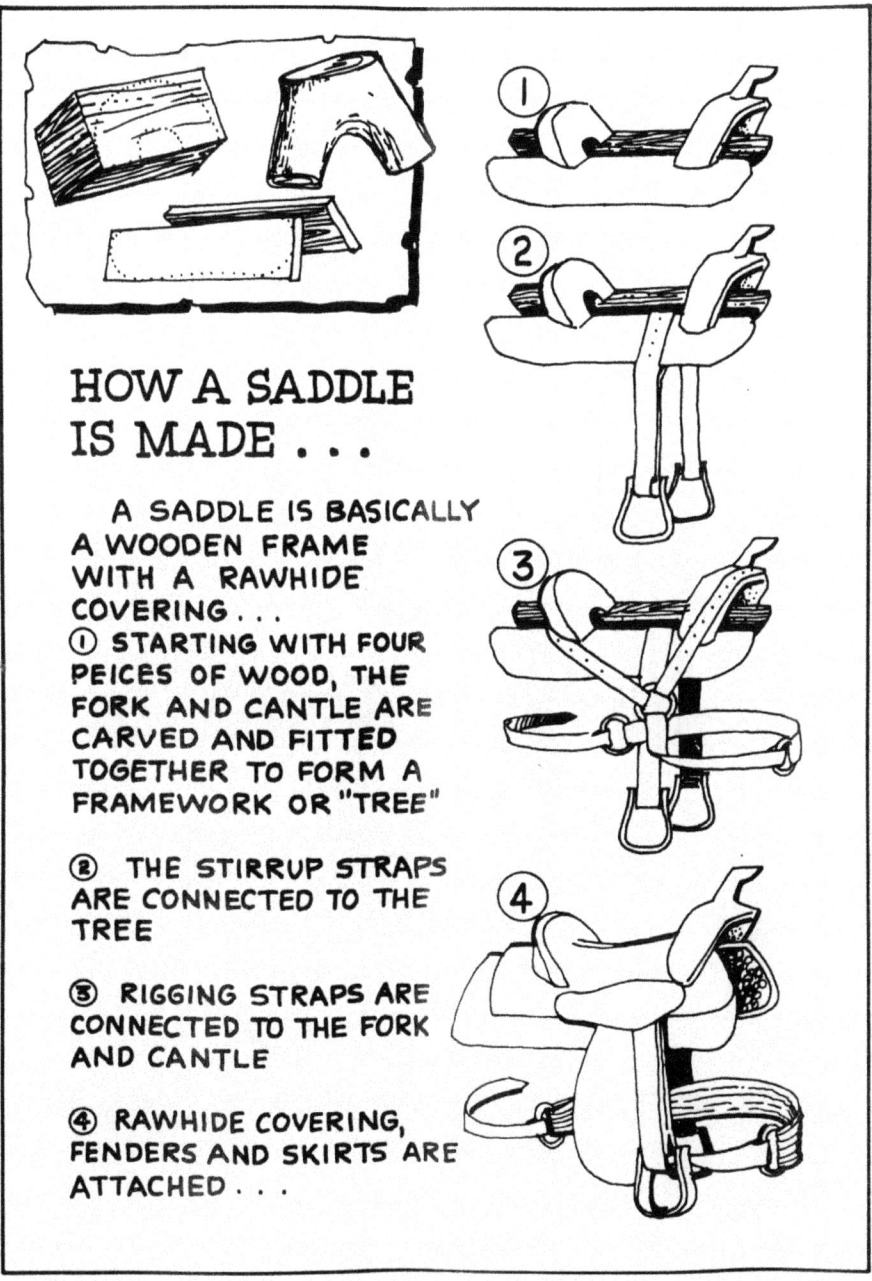

HOW A SADDLE IS MADE...

A SADDLE IS BASICALLY A WOODEN FRAME WITH A RAWHIDE COVERING...

① STARTING WITH FOUR PEICES OF WOOD, THE FORK AND CANTLE ARE CARVED AND FITTED TOGETHER TO FORM A FRAMEWORK OR "TREE"

② THE STIRRUP STRAPS ARE CONNECTED TO THE TREE

③ RIGGING STRAPS ARE CONNECTED TO THE FORK AND CANTLE

④ RAWHIDE COVERING, FENDERS AND SKIRTS ARE ATTACHED...

Opposite, above and following page: "The Cowboy's Gear: Part I, Saddles," from "The View from Persimmon Hill," written and illustrated by Ross Hess.

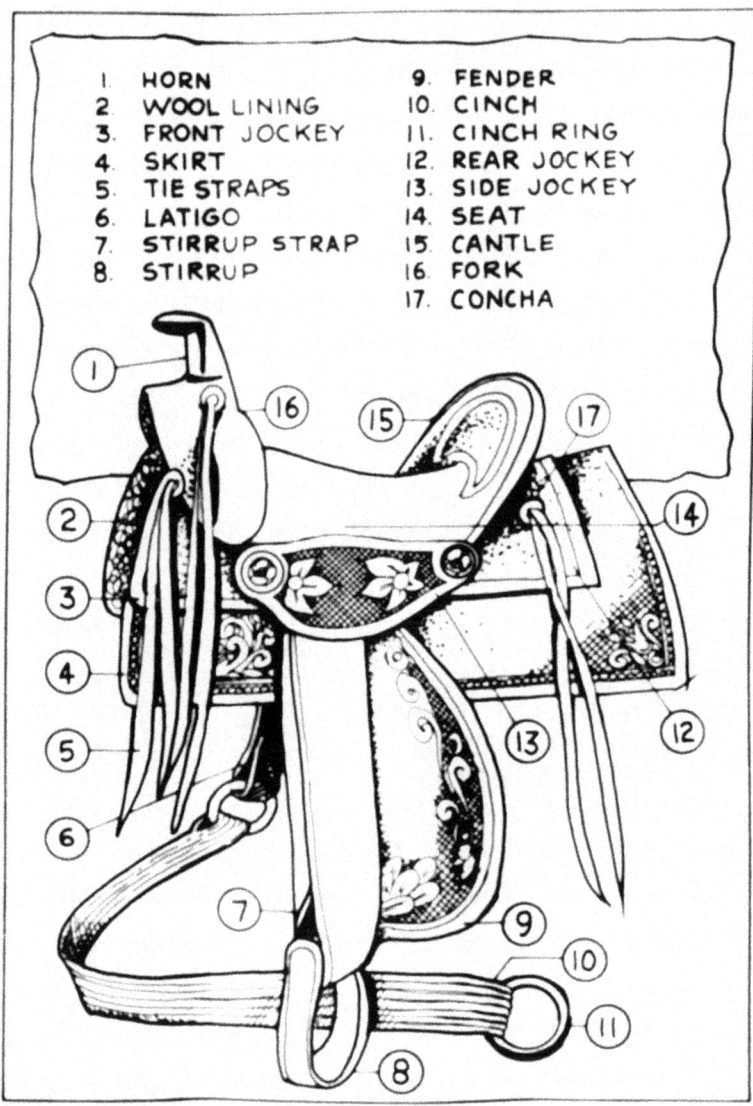

for example, provides extensive discussion of its components and rigging.[28]

Daddy's description of the possessions of the cowboy demonstrates the loving detail of each discussion and illustration. "The Cowboy's Gear, Part II: Possessions" reads:

> Life was simple a hundred years ago ... particularly for the cowpoke ... here was a man whose constant contact with nature gave him everything he needed

10. "The View from Persimmon Hill"

... the sky above with sun, moon and stars was his timepiece, his compass, and roof over his head. Things which we now think to be necessary were not to a cowboy ... if he were herding cattle, he would shave only after completing the months long trip! The Westerner enjoyed certain simple habits, one of which was tobacco ... if he smoked, chances are it would be a "quirly" made from the necessary ingredients of Bull Durham, cigarette paper, and spit. Wooden matches were available then, as was the "cable twist" chewing tobacco. Transportation being what it was then, it might be months or even years before one would see his family ... many carried tintypes of their loved ones. The cowboy had little faith in the "greenback," so if he carried money, it would be gold or silver coin. A cowboy would always carry a knife. Knives were used for everything from skinning game to picking teeth! The pocket knife was most common; some carried the famous "bowie" knife.[29]

His discussion of dress is lovingly detailed:

The average cowboy around 1880 was not a style setting or a glamorous figure. He was conservative, and the clothing he wore reflected this attitude ... usually gray or black, and made of rough fabrics. Duds which are seen nowadays came into being only after the advent of wild west shows and rodeos which glamorized cowboy clothing. Standard chapeau in the old west was black felt and wide brimmed ... until John B. Stetson began in the 1860's. His hats sold for about $15 ... 2 weeks pay for the cowpoke! Sometimes hats were decorated with leather or horsehair bands. The only colorful part of the cowboy's clothing was his bandanna, which would be red or blue ... sometimes it would have a printed pattern ... boots were the most expensive item ... about $30, and were sometimes, but not frequently decorated. Guns, of course, were an important item, and cowboys usually carried one. Gloves were important too. They not only provided warmth for the wearer, but also prevented rope burns and brush scratches. The style in spurs ranged from the simple 4 pointed Texas spur to the elaborate Mexican which had rowels six inches in diameter![30]

"The View from Persimmon Hill" and "The Western Adventure" adopted stances that were politically courageous in the context of the South in the 1950s. My father discussed the important contribution of African Americans, for example, in the history of the West:

Few people are aware of the important contributions made by negroes to the development of the west ... it has been estimated that perhaps ⅓ of the cowboys who worked the Chisholm trail were negroes.... Bill Pickett, a negro, invented bulldogging! They fought and died under General Custer! A negro arrested Billy the Kid and brought him in for questioning during the Lincoln County Range War! Negroes were with Coronado, Lewis and Clark and Fremont!! Negro troopers guarded the boundary against sooners in the run of '89! Negro troopers captured Geronimo, and guarded him at Fort Sill, Oklahoma.... Pioneers on the Oregon trail rode in wagons built by a negro ... Hiram Young. The famed tenth cavalry—an all–Negro Unit! A negro was adopted by the Crow Indians and became a great war chief!![31]

Daddy also discussed the unique contributions of Bill Pickett:

> Bulldogging was the invention of a fellow named Bill Pickett ... a colored cowboy who worked for Zack Miller's 101 Ranch.... One afternoon Bill had been trying to rope a bull—with no success... He finally became disgusted. Jumping from his horse, Bill grabbed the bull by the horns and wrestled him to a standstill. He finally subdued the bull by clamping down on the snout with his teeth and hanging on! ... Pickett's feat was called bulldogging because of the European practice of training dogs to hold bulls at bay by biting their noses ... *bulldogs*! Bill Pickett continued his career with the "101 Ranch Roundup" for many years, and once won a $25,000 bet by throwing a Spanish bull and holding it down for fifteen minutes! Nose biting soon lost its popularity, but bulldogging thrived, and has become the major event in rodeos everywhere![32]

My father's column similarly acknowledged the experience of American Indians.

> To the white man, the buffalo was just an odd looking curiosity of North America ... he never understood the buffalo, or the Indian who depended on them for everything. To the Indian, the buffalo was life ... it provided his food, his clothing, and his shelter. Bones were used to make tools, and buffalo chips were burned to provide heat. Charms, medicines, and musical instruments were made of ingredients provided by the buffalo ... the Indian could not exist without him.... And so the Indian worshipped the buffalo ... every western tribe had ceremonies devoted to the shaggy beasts [image of Mandan buffalo dancer.]... True, the Indian killed the buffalo, but never was he wasteful, for he realized his total dependence upon the life-giving animal. The buffalo ... in 1800 numbered 100 million! Had they been lined up, 6 abreast, would have reached from New York to San Francisco! 1880 saw only hundreds left. It is little wonder then that the Indian hated and fought the white man who came and slaughtered the buffalo ... for in so doing he destroyed the existence of the redman![33]

In a social context of homogenizing and derogatory representation, "The View from Persimmon Hill" and "The Western Adventure" offered a vision of history that acknowledged the presence, legitimacy, and interconnected culture of white settlers, American Indians and African Americans.

The I'n-Lon-Schka

In emphatic contrast to the studious respect or the mercenary indifference of the dominant culture lies the self-representation of the Osage—or rather, the representations produced in honor of *Wah-Kon-Tah*, God, aspects of the natural world, the elders, and the community as a whole. For the Osage, the *I'n-lon-schka*, an offshoot of the Grass Dance ("Pony Smoke") dance, contains rich symbolism maintained by a hierarchy of

Bulldogger Bill Pickett, a cowboy with Zack Miller's 101 Ranch (© Dickinson Research Center, National Cowboy & Western Heritage Museum, Oklahoma City, Oklahoma).

participants, and serves to strengthen, reunite, and reinforce in traditional ways community as a whole. Other dances are dedicated to specific ceremonial intentions: my first Osage dance, the ceremony in June of 2013, for example, was dedicated to the crowning of the Osage Princess, Autumn Williams. Her family, prior Princesses, and important members of the *I'n-*

I'n-lon-shcka dancers, Hominy, Oklahoma, with roundhouse and dance arbor, 2014 (courtesy Benny Polacca/*Osage News*).

lon-shcka committee, were acknowledged and given piles of Pendleton blankets, and both traditional and "fancy" dances were conducted for the community and invited guests.

The *I'n-lon-schka*, however, is the single, defining ceremonial event of the nation. Not only does the *I'n-lon-schka* serve to bind the community together socially, but it also recalls elders and traditional customs, reinforces religious beliefs and practices, acknowledges individuals who have contributed to the community, reminds young participants to have "respect for the drum, their elders, those in authority, those who have gone before them, and their fellow men,"[34] and above all, emphasizes harmonious existence and the possibility of social and spiritual growth.[35] As Alice Callahan states in her definitive text on the *I'n-lon-schka*, emphasis is placed on the dance "because the I'n-Lon-Schka will go on, and the spirits and memories of those who went before are still there and prepare the people for another world."[36] This is so despite the fact that the four-day ceremony, based upon dances acquired from other nations, transmitted through oral tradition, and transformed in dress, architecture, and framing belief system, has endured "the loss of some of the text of many of the older songs and ... precise knowledge of the sequence of the songs ... [as well as] of the ritual connected with the dance."[37]

The modern *I'n-lon-shcka* was introduced in the late nineteenth century, when it contained aspects of ancient religion, such as sacred medicine bundles, the use of tobacco and cedar smoke, and giving away of blankets, ponies and food.[38] Among the *I'n-lon-schka* and *Hethuska* societies of the Kansa (Kaw), Omaha, and Ponca people, and the Iruska society of the Pawnee, ceremonies and dances were presided over by "officers chosen to wear crow belts, feather bustles symbolizing crows flocking over a battlefield," as well as roaches resembling those worn by the Osage.[39] In the nineteenth century, the dancing ceremony spread; "[w]hen the Northern Plains tribes received it in the 1860s, they called it the Omaha Dance in recognition of its southern origins. It was also called the Grass Dance, after the braids of sweet-smelling grass worn in the bustles."[40]

The Osage received the Crow/Omaha/Grass Dance in the mid–1880s to early 1890s, approximately the same time as the Ghost Dance, a round dance derived from the Northern Paiute of western Nevada.[41] In the mid–1880s, "three members of the Kansa (Kaw) tribe visited the people of the Wah-xa Koh li division of the Osage [near modern-day Pawhuska] to offer them ... [the 'Helucka Watchi' dance, received by the Kansa from the Ponca people."[42] An Osage man named *Mozhon Okashe* accepted a drum from the Kansa on behalf of his son, Ben Mashunkashey (Allotee #457), who became the first Osage *I'n-lon-shcka* Drum Keeper for the Pawhuska District.[43] The dances were often combined; the adapted Crow Dance (known as the Charcoal Dance by the Osage, after the dark paint warriors used in preparation for warfare)[44] was performed in the afternoon, and the Ghost Dance at night, although by 1893 the Ghost Dance was gone. In the late nineteenth and early twentieth centuries, among the prairie tribes of Oklahoma and Nebraska—the Osage, Omaha, Ponca, and Pawnee—the Grass dance acquired elements of the *Midewiwin* (the "Dream" or "Drum Dance"), a ceremony centering on a large drum and offering revitalization features similar to the Ghost Dance[45]:

> This version, called the Straight Dance, dispensed with the crow belt, while retaining much of the ritual and many of the officers of the Inloshka societies ... it remains relatively conservative in choreography and costume. The dance's footwork is the basic toe-heel step and its motions are those of the feast-stalking aspect of the Grass Dance. The Straight Dance costume echoes its origins in the dress clothing of the prairie peoples: cloth shirt and leggings (both decorated with ribbon-work applique), crossed-beaded bandoliers, a headdress of deer-hair roach and an eagle-feather or otter-fur turban, and otter-fur trailer.[46]

The Gourd Dance, which grew out of early warrior society ceremony, is still used by revived men's societies; its name derives from the dancers' rattle.[47] Many of the songs, considered the most important aspect of ceremony, were also derived from the Ponca and Kaw.[48]

The ceremony known as *I'n-lon-schka* was therefore distilled from an interchange of traditional Osage practices with practices of other prairie peoples (what one elder described as a "circle of knowledge"),[49] as well as revivalist practices initiated as a response to catastrophic social change. Among the Osage, separate drum and dance organizations were established in Pawhuska and Hominy after being introduced by the Kansa; in the Gray Horse district, by the Ponca; and in the former division of Heartstays, near Barnsdall, now consolidated into Pawhuska.[50] The ceremony was known by white settlers as the "Pony Smoke" dance at the time that the Osage joined in the *I'n-lon-schka* with neighboring peoples (the Pawnee, Otoe, Ponca, Kansa, and Delaware, among others). The "Pony Smoke" was characterized by the reciprocal exchange of gifts, such as blankets, food, and most notably, ponies; special elbow-shaped stone pipes, distinct from those previously used by the Osage, were associated with the ceremony.[51]

As the Native American Church gained followers, the *I'n-lon-schka* dance began to fade in popularity, and its association with intertribal exchange and pipe sharing died away. The dance almost vanished in the Hominy district; the Drum Keeper left the drum hanging at the roundhouse near my Grandmother's home, "after several years of failed attempts to pass the drum to a new keeper."[52] Pawhuska and Barnsdall experienced similar declines. Only with an effort by prominent Osage who were also members of the Native American Church to sustain the dance did it experience resurgence.[53] Today the *I'n-lon-schka* is the crux of present-day artistic performance and honorary events at which traditional art objects are employed, held in June in the three Districts—Grey Horse, Hominy, and Pawhuska.[54]

At the heart of the *I'n-lon-schka* ceremony is the drum, always played by men, with women seated a few feet behind them to support their drumming and singing, and offer vocalizations of their own. Although the ceremony has become Christian in its opening and closing prayers, it is nonetheless said that "the drum is used to communicate with the Great Spirit," and is "the center and hub of the people, because it carries ... their songs, their life, their history"[55]; its throbbing beat throughout the ceremony, punctuated by high-pitched song, resonates powerfully through the body of participant and observer alike, and serves to cue "repeated verses; choruses; types of song, such as the war songs [prayer songs, mourning songs, warrior songs, calling songs, and family songs]; and stopping points," including signals for the Tail Dancers,[56] a group of four to six men who are honored as the best dancers (formerly, the best warriors) and "outstanding young men" and who dance together at short intervals

Alexis Madden and her father, David, perform competitive dancing in *I'n-lon-schka* style dress. His cloth shirt features ribbon work and the leggings beaded ornamentation, and he also wears arm and leg bands, otter-fur bandolier, and a roach headdress (courtesy Tara Madden).

throughout the ceremony.[57] One of the most powerful moments I experienced at the *I'n-lon-schka*—beyond even the brilliant costumes, the hypnotic repetition of movements, the silent support of the witnessing audience sweltering in the heat, the jingling bells and the embodied experience of the drum—was the warrior song, consisting of "sharp, accented

Top: I'n-lon-shcka dancers, Hominy, Oklahoma, outside roundhouse, 2014 (courtesy Benny Polacca/*Osage News*). *Bottom:* I'n-lon-shcka dancers Andrew Dreadfulwater, Nathan Dreadfulwater, Daniel Madden and David Madden, Hominy, Oklahoma, 2014 (courtesy Tara Madden/*Osage News*).

drumbeats that explode unexpectedly from the drummers' circle and signal a faster tempo for the dancers."[58] According to Callahan, "[t]hose songs of triumph and victory direct the thoughts of the men of the tribe to that unseen source of all power which enables human beings to act their part in life."[59]

Through the majority of the ceremony, elaborately attired male dancers circle the drum, employing a controlled, dignified, and repetitious series of steps, which stand in marked contrast to the dramatic movements of the "fancy dancers," some of whom are hired to perform at the fringe of the arena. Originally reserved for "full blood" Osage men, the dance today welcomes Osage men and women who respect the ceremony, and young children learning the steps by following, although "men remain the more important dancers," with a wider range of movement and vocal expression, and women and girls step only at the farthest rim of the arena.[60] Although I was told that the dancers do not pray while they perform, Callahan maintains that, unaware of the onlookers, the dancers "receive a spiritual strength" in their performance.[61] Having witnessed both performances, I can affirm her suggestion that the Osage *I'n-lon-schka*, "which they perform annually[,] is never commercialized and retains the ancient dignity free from powwow histrionics," as well as being performed in complete

I'n-lon-shcka dancers, Gray Horse, Oklahoma, 2014 (courtesy Benny Polacca/*Osage News*).

and traditional attire, due to their relative economic prosperity.[62] The most fascinating aspect of the performance are those individuals who retain a residual tie to their ancient gens, or clan, and perform with idiosyncratic movements suggesting the clan's totem—a large bird or mammal, for example.

The *I'n-lon-schka* is characterized by extensive, highly organized planning, a hierarchy of participants, expensive and elaborate attire and adornment, generous dinners of traditional food—fried bread, beef soup, ground corn, fried meat pies, buffalo stew—prefaced by prayers and speeches of welcome, and the honoring of individual participants and families with generous acknowledgements and gifts, often Pendleton blankets, and formerly food, horses, and other goods.[63] Women participate, therefore, not only in their elaborate attire and elegant, restrained movement around the perimeter of the dance, but as well in the organization of the ceremony throughout the preceding year, the accommodation of incoming family and visitors, and the preparation of food.

The preeminence of the *I'n-lon-schka* in Osage culture is affirmed by Frederick Morris Lookout, a former Drum Keeper in Pawhuska, who assumed the honored "position of Head Singer on each of the three Osage E-Lon-schka committees."[64] Lookout describes the dance as "an extraordinary social device that transmitted a powerful spiritual foundation … perpetuat[ing] all of our cultural values, and subsequently provid[ing] the only sense of tribal unity we have … it is the strength of the Elon-schska, its vitality and flexibility, which has enabled the Osage ceremonies to survive."[65] From a theoretical perspective, as Steedman states in *Dust: The Archive and Cultural Memory*, "performances function as vital acts of transfer, transmitting social knowledge, memory, and a sense of identity through reiterated behavior."[66] Although an Osage commentator, noting the survival of the ceremony for over a century of economic and social change, stated that young dancers carry on the *I'n-lon-schka* performance "the best way that they can,"[67] and though the *Watsipxa* or "Crier" echoed this perception at the end of the 2014 ceremony in stating, "we do the best we can in following our elders," it is clear that the spiritual power, the unifying force, and the social cohesion created by *I'n-lon-schka* performance is extended through constant reiteration.

Even for the non–Osage, the *I'n-lon-schka* ceremony can be profoundly transformative. I attended my first Osage ceremony with a medicine man for the Paiute and Modoc people, Pbonchai Tallman, and had the honor of staying with Paula Farid and her daughter, Amy Farid, as they prepared for days of ceremony. In an interview, Tallman relates the impact the experience had on his medicine:

> We arrived at the Osage Nation, and we drove around until we came to this thing that was the archives building ... when I was talking to Pauline she said, what's your name, and I said Pbonchai, Tall Walking Spirit. And she said, "Oh, I think I've heard of you, you're from the west, right? I don't know much about you, but I do know one thing. You're to receive your confirmation on bear medicine. We went over to this building [for the *I'n-lon-schka*], and when we went in there, we told them that we were guests of Paula [Farid, member of the Five Woman Osage Council], and Pauline, and they set us down ... and they had beautiful dancers, and they did everything very very nicely. And then, when we were sitting there, I felt pulled up to the clouds, and there was this old man, and six Medicine Men, and they were twirling around, and the old man said, "Did you enjoy your dance?" I said yes, and he said, "We'll have to do it again sometime," and smiled at me. And he put me through some other things. And then all of a sudden I was in a lodge, I wasn't on the clouds any more. And the old man said, here are your instructions, never to be repeated again. And there were two young men standing behind me with full bear capes on. And then I went out [from the clouds] with my instructions. And I've been blessed with the ability to heal, and I've been doing all of my callings, and I've been successful. And then we went on a quest the next day to go find your Grandmother's house. And there was magic going on, I could feel your spirit healing as we went in ... while we were at your Grandmother's house, we met the people who were living there, and you got lots of healing that day. Then we went to Pawnee, and we found Pawnee Bill's house, and we sat on the porch, just you and me, and we had the nicest conversation. We really enjoyed each other, and looked around and saw the day.[68]

Although articulated in non-academic language, the experience of Tallman, an American Indian elder, is of profound significance. The Lakota scholar Vine Deloria, Jr., stated in 1982,

> the realities of Indian belief and existence have become so misunderstood and distorted at this point that when a real Indian stands up and speaks the truth at any given moment, he or she is not only unlikely to be believed, but will probably be publicly contradicted and "corrected" by the citation of some non-Indian and totally inaccurate "expert." More, young Indians in universities are now being trained to view themselves and their cultures in the terms prescribed by such experts rather than in the traditional terms of the tribal elders. The process automatically sets the members of Indian communities at odds with one another, while outsiders run around picking up pieces for themselves. In this way, the experts are perfecting a system of self-validation in which all semblance of honesty and accuracy are lost. This is not only a travesty of scholarship, but it is absolutely devastating to Indian societies.[69]

Pam Colorado, an Oneida academic, states, "The process is ultimately intended to supplant Indians, even in areas of their own customs and spirituality. In the end, non–Indians will have complete power to define what is and is not Indian, even for Indians. We are talking about the absolute ideological/conceptual subordination they already experience."[70]

In this context, the view of a Native American Medicine Man—Tallman is Paiute, the people who contributed the Ghost Dance to the Osage—should be considered with the authority it deserves.

> My first impression was they must be fairly wealthy to afford an arbor like they had—all steel frame and big and nice. And then I noticed everybody had similar costumes—the women dressed in long dresses with capes and jangle. They were very very beautiful. And the men dressed with porcupine roaches on their hair and eagle feathers on top. Everybody had an eagle feather. And then they danced in a counterclockwise direction around the drums in the center ... seeing three hundred Native American men all dancing in unison, and women on the sides all dressed similarly and all dancing in unison. And everybody was included. There were old men out there, and there were first graders out there, little children. Everybody danced. So they are including their elders, which impressed me. They only have *I'n-lon-schka* once a year. I don't know if they have any other ceremonies! Nobody mentioned anything. I liked the participation and the enthusiasm, even though they weren't showing outright, you could tell everybody was enjoying the ceremony. I wasn't able to discern what the movements and ceremony were actually about. But it was very beautiful. They were fixing fairly elaborate meals for everybody. Everybody ate well. And

Amy Farid, daughter of Paula Farid, dressed for *I'n-lon-shcka* on the Osage reservation, Pawhuska, Oklahoma, 2014 (courtesy Paula Farid).

Nathan Dreadfulwater and Daniel Madden at *I'n-lon-shcka*, Hominy, Oklahoma, 2014 (courtesy Tara Madden/*Osage News*).

it was also social time. People who hadn't seen each other for a while, you could see people reconnecting relationships. It was a good thing. Their hospitality and their desire to live the Way and bring back customs into their society really touched my heart. It's almost like watching the rebirth of a nation. We [also] went to their sacred church [the roundhouse] where they still have sacrament. It was good to see that some of the old ways are still preserved ... an awesome sight to see. God bless the Osage!

My experience of witnessing a sacred ceremony not open to the public is both an honor and a complex intellectual experience. George Tinker, an Osage scholar and author, has spoken strongly about the "emergence of Indian ceremonial traditions into the larger public consciousness," which he argues "has generated a sexy appeal of the exotic among the spiritually exhausted colonizer community."[71] Tinker argues that it is difficult for non–Indians to comprehend aspects of ceremony, which "makes it necessary for Indian structures to remodel themselves culturally" to be inclusive; non–Indian participants, he claims, "experience only the illusion of Indianness and the illusion of spiritual power ... to the extent that the experience is real, it is no longer in any way Indian."[72] Additionally, as he rightly indicates, "spiritual knowledge is not the universal right of all citizens in the national community ... different clans or societies have particular responsibilities for parts of a national ceremony and thus possess particular knowledge not necessarily shared by all in the community," and certainly not the right of those outside the culture to "know." Essentially then, for Tinker,

> white participation in Indian community ceremonial actions contributes to the ongoing destruction of Indian culture, ceremonies, and communities ... [and] reinforces the notion of white privilege ... we hurt our white relatives and friends when we naively invite them into our private, community ceremonial life. We are only encouraging the final act of colonization and conquest.[73]

Tinker goes so far as to argue that,

> even in those cases when a non–Indian has a clear invitation from an Indian participant, the question must be raised whether the Indian person has the right to extend the invitation ... since the ceremony is a community event and all participants affect the entire community.... [In addition,] Any non–Indian who is so invited needs to question seriously whether the invitation is even remotely valid and genuine—even if it comes from a high-status elder or leader. And perhaps the non–Indian should also question his or her own motives for having any interest in experiencing somebody else's intimate spiritual relationships.

In my experience of the *I'n-lon-shcka*, however, the clarity, validity, and motives of those who invited me appeared to be immaculate. In extending an invitation to me, a white scholar, to join her family, the respected elder Paula Farid ensured that the history and ceremony of the Osage would continue to be acknowledged, but the ceremony itself did not change or adjust to accommodate visitors; non–Osage attendants had to sit far outside the arbor on benches in the rain, and nothing of the meaning of the ceremony was explained. Rather than springing from an interest in exoticism or colonization, my intention was to learn more about the centuries-long relationship between my family and the Osage, and document the traditions that persist.

In attending the *I'n-lon-shcka*, I had no illusions about participating in, or receiving or fully understanding, Osage spirituality. Indeed, I am left with the same questions that concluded Alice Anne Callahan's text devoted solely to the *I'n-lon-schka*: what is the meaning of the drumming and songs to the participants, particularly the women? What layers of religious or historical meaning continue to be conveyed in the *I'n-lon-schka*? What fragments of song, dance, attire, and prayer persist throughout the history of the Osage?[74] To some extent, one must be a participant to begin to understand and experience the overwhelming sensation of the ceremony: as Joy Harjo, a Muskogee author and performer, has stated, "[w]hen I am home in Oklahoma at the stomping grounds, we may talk about the complexities of meaning, but to comprehend it, to know it intimately, that intricate context of history and family, is to dance it[.]"[75]

The *I'n-lon-schka* cannot replace the extensive, original faith which once threaded through every aspect of Osage life, nor is that the intention of the ceremony, which today is introduced with Christian prayer. Centuries ago, at dawn, at mid-day, and at sunset, for acts of peace, war, planting, and naming, spiritual ceremonies were conducted related to nature, and intended to honor and mirror *Wah-kon-ta*. In 1829, a white observer stated that "[t]hese Indians have a native religion of their own and are the only tribe I ever knew that had. At break of day every morning, I could hear them at prayer for an hour. They appeared to be as devout in their way as any class of people."[76] Again, in 1940, a Baptist missionary, the Rev. Isaac McCoy, stated, "It has been reported that the Osages did not believe in the existence of the Great Spirit. I was astonished that anyone who had ever been two days among them … should be so deceived. I have never before seen Indians who gave more undoubted evidence of their belief in God."[77] The dance also cannot serve as a replacement for the Native American Church, which still persists in some towns.

Yet the current dance—which has grown to an average of 700 participants and 2,000 atttendees in Pawhuska alone—has acquired its own trajectory and power. In the old Osage faith, the cosmos "moved in endless cycles of birth, decay and death, its eternal renewal guaranteed by a supreme power, Wah-Don-Dah, the creative and organizing principle."[78] Adherence to appropriate ritual forms included an acceptance of death and change as part of an overall pattern of order, "[b]ut, paradoxically, this did not entail strict rigidity in these practices. Close observation of the natural world ... reveal[ed] changed circumstances which, from time to time, would require amendment of the ritual forms."[79] The ability of the Osage—unique in their centuries-long interaction with a foreign culture, within which their subjectivity was shaped—to survive, adapt, and recreate ceremony and spiritual practice is, in this light, of a piece with their ancient belief in the mutability of the cosmos. The ceremony, which occurs in the agricultural growing season of June, once was the Osage's most important spiritual season,[80] and one's sense is that it signifies constant renewal, rejuvenation, and the reincarnation of the ancient made fresh, relevant, and even eternal.

11

"The most beautiful blazing blue sky and emerald green fields": Memories, Diaspora and the Sense of Place

In *The Man Made of Words*, N. Scott Momaday describes the importance of place. "None of us lives apart from the land entirely; such an isolation is unimaginable. We have sooner or later to come to terms with the world around us ... the physical world, not only as it is revealed to us immediately through our senses, but also as it is perceived truly in the long turn of seasons and of years."[1] For both Osage and ancestor, place has a resonance and a depth, a sense of profound personal identity and connection with individual body and selfhood that resonates as sound does within the physical body. My Aunt Camelia Berry describes that space:

> Open land in Oklahoma still is beautiful. In the spring it is a Paradise ... a 40 million-acre sea of grass.... The most beautiful blazing blue sky, emerald green fields, crisp breezes, can turn cold, with threatening sky, torrential rain and wind and the roar of a tornado seen or unseen in the dark, leaving desolation and death in its wake. In winter a soft mild overcast, weak but comforting sunshine, can turn overnight into a slashing sleet storm that coats every tree branch and every blade of grass with ice that glitters like crystal and diamonds in the innocent sunshine of early morning ... [there are] rivers, streams, and creeks, all sleepy, sandy and shallow with inviting quiet swimming holes and easy fording places. The sandbars blaze in the brilliant sunshine, the blue of the sky makes puddles turquoise blue.... Those lovely pools can be quicksand, deep enough to swallow wagons and teams. The swimming holes have deep unseen currents.[2]

Osage author John Joseph Mathews describes the land with affection too, but with a softer perspective on its unpredictability:

> The impression was one of space: whispering space.... It was wild[, but] never silent. In summer the grasses whispered and laughed and sang, changing to mournful whispers during the autumn, then screaming like a demented woman when winter turned the emerald to copper. In the spring the breezes talked confidentially of the mating season, burdened with the scents of the earth and carrying the voices of the curlew, the sandpiper, and the killdeer, the meadowlark and the sonorous booming of the prairie chicken[3] ... in the blackjacks ... the prairie breezes seemed to have become entangled and died. Here life seemed to murmur, almost whisper.... The leaves rattled slightly, lazily, and made moving patterns on the sparse grass. There were the sleepy voices of birds: the sad call of the woodphoebe, the jerky notes of a brown thrasher, and a mockingbird singing persistently from the top of a dead tree wasting his voice on a somnolent world.[4]

Jackson describes a range of peoples for whom nothing is more important than the sense of place: for them, identity derives from the place where one has the right to stand; for them, "to be without country is not to belong, to be bereft of the ontological ground of human being."[5] In this chapter I will discuss the connection of the Osage and the settler to the land in Oklahoma—a connection that emerges as not merely material or sentimental, but as a profound aspect of spiritual orientation toward a higher sense of meaning in cultural and individual life.

The Osage and the Sense of Place

In his memoir discussing the experience of growing up in Pawhuska in the Depression era, leaving Oklahoma as a Rhodes scholar, and returning to receive his Osage name, *Nom-peh-wah-the*, Carter Revard invariably returns to space and place. Revard describes his home in Buck Creek Valley, where there were

> knee-deep wildflowers and bluestem hay to the eastern prairie hills ... a bluewater pond [was there] for cattle, and fish came into it, and willows began growing and elms and hackberries along its dam, and there were persimmons and buttonbush and such up in its swampy top areas where the redwing blackbirds perched ... on the meadow and with the elm, catalpa, poplar trees around a house where birds would have only those trees except for the willows of the pond a quarter mile away, our trees were where the orchard orioles, robins, turtledoves, scissortails, bluebirds, kingbirds, dickcissels came to perch.[6]

In a text that focuses upon retrieving identity and Osage spiritual ceremony, Revard irresistably and repeatedly invokes the land, his home within it, and the relationship of these to spiritual beliefs. The emphasis on land and place emerges in his discussion of the Osage origin *wi-gi-e*, or prayer, that served as a central aspect of virtually all ceremonies and clan traditions:

> the Osages came from the mid-heavens, the stars, to become a people on this earth. In this journey they were directed by various powers through three "divisions" of the heavens, where they found no place to become a people, but in the fourth "division" they met "the Man of Mystery, the god of the clouds.... He said to them: "I am a person of whom your little ones may make their bodies. When they make of me their bodies, they shall cause themselves to become deathless."[7]

According to the prayer, the Osage people approached a buffalo bull, "who also said they could make their bodies of him, and proceeded to throw himself upon the ground so that there sprang up for their use as medicine and food certain plants[.]"[8] Thus, as Revard indicates, the Osage chants, embedded within ceremony, show a deep connection between life itself and the "willing sacrifices for food and clothing and ceremonial regalia" made by animals "as part of the sacred agreement made as Origin Time human and non-human beings of this world[.]"[9]

Belief in a universe comprised of dual realms, the physical and the spiritual, is consistently envisioned as the product of a "begetting" between the earth (*Hon-ga*, "the Sacred One") and the sky (*Tsi-zhu*, "Household.")[10] The sky and earth realms were subdivided into twenty-four *ton-won-gthon*, or clans, associated with "life symbols which included animals, plants, heavenly bodies and natural phenomena such as clouds and lightning."[11] Ceremonies for the initiation of new chiefs and the issuing of Osage names invoked the union of earth and sky; prior to the reduction in numbers of the tribe and intermarriage with settlers, marriage had to be between members of sky and earth, reiterating and reenacting the tribe's origins.[12] Each clan in turn—the Black Bear or Thunder clan, for example—had its own version of the origin story that conformed to nature and to the duality of origin. The version of creation told by Black Dog (*Shon-ton-ca-be*) c. 1900, for example, focuses upon the elk, but again returns to the land:

> Way beyond ... a part of the Wazha'zhe lived in the sky. They desired to know their origin, the source from which they came into existence. They went to the sun. He told them that they were his children. Then they wandered still farther and came to the moon. She told them that she gave birth to them, and that the sun was their father. She told them that they must leave their present abode and go down to the earth and dwell there. They came to the earth, but found it covered with water. They could not return to the place they had left, so they wept, but no answer came to them from anywhere. They floated about in the

air, seeking in every direction for help from some god; but they found none. The animals were with them, and of all these the elk was the finest and most stately, and inspired all the animals with confidence; so they appealed to the elk for help. He dropped to the water and began to sink ... [but then called on the winds for help; the winds] carried the water upward. At first rocks only were exposed, and the people traveled on the rocky places that produced no plants, and there was nothing to eat. Then the waters began to go down until the soft earth was exposed. When this happened the elk in his joy rolled over and over on the soft earth, and all his loose hairs clung to the soil. The hairs grew, and from them sprang beans, corn, potatoes, and wild turnips, and then all the grasses and trees.[13]

The emphasis on land in the origin story is echoed in Osage ceremonies related to planting. The name for the month of April means "planting" in Osage; it was believed that, at this time, Mother Earth and Grandfather, the Sun, came together "for the coming of the fruits of the earth[.]"[14] When Osage women planted seeds in the ground, they stamped the earth down with their feet: the left foot represented the sky people, and the right, the earth. After planting, Osage women sang prayers that united the importance of ground, growth, and dwelling:

> I have made a footprint, a sacred one.
> I have made a footprint, through it the blades push upward.
> I have made a footprint, through it the blades radiate.
> I have made a footprint, over it the blades float in the wind.
> I have made a footprint, over it the ears lean toward one another.
> I have made a footprint, over it I pluck the ears.
> I have made a footprint, over it I bend the stalks to pluck the ears.
> I have made a footprint, over it the tassels like gray.
> I have made a footprint, smoke rises from my lodge.
> I have made a footprint, there is cheer in my lodge.
> I have made a footprint, I live in the light of day.[15]

In this way, Osage women enacted N. Scott Momaday's statement, "I exist in a landscape, and my existence is indivisible with the land."[16]

In the Osage naming ceremony that took place at the center of each village, the connection between the people and the land is also reiterated. As Revard states,

> When a child was to be given its sacred name, all the twenty-four clans were assembled in a circle or oval, with the child seated at the East where the Sun rises, and looking to the West where the Sun sets: his path in life was to be like that of the Sun, rising in power and traveling always irresistibly across the sky, going down in beauty as the stars and moon came out, and returning each dawn.[17]

During the naming ceremony, "the assembly of the Clans, that is, persons who had made their bodies of these great beings"—the animals encountered in the Creation story, such as the mountain lion and black bear—"and the circular arrangement of these Clans, oriented east-west, sustained the child being named as a member" of the nation. Thus, "[g]athering into this child-naming, or village-dwelling, or dancing circle ... was viewed by the tribal elders as a symbolic embodying of the great cosmic order of Earth and Sky and Water."[18] In the ceremony to install a new chief and the ceremony known as the Hearing of the Sayings of the Ancient Men, the emphasis on nature and place was reiterated: the Rite of the Chiefs "not only named a new chief, but recited the history of their becoming a nation: how Osages came from the stars and chose bodily forms, created tribal organizations that symbolized their history and cosmic order, chose certain animals as clan patrons, chose certain foods and names tied into myth and history." The Hearing of the Sayings rite "expresses the origin of the people as a begetting of life between 'two great fructifying forces—namely the sky and the earth,' with life continuing forever to proceed from this begetting."[19]

The Family and the Land

My family also had a close association with the land. For all of his material prosperity and extravagance, the patriarch of the Mullendore family, Erd Mullendore, attached importance above all else to land he perceived as his own:

> Mr. Mullendore was always a farmer and rancher. He always devoted most of his time to that phase of his holdings, leaving the banking and oil problems to others. His farm here, and his ranches in the Osage got most of his time, and he led a hardy, active life until the very end. While he was ill, and unable to go about his farm even in his last illness, he would often get into his car, and be driven over to his farm by his daughters—"he wanted to see the cattle," he would tell them.[20]

As late as 1970, E.C.'s grandson, E.C. Mullendore IV, was honored at the Mullendore ranch in the traditional Osage rite. Each Osage clan traditionally had its own priest, or *Xo-ka*, who selected names according to clan history, gender, and the birth order of the child[21]; as the great-grandson of an Osage chief, E.C. Mullendore IV was honored by Fred Lookout, the last of the Osage "full blood" chiefs, with the name of *Xhiu-tha-ga-he* (Eagle Chief). *Xhiu-tha* means "Eagle" lake, as the Mullendore ranch was located in the Huiah dam region of Osage county.[22]

Love for the land despite an active civic career seems to be a family characteristic. James E. Berry, who later became lieutenant governor of

Oklahoma, recalls his father participating in the Land Run and building a two room house: "I took it upon myself to keep the family well provided with fish, and game, which was plentiful in that vicinity[.]"[23] My fond memories of my Uncle Everett before his death mirror these accounts: to the end of his life my Uncle Everett despite being president of a bank and a prominent and active citizen of Pawnee, spent hours driving to The Place near Hominy and the Osage—in my memory, wearing an elegant suit and cowboy boots, jolting his expensive car over bumps in the pasture at The Place, and proudly pointing out the cattle across a vast landscape of green fields, dark groves of blackjack trees, outcroppings of red sandstone and a view of the two thousand acre ranch as far as the eye could see.

For my mother, a sense of place, "The Place," was always foremost in her recollections and perceptions of the world. A photograph of her as a small child depicts a determined, tiny girl with smoothed-back curls reading a book; most noteworthy about the photograph are her cowboy boots, which, she states, she insisted upon wearing, her connection with The Place, her place. Her memories of the early time when she played with

Catherine Berry Hess in studio portrait wearing cowboy boots, Hominy, Oklahoma, circa 1941 (courtesy Catherine Berry Hess).

11. "The most beautiful blazing blue sky and emerald green fields" 185

the hired hands, rode her pony, read alongside her dog Bird, and walked the red hills finding arrowheads were a backdrop not only to her life but mine as well, the star by which present time and place were measured. Her memories crept into the column she wrote for the Iowa *Des Moines Register*, "Old Fashioned Thrift," which my father illustrated, and describing skills such as growing gardens, making bonnets, and creating cough remedies[24]; each in their own right, and together, they brought forward into other spaces and times the world their writing describes.

My own attachment to place has followed me through a lifetime: childhood memories, the eruptions of emotion when family members moved or died, tantalizing fragments of stories shared by my family, sensations beyond words in physically experiencing the region I left behind. The journey I took to the Osage nation and to The Place forty-five years after being there before awakened so many embodied memories and sensations—the smell of sweetgrass, visions of wide open vistas of ranchland and trees, the sounds of birds and the burbling of rivers, all of which remain a part of my identity, although most were previously forgotten. Lloyd states, "Childhood memories are always vivid, but what astonishes me about these is that they encompass the experiences of a relatively short time."[25] My mother's occasional stories, and the few visits I made to Osage territory, "cannot [fully] explain the attraction."[26] For Roger Lloyd, for Dennis McAuliffe, for Carter Revard, for me—the happenstance geography of our birth cannot fully explain the profound sensation of belonging and place evoked by that "hot sun, the prairie weeds casting up clouds of yellow pollen, the distant horizon, [and] the bright air[.]"[27]

The loss of land has been great for both family and the Osage. A farmer wrote of the open grasslands in 1893, "[t]he prairies are gone. I held one of the ripping, snarling, breaking plows that rolled the hazel bushes and wild sunflowers under[,] … and so there comes into my reminiscences an unmistakable note of sadness."[28] It is at once indescribably pleasurable and heartbreaking to visit the Tallgrass Prairie Reserve—owned by the Osage, then purchased from them by a white fianancier and ultimately sold to the Nature Conservancy—knowing that it is all that remains of the unplowed prairie that once stretched across 142 million acres of the United States. The sweet smell of the grass, the variegated waves of flowers, the rushing sound of the wind and birds, the sight of massive bison, their pelts shedding in the spring—it is devastating to feel at once finally at home, and to understand that this land, which once stretched across the United States, is gone. The Osage's dispensation of the property, so very near the Tribal Museum, is hard to understand: while many of the land sales, including that of the Conservancy region, involved

Tallgrass Nature Conservancy, near Pawhuska, Oklahoma, 2014 (author's photograph).

fraud,[29] the Osage nonetheless sold holdings which were unoccupied, and covered the pristine prairie with oil wells, which are today subject to the will of major contributors to the Conservancy. One of the board members, Norman Schwarzkopf, a member of the Conservancy Board with authority over the handling of land and mineral rights, was adopted like Frank Phillips before him as an honorary Osage, inducted on the day the Conservancy was opened.[30]

The Place is now gone, too. In the confusion of the real estate market of 2010, sweet-talking real estate agents deceived my elderly parents, and the ranch is gone. Its loss feels particularly heavy as one walks the red soil, stony outcroppings, and grass waving in the wind as far as the eye can see; the old stone barn, standing ever ready for use, near the site of my mother's old house, now destroyed, is heartbreaking; the old Cross Bell brand, now long out of use, hangs, partly visible. The old cowhands in their boots, the women with beautiful dresses, the jingling harness of the horses, the long and shorthorn cattle, all are gone, as are the American Indian people who once lived there; all that remains are the oil wells.

Almost a hundred years ago, my Grandmother was struggling to give birth to my Uncle Everett, Jr., and my Grandfather Everett, Sr. stopped a train to bring the family physician back to The Place, where my uncle was born.[31] My mother rode a horse with Everett to the one room schoolhouse at McVey.[32] She drove into Wynona to buy ice cream with the family. At The Place, she listened to the radio, talked on the phone on a party line, tossed knives in a throwing game with hired hands, and escaped into her own world by riding out into the hills on her horse, Smokey,[33] never dreaming of the complexities of life to come. Now I understand the thoughts in my mother's mind when she sang to me as a child Woody Guthrie's song "Oklahoma Hills."

Conclusion

In a sense, this textual journey has been a retracing of my ancestry and my sense of place, retelling their story and mine, and regaining a sense of mutuality that has healed my own sense of loss of place. For those whose life histories have drifted astray from the cultures and histories of their family before them, as Jackson states, there is "a sense of pathological loss."[1] Roger Lloyd notes that the academic attempt to reconstruct the pre-contact lives of American Indians is driven by more than "scholarly curiosity," but also an inchoate sense that "in recapturing something of these primitive communal lifeways we can connect with something from which we have been severed"[2]; according to Lloyd, disconnection from nature, from community, and from shared labor, leads to alienation—"leav[ing] us feeling empty, denatured in fact, and committed to a place in the world which sometimes feels pretentious and false, although we can't say exactly why."[3]

In reconnecting with community, in hearing the stories of ancestors in their own voices, we are reminded that there is more connection among disparate cultures, more intersubjectivity, than we could have imagined. In Jackson's view, the self genuinely has no reality except in relation to others; it arises from interaction with others, and is enabled by interconnection, even with a culturally distant, imagined or ancestral community.[4] Although we arrive in the world as if it were predetermined, a "sedimented world of ancestral acts and foregone conclusions,"[5] we have choices in interacting with others; we recreate the world with each choice. And that action is the essence of anthropological understanding, of understanding those who seem far from us in culture or in time—finding them amusing, heroic, close to our hearts. As Jackson states, the "plurality is not inimical but necessary to our integrity ... inspiring us to accept and celebrate the manifold and contradictory character of existence in the knowledge that any one person embodies the potential to be any other."[6] In experiencing the world of ancestors through stories, images, and archival records, through journeys to places with which we are connected, and through the senses, we can experience an embodied anthropology, in which, at moments, absolute conceptions of difference are erased: "one may thereby be led to an understanding of how those rare moments of erasure and effacement occur when self and other are constituted in mutuality and acceptance[,] rather than violence and contempt."[7]

At the end of writing this book, I watched an old, forgotten video from the archive. For just a few moments, I was there. There, at The Place, was my beloved Uncle Everett Berry, and my Grandmother, now passed away; there was my mother, so beautiful and shy; there was my sister, all sweetness and blue eyes; and there I was, a touseled, black-haired, wild-eyed baby. I could not comprehend then that that moment would be gone forever; my Daddy, so handsome, in slicked-back hair, perfect dark suit and slim tie, my cousins as children, and the ponies and barn at The Place. When the soundless video abruptly ended, it was a physical shock; there was no more to be seen; the rest was lost in time. But whenever watched, the moment reinserts itself freshly in memory; the old video preserves the memory, the smiles, the gestures, even the smell of the wind; and the sense of place, riveting and surreal. And this, this always, is the power of the archive.

Appendix:
Ross Hess's Writings

The following are extracts from Ross Hess's column "The View from Persimmon Hill."[1]

"The cowboy's life was mostly hard work, poor pay, and long hours.... He had little time or opportunity for pleasure. But there were some rewards.... One of the best things about the cowboy's life was meal time. This was not just a time to eat, but for music, tall tales, and other distractions to relieve the monotony and loneliness of punching cattle ... and the outfit that had a good cook never had any difficulty in recruiting new hands ... one of the favorite foods of the cowboy was an item commonly called "sowbelly" and though it may sound unappetizing, par boiled and fried it was *delicious*! Sowbelly can still be found in some grocery stores, packaged and labeled ... salt pork. And the person who has never tried this crisp, tasty treat has missed out on one of the *finer* things in life!"

"Chisholm! 1965 marks the 100th anniversary of the Chisholm Trail.... A term which has come to be synonymous with West. This is the story of its beginning. Strange as it may seem, Jesse Chisholm was not a cowboy. But an *Indian* and he probably never saw Texas! He was born in Tennessee, and moved West with his mother, a Cherokee Indian, over the trail of tears. Jesse traded with Plains Indians for hides, and freighted them from (what is now) Oklahoma City to Wichita, Kansas.... The herd from Texas was driven to California.... When the herders came upon Jesse's wagon tracks ... they decided to follow the tracks, and wound up in Abilene, Kansas. Today U.S. Highway 81 follows the route of the cattle herds ... and, here and there, traces are still visible of the century old "Chisholm Trail!"

October 3, 1965: "Texas Longhorn. People are sometimes mislead by glorified accounts of the cowboy's life ... had it not been for this beast, that life would never have existed. No other breed of cattle could withstand the climate and the long drives to market ... the longhorn dictated life in the southwest for more than thirty years. The Texas longhorn was the descendant of Andalusian stock brought to the American continent in 1541 by Gregorio Villalobos, the West's first cattle rancher. Strays which ran wild multiplied so rapidly that by the middle 1800's they numbered in the millions. As one Texan put it ... 'The Civil War ended just in time. In another year the whole state of Texas would have sunk from the weight of the steers!' Millions of longhorns were driven to rail points in Kansas during the 70s and 80s to supply the eastern demand for beef. Towns such as Dodge City and Abilene owed their livelihood to the trail herds, and the way of life led by 'waddies' sparks the imagination even today. By 1900 the era of the longhorn was ended, and today he is seen only in wildlife refuges or in city zoos!"

September 12, 1965: "The most important item of equipment carried by a man in the early west was his hand gun ... when a man traveled west during the late 1800s, he left behind all forms of organized law. In many cases his skill with a pistol became his judge, jury and executioner. The favorite weapon of cattlemen, outlaws, and lawmen was the colt single action frontier revolver, model 1872 ... also known as the colt army revolver, it was carried by many of the famous gunfighters. (Hickock, Earp, Bonney, Holiday, Hardin) But people in the west called it the 'peacemaker,' and it worked hard to earn the title!" [Picture of cemetery.]

"In all the West no one was so well known, so much written about, or so willing to tell of his own exploits as the two gun, curly locked, frontier marshal ... Wild Bill Hickock ... by his own admission was the greatest fighter in the west, with the possible exception of John Wesley Hardin who outdid him once in Abilene. This hero of the old west claimed to have killed more than 100 men, 50 of them in *one battle* with *50 bullets*! On one occasion Wild Bill was purported to have done in 9 men in hand-to-hand combat, and walked away after receiving a load of buckshot and being stabbed 13 times! ... Truly an outstanding example of raw courage, steel nerves, and cool confidence.... This is the same J.B. Hickok who was fired from his job as sheriff of Abilene after a gunfight in which he killed his own deputy who was running to Hickok's rescue! Friend and staunch admirer: Calamity Jane—a rootin', tootin' pistol packin' mama who helped Hickok to achieve fame. She was true to the very end ... her last request was that she be buried by Hickok's side—a wish which was granted ... this card hand [Ace of clubs, Ace of spades, 8 of spades] is referred to by poker players as the 'dead man's hand.' ... the hand that J.B. 'Wild Bill' Hickok held one day in 1876 when

... he was shot in the back by a notoriety seeker. The weapon misfired 5 times before the fatal bullet struck him down!"

"A cowpoke working cattle every day could get pretty tired of beans and bacon ... to whet the appetite of hungry cowpokes, one oldtime dough-twister concocted a very special stew ... which gave his boys something to look forward to at chow time.... The stew was all meat, made from a young calf, and nothing was left out ... brains, liver, heart, sweetbreads and tenderloin ... everything but bones went into the pot.... The stew's name came from a hungry puncher who, when he discovered what it was made of, remarked ... this is a @!!!* stew!! And so it is called even today, except that in polite company it is simply referred to as sonofagun stew!"

"The Western Adventure": "Winchester repeating rifle—Cal. .44—model 1873. Other Winchester weapons: Winchester made Spencer rifle, the henry rifle, volcanic repeating pistol. Oliver R. Winchester first began manufacturing rifles in his New Haven, Connecticut factory in 1857.... Winchester's first big success was the henry rifle, first made in 1860. It was a fifteen shot repeater which was carried by Sherman's troops in Georgia ... the Confederates called it 'that d____d Yankee rifle that's loaded on Sunday and fired all week!' But Winchester's name did not become famous 'til after the war when he designed a new type repeating rifle ... which became known as 'the gun that won the west.' The Winchester was a prized possession ... anybody who could afford one, or steal one—had one! A later model, the Winchester 1894, is still manufactured and sold ... and is a favorite of western sportsmen!"

'The fastest gun in the West' has for years been the favorite topic of screen writers and western novelists.... A list of nominees for the dubious title of 'fastest gun in the west' might well include the names of Billy the Kid, Wild Bill Hickok, William Longley, and Ben Thompson ... but for sheer viciousness, none could compare to the most deadly gunman of all—John Wesley Hardin. The son of a circuit riding Texas preacher, Hardin dedicated his life to violating the fifth commandment. He used his .44 the first time ... on a negro ... 'who came at me with a big stick...' at the age of fifteen! In the following ten years, Hardin gunned down no less than forty-two men—including sheriff Charlie Webb ... for whose death Hardin was tried and convicted of murder. He was sentenced to 25 years imprisonment. After serving 16 years, Hardin was paroled ... and led a reformed life—studied law—even taught Sunday school. But Hardin's romantic inclinations led to an argument with an el paso lawman ... John Selman—who caught him unaware in a dice game and ended the gunman's life with a bullet in the back."

"The rodeo is fast becoming one of the most popular spectator sports in America ... the thrills of a rodeo are unmatched by any other sport ...

rodeoing began with cowboys who, having finished a roundup, would compete to show their skill with animals. Roundups soon became unnecessary, but the cowpokes found that people would pay money to see them have fun, so rodeos continued.... Rodeos today are held in most of the 50 states, and have become a major entertainment attraction. New events have been added to increase interest, including barrel racing, clowns, and trick riding. The word rodeo is Spanish—pronounced roDAY'o ... but the person who says rodayo at a *rodeo* is apt to be viewed with contempt by the loyal rodeo fan! National finals RODEO Dec. 4th—Dec. 11th New Fairgrounds Arena Oklahoma City."

"How to get from East to West was a major problem to the early settlers.... There were many ways of going west in the early 1800s. One could walk ... or go by wagon train ... or on horseback. But those who preferred luxury rode the Concord Coach. Designed and built in Concord, New Hamshire. Wt. empty—3,000 lbs. Body—hickory wood Suspension—leather No. seats—3 Crew—Driver and shotgun messenger Normal passenger load—9 Maximum passenger capacity—25 Maximum speed—18 MPH Cruising speed—10 mph Cost not including accessories—$1,000 Fare (St. Louis to San Francisco)—$200 Concord Coaches were in use in the 1700s, and became so popular that the first railroads modified them for use as passenger cars! ... when the west opened up, the concord was pressed into service as the fastest and most comfortable cross-country conveyance ... if there were no floods or blizzards, no Indians to fight and no breakdowns, one could, by riding day and night with few rest stops and little sleep, reach California from St. Louis in only *25 days*!"

"The builders of the first telegraph line through the west had little idea of the problems in store for them. Foremost among their troubles were routine attacks from hostile Indians, and fugitive criminals, as well as floods and raging prairie fires ... on the treeless plains the animals used the poles as rubbing posts—destroying them by the thousands! They actually seemed to *enjoy* the sharp spikes which were driven into the poles to discourage them!! Even after death the buffalo returned to haunt the hapless repair crews ... who found that the Indians who cut the wires would retie them with *buffalo hide* ... making the break impossible to detect!"

"The Hereford: first brought to this country from England in the year 1789 ... the first Herefords were shipped to Texas in 1860 and since have dominated the beef cattle industry. With longhorn cattle, all a rancher had to do was round them up, slap a brand on them, and trail-drive them to Kansas—where they brought a 1000 percent profit! ... but people soon began to demand better and cheaper meat, so many ranchers started importing Herefords to 'beef up' production ... most Texans didn't like the whiteface cattle—they just didn't look like critters ought to look! And, when they were mixed with the longhorns, they soon became footsore—many were literally walked to death! The Texans soon began calling them 'tenderfeet' ... the term has come to mean any inexperienced Westerner!"

"The Pony Express. The first pony express rider left St. Joseph, Missouri on April 3, 1860 ... and rode into history.... The Pony Express lasted only 18 months, but this romantic era found courageous riders braving blizzards, floods, heat, cold, and hostile Indians to carry the mail 650,000 miles while only *once* losing a letter! Riders were rugged and durable—but *light*. Total weight of rider, mail sack, mail and saddle was never more than 165 pounds! Letters were carried in a leather 'mochilla' which had 4 mail pouches ... couriers carried a horn to alert station masters of their arrival ... the riders only protection was a pair of pistols ... rifles were much too heavy! Saddles were just leather covered frames, and weighed only 13 pounds! Most famous of the pony riders was William F. "Buffalo Bill" Cody, who once rode *322 miles* in one stretch to see the mail through!"

"A popular subject of Western writers is the story of the settlement of that great frontier ... and this is rightly so.... Today we are harvesting the rewards of the efforts expended by thousands of un-named individuals who took part in that glorious and eventful drama ... the settlement of the American West. We can hardly imagine the frustrations, the struggles, the hardships, and the loneliness which they endured... we can only appreciate the legacy which is ours ... the pioneers had to build where nothing had been built ... invent fencing where no rails existed ... use hay or cow chips in stoves where there was no timber or coal... even invent new vehicles in which to travel west ... or a wind-pump where there was no water.... But most of all, their success was achieved through stoic heroism—such as the Mormons who, to reach Utah, *walked 1500 miles, pushing hand carts!*"

"Levi Strauss was a member of a New York tailoring family who went west at the beginning of the California gold rush ... when Levi Strauss arrived in San Francisco in 1849, he had every intention of making and selling tents to gold miners ... but the miners didn't need tents, they needed work pants.... So Levi made trousers out of his tent cloth, and the result was an immediate sell-out! Thread was not strong enough to hold pockets in rough wear, so Levi used rivets to strengthen them.... *He began mass production, and by 1870 'Levi's' were sold throughout the west.* The blue canvas cloth, copper rivets, leather waist-band tag, and orange thread became standard by 1870, and patented by 1908 ... today's levis are much the same as a hundred years ago, and wearing them is a western tradition!"

Cartoons by Hess addressed such topics as Billy the Kid, Belle Starr, the discovery of gold at Sutter's mill, Butch Cassidy, Jesse James, Edward Creighton,

George Maledon (the hangman in Ft. Smith, Arkansas), James Bowie (defending the Alamo along with Davy Crockett, he was "so weak from pneumonia that he could not rise from his bed ... yet he wielded his famous blade, and stacked up *nine* of the invaders before he fell!").

"People have always wondered about the origin of Western town names. Some were named for Indian tribes, rivers, etc.... Others were more unique. One such town is located on the slopes of Mt. Davidson in Nevada. This area had been the site of Mormon settlements as early as the 1840s, and thousands of prospectors passed in the 1850s on their way to the rich gold fields in California ... the same prospectors rushed back in 1859 to work the most fabulous silver bonanza ever discovered ... the Washoe diggings— later to become known as the *Comstock Lode*.... A town sprang up and mushroomed from 5 to 10 to 15 and finally, *25,000 people*. But the town had no name ... and nobody much cared what it was *called* as long as the silver lasted ... until one night a drunken no-good called Virginny Finney staggered out of a saloon, tripped, and smashed a full bottle of whiskey ... to still the laughter of his mirthful friends, Finney regained his composure and proclaimed to all present ... I Christen this place ... Virginia! The title stuck, and the town that had no name became ... Virginia City, Nevada. Today Virginia City has been restored and is one of Nevada's most colorful tourist attractions."

"Cattle brands were an important part of the early West. These 'signatures' were known and respected ... at least by most people.... In their earliest use, brands were applied to an animal simply by tracing the design with a hot spur, or other metal instrument ... a 'running iron.' These brands were crude, and easily modified or defaced by cattle rustlers. Sometimes the intentions of vagrants who carried running irons were questioned, and the result was often a hung decision! Because of this, 'fixed irons' came into use by cattlemen, and the mere possession of a running iron was a crime! Today all brands are registered in the state where they are used, and a booklet is published to aid in identification. Despite this, cattle rustling is still a problem. In 1965 alone, several *thousand* cases were reported! This chart shows how a single character can be modified to form many different brands. In all, more than 300,000 brands have been used: R, walking R, drag, flying, backward, rocking, double, bar, slash, running, box, diamond, circle, crazy, lazy."

"Some miners in Denver once decided to play a practical joke on an eastern newspaper editor who had just arrived in town ... the editor was scheduled to visit a nearby mine ... where the miners had made preparations for his visit by thoroughly "salting" the mining area with gold dust and nuggets fired from a shotgun ... when the editor arrived at the mine he ceremonially washed some dirt about in a pan, and was amazed to find gold on his very *first* try! He then announced to those present ... Gentlemen, I have worked with my own hands, and seen with my own eyes. The news of your rich discovery shall go all over the world, as far as my paper can waft it! And so it was! For this practical joke, as much as anything, influenced this editor to write many glowing accounts of the riches and opportunities to be found in the west ... and the famous words, "Go West Young Man!" gained immortality for ... Horace Greeley!"

"Meeting of the Rails: May 10, 1869. When the Union Pacific Railroad met the Central Pacific at Promontory Point, Utah in 1869, it was the most celebrated event of the time. This is the story of the unique method used to announce the event. The telegraph wires at promontory point were connected to the rails ... telegraph lines lead from promontory point to every city in the nation, where they were connected to various devices which would be set off by the electric signal generated each time the last spike was struck ... by noon of May 10th all was ready.... Minutes ... then hours ticked by as the nation waited.... Finally, at 2:43, word came. 'We have got done praying ... ready now.' The last spike was placed and ... Throughout America whistles, roaring cannons, and bells announced the completed pacific railroad. The celebration lasted for days. *Small wonder!* Travel time from New York to San Francisco was cut from four weeks to less than seven days!"

"The pioneers who settled the west had a space capsule too ... with which they traveled through western space ... it was called a 'prairie schooner,' and in many respects was like today's space vehicles ... sturdy, compact, designed to do a job, and with very little provision for comfort—every square inch was needed for necessities, and everyone, including the driver, walked! In some ways the risks were greater than those of the astronaut ... and their only 'ground control' was a limitless faith in divine providence! Components: tongue, doubletree, canvas "sheet," tool box, brake mechanism, brake arm, bows to support canvas, tar bucket (for greasing wheels)."

"This week's story concerns a form of entertainment that was unique to the old west. Entertainment then wasn't as varied as it is now, but ... Things in the west were never dull! Those who enjoyed nightlife had a choice of poker, faro, or dice games, and, of course, there was plenty of 'red eye.' If things ever did become monotonous, it wasn't long before a new twist would be added to an old game ... such was the case with horseback pool. Upon at least one occasion a player interrupted his game to put three bullet holes in a heckler. And while the intruder was being carried away, calmly finished his game!"

Chapter Notes

All citations labeled "Archive" are excerpted from two volumes of letters, photographs, wills, genealogies, newspaper clippings, and typed reminiscences collected by family members under the supervision of Everett Berry, Jr. (my uncle) between 1960 and 2000. Sources for materials within these unpublished volumes (of which three sets were created) often contain no date, no page, and sometimes no author, but the information was verified in interviews with my mother, Catherine Berry Hess, in 2013.

Preface

1. Paul Stoller, *Sensuous Scholarship* (Philadelphia: University of Pennsylvania Press, 1997); Michael Jackson, *Minima Ethnographica: Intersubjectivity and the Anthropological Project* (Chicago: University of Chicago Press, 1998).
2. *Ibid.*
3. Stoller, xv.

Introduction

1. Arlette Farge, *The Allure of the Archives* (New Haven, CT: Yale University Press, 2013), 4.
2. *Ibid.*, 5.
3. *Ibid.*
4. *Ibid.*
5. See Carolyn Steedman, *Dust: The Archive and Cultural History* (New Brunswick, NJ: Rutgers University Press, 2001), 1–16.
6. Ann Laura Stoler, *Along the Archival Grain: Epistemic Anxieties and Colonial Common Sense* (Princeton, NJ: Princeton University Press, 2009), 1–2.
7. Farge, 4; Stoler, 2.
8. Stoler, 2.
9. Camelia Uzzell Berry, *Oklahoma Prairie Plowed Under: The Story of Berry Brothers in Indian Territory* (Cortez, CO: Colorado, 1988), 210–211.
10. *Ibid.*
11. Willard Hughes Rollings, *The Osage: An Ethnographic Study of Hegemony on the Prairie-Plains* (Columbia: University of Missouri Press, 1992), 285.
12. Stoller, *Sensuous Scholarship*; Jackson, *Minima Ethnographica.*
13. *Ibid.*
14. *Ibid.*
15. Dennis McAuliffe, Jr., *Bloodland: A Family Story of Oil, Greed and Murder on the Osage Reservation* (New York: Random House, 1994), 92.
16. *The Last Run*, "Father and Son Made the Run," by T.N. Berry, n.p., n.d. Archive.
17. Transcription of phone call between Martha Brown and Virginia Berry Harrison (deceased), 1987. Archive.
18. The term Osage has been spelled variously in the possessive and plural in the literature. For clarity's sake I refer to discus-

sions of the Osage in the singular throughout. Many Osage words, such as *I'n-lonschka* and *Wah-Kon-Tah*, are also spelled variously. I retain the above spelling for clarity throughout this text, except within the quotations of others.

19. Farge, 5.
20. M. Annette Jaimes, "Federal Indian Identification Policy: A Usurption of Indigenous Sovereignty in North America," in M. Annette Jaimes, ed., *The State of Native America: Genocide, Colonization, and Resistance* (Boston: South End Press, 1992), 10; Gerald Vizenor, *Fugitive Poses: Native American Indian Scenes of Absence and Presence* (Lincoln: University of Nebraska Press, 1998), 27.
21. Steedman, 5.
22. There is a vast literature on the "Other." See, for example, Olu Oguibe and Okwui Enwezor, ed., *Reading the Contemporary: African Art from Theory to the Marketplace* (Cambridge: MIT Press, 1999).
23. Barbara Bender, "Place and Landscape," in Christopher Tilley, Webb Keane, Susanne Kuechler-Fogden, Mike Rowlands, and Patricia Spyer, *Handbook of Material Culture* (London: Sage, 2006), 304.
24. *Ibid.*, 305.
25. John Joseph Mathews, *Wah'Kon-Tah: The Osage and the White Man's Road* (Norman: University of Oklahoma Press, 1932), 19.
26. Camelia Berry, 110.
27. Bender, 306.
28. Jackson, 15.
29. Roger Hall Lloyd, *Osage County: A Tribe and American Culture, 1600–1934* (Lincoln, NE: iUniverse, 2006), 3.
30. Bender, 305.
31. *Ibid.*

Chapter 1

1. *Osage Indian Tribe Centennial Celebration: 1872–1972* (Tulsa, OK: Acorn, 1972).
2. *Ibid.*
3. For an account of the misrepresentation of American Indian history, see Frederick E. Hoxie, "Missing the Point: Academic Experts and American Indian Politics," in Daniel M. Cobb and Loretta Fowler, ed., *Beyond Red Power: American Indian Policies and Activism Since 1909* (Sante Fe, NM: School for Advanced Research Press, 2007): 16–32.
4. Some scholars estimate that 99 percent of the American Indians were killed. See Ward Churchill. Lenore A. Stiffarm with Phil Lane, Jr., "The Demography of Native North America: A Question of American Indian Survival," in Jaimes, 37.
5. Willard Hughes Rollings, *The Osage: An Ethnographical Study of Hegemony on the Prairie-Plains* (Columbia: University of Missouri Press, 1992), 1.
6. Victor Tixier, John Francis McDermott, ed., Albert J. Salvan, trans., *Tixier's Travels on the Osage Prairies, 1839–40* (Norman: University of Oklahoma Press, 1940 [France: Clermand-Ferrand, 1844]), 129.
7. McAuliffe, 41.
8. *Ibid.*
9. Rollings, 3.
10. Roger Hall Lloyd, *Osage County: A Tribe and American Culture* (New York: iUniverse, 2006).
11. McAuliffe, 40.
12. Alexandra Harmon, "Osage Oil Owners," in *Rich Indians: Native People and the Problem of Wealth in American Society* (Chapel Hill: University of North Carolina Press, 2010), 171.
13. *Ibid.*
14. Garrick Bailey and Daniel C. Swan, *Art of the Osage* (Washington: St. Louis Art Museum in Association with University of Washington Press, 2004), 3.
15. *Ibid.*
16. Lloyd, 46.
17. *Ibid.*, 16.
18. *Ibid.*, 19–20.
19. *Ibid.*, 21.
20. Lloyd, 46; Bailey, 4.
21. Lloyd, 46.
22. Bailey, 5–6.
23. *Ibid.*, 4.
24. *Ibid.*, 4.
25. Interview with Paula Farid, Pawhuska, OK, November 5, 2013.
26. Bailey, 5.
27. Burns, 103–104.
28. Lloyd, 59.
29. *Ibid.*,104.
30. McAuliffe, 40.
31. Burns, 131–32.
32. Lloyd.
33. *Ibid.*, 64.

34. Lloyd, 114.
35. According to Hogan, "Chief White Hair was originally called Gra-to-moh-se (Iron Hawk), a six-feet-seven inch or six-feet-eight inch Osage brave. He got the name Paw-hui-skah or White Hair in an interesting way. At the Battle of Wabash on November 4, 1791, one of the worst defeats the Americans ever suffered from the Indians, General Arthur St. Clair led 3,000 American soldiers to put down an Indian uprising. The Osages allied themselves with the other tribes to fight the whites. The young Osage named Gra-to-moh-se, believing he had killed an American officer, leaned over him and grabbed his hair to scalp him. In those days officers wore perukes, the powdered wigs of the British courts. When the officer's white wig came off in the Indian's hand, Gra-to-moh-se screamed, amazed at how easily the white man's scalp had left his head. The scream awakened the wounded officer who also screamed, seeing that he was about to be scalped. The Indian thought he was witnessing a man rising from the dead. In the confusion, the American was able to run away, leaving the Indian amazed and still holding the white wig. From that day forward Iron Hawk was known as White Hair or Paw-hui-skah and he wore the white wig for the rest of his life, thinking it would protect him against death." Lawrence J. Hogan, *The Osage Indian Murders: The Story of a Multiple Murder Plot to Acquire the Estates of Wealthy Osage Tribal Members* (Frederick, MD: Amlex, 1998), 29.
36. McAuliffe, 39.
37. Jefferson, cited in Lloyd, 115.
38. Lloyd, 75.
39. Janet Berry Hess, *Art and Architecture in Postcolonial Africa* (Jefferson, NC: McFarland, 2006).
40. See, for example, Bender, 307.
41. Lloyd, 119.
42. *Ibid.*
43. *Ibid.*, 122.
44. Rollings, 213.
45. *Ibid.*, 93.
46. *Ibid.*, 93–94.
47. *Ibid.*, 94; Lou Brock, *The Osage Timeline* (Pawhuska, OK: Osage Tribal Museum, 2013), 11.
48. Brock, 12.
49. Ward Churchill and Glenn T. Morris, "Key Indian Laws and Cases," in *The State of Native America: Genocide, Colonization, and Resistance* (Boston: South End, 1992), 14.
50. Lloyd, 153.
51. *Ibid.*
52. *Ibid.*, 155.
53. Eliza Whitmire, 1938, in Patrick Minges, *Black Indian Slave Narratives* (Winston-Salem, NC: John F. Blair, 2004), 34.
54. McAuliffe.
55. Rollings, 6.
56. *Ibid.*, 7.
57. *Ibid.*, 114.
58. Lloyd, 111.
59. Frances W. Kaye, "Little Squatter on the Osage Diminished Reserve: Reading Laura Ingalls Wilders' Kansas Indians," *Great Plains Quarterly* 20, issue 2 (2000): 128.
60. Burns, 300.
61. McAuliffe, 38.
62. Burns, 301.
63. *Ibid.*, 301.
64. Kaye, 130.
65. *Ibid.*, 136.
66. A subsequent Indian agent, Laban Miles, brought his nephew, the future President Herbert Hoover, to attend Osage schools. *Ibid.*
67. Lloyd, 244.
68. *Ibid.*, 288.
69. *Ibid.*, 340–41.
70. *Ibid.*, 398.
71. Hogan, *The Osage Indian Murders*, 20; Brock, 29.
72. Hogan, 21.
73. *Ibid.*
74. Lloyd, 385. "'Mixed blood' Indians received title by fee simple patent; 'full bloods' were issued 'trust patents,' meaning they had no control over their allotted property for a period of twenty-five years." Rebecca L. Robbins, "Self-Determination and Subordination: The Past, Present, and Future of American Indian Governance," in Jaimes, ed., *The State of Native America*, 93.
75. Wilson, in Osage Tribal Museum handout, Osage Tribal Museum, Pawhuska, Ok., 2014. For more information on grass leasing by the Osage, see Robert M. Burrill, "The Establishment of Ranching on the Osage Reservation," *Geographical Review* 62, no. 4 (1972): 524–543.
76. Callahan, 12.
77. Burill, 534–35.
78. Robert M. Burrill, "The Osage Pas-

ture Map," *The Chronicles of Oklahoma* 53, issue 2 (1975): 207.
79. *Ibid.*, 211.
80. Churchill and Morris, 14.
81. Hogan, 24–25; Callahan, 15.
82. Hogan, 24–25.
83. *Ibid.*, 29. The auctions "only gave successful bidders the right to drill for oil. There was no guarantee that they would find it and, if they did, they then had to pay royalties on what the well yielded" (33).
84. "Total revenues [to the Osage] in 1923 … were more than $27.6 million… an allotted Osage in 1925 had buying power equivalent to a million dollars or more in the 1990s" (174, 177).
85. Brock, 408.
86. *Osage Indian Tribe Centennial Celebration of 1872-1972.*

Chapter 2

1. Jackson, 1.
2. *Ibid.*
3. *Ibid.*, 2.
4. *Ibid.*, 7.
5. *Ibid.*, 4.
6. *Ibid.*, 7.
7. *Ibid.*, 5.
8. *Ibid.*
9. Richard Dyer, *White* (New York: Routledge, 1997), xiv.
10. *Ibid.*
11. McAuliffe, 107–108.
12. Custer, in Sherman Alexie, *New Shirts and Old Skins* (Los Angeles: University of California Press, 1993), 36–38.
13. Jackson, 10.
14. Jackson, 15.
15. *Ibid.*, 10.
16. *Ibid.*, 4.
17. *Ibid.*
18. *Historical and Biographical History of Oklahoma*, 1901, n.p. Archive.
19. Lloyd, 233.
20. Gerald Vizenor, *Fugitive Poses: Native American Indian Scenes of Absence and Presence* (Lincoln: University of Nebraska Press, 1998), 11.
21. *Ibid.*
22. Camelia Berry, 12.
23. *Ibid.*
24. Jackson, 9.
25. Camelia Berry, 169.
26. *Ibid.*, 176.
27. *Ibid.*, 218.
28. Ward Churchill, cited in Jaimes, "Sand Creek: The Morning After," in Jaimes, 5.
29. Unattributed, n.d., Archive.
30. Murray R. Wickett, *Contested Territory: Whites, Native Americans and African Americans in Oklahoma, 1865-1907* (Baton Rouge: Louisiana State University Press, 2000): 5–6.
31. *Ibid.*, 6.
32. Cited in Wickett, 15.
33. Minges, 39.
34. *Ibid.*, 102.
35. *Ibid.*, 42, 45.
36. Ned Thompson, cited in Mingus, 136.
37. M. Annette Jaimes, "Federal Indian Identification Policy," in Jaimes, 126.
38. Churchill and Morris, 14.
39. Jaimes, 130. See Linda Williams Reese, *Women of Oklahoma: 1890-1920* (Norman: University of Oklahoma Press, 1997), 53. ("By the 1910 federal census only one-third of the total Indian population in Oklahoma claimed to be full-blood.")
40. *Ibid.*, 129.
41. These parties lasted until 1980. Callahan, 12.
42. Terry P. Wilson, "Osage Indian Women During a Century of Change, 1870–1980," *Prologue* 14, issue 4 (Winter 1982): 188.
43. *Ibid.*
44. Hogan, 26–27.
45. *The Osage Timeline*, 55.
46. Joshua A. Krisch, "When Racism Was a Science," *New York Times*, October, 2014, p. D6.
47. Reese, 150.
48. *Ibid.*, 151.
49. Robert B. Porter, cited in William Glaberson, "Who Is a Seminole, and Who Gets to Decide?," *New York Times*, January 29, 2001, p. A1.
50. *Ibid.*, A14.
51. *Ibid.*
52. *Osage Timeline*, 55.
53. Peter La Chapelle, *Proud to Be An Okie: Cultural Politics, Country Music, and Migration to Southern California* (Berkeley: University of California Press, 2007), 22.
54. *Ibid.*, 23–24.
55. *Ibid.*, 27–28.
56. Burns, 446.
57. Camelia Berry, 15.
58. Jackson, 5.

59. Momaday, 27.
60. Jackson, 12.
61. *Ibid.*, 16.
62. Stoller, xv–xvi.
63. Unattributed, n.d. Archive.
64. W.E. Berry, n.d. Archive.
65. David Hess, *The Ancestors of the Hess Family of Anadarko* (published by the Hess family, 2004), 18. My Great-Great-Grandfather on my father's side was from Baden, Germany, and immigrated to New Orleans, moving then from Ohio to Oklahoma.
66. Jackson, 12.
67. R.D. Laing (1965, chap. 3), cited in Jackson, 16.
68. Jackson, 16–17.
69. Interview with Catherine Hess, Lincoln, CA, December 29, 2013.
70. Jackson, 137, 132.

Chapter 3

1. Antoinette Burton, ed., *Archive Stories: Facts, Fictions, and the Writing of History* (Durham, NC: Duke University Press, 2005), 2.
2. *Ibid.*
3. *Ibid.*, 6.
4. Farge, 5.
5. *Tall Tales and Historic Adventures: David Duncan, Legendary Longhunter*, p. 6. Archive.
6. Camelia Berry, 3.
7. *Ibid.*, 8.
8. *Ibid.*, 9.
9. Camelia Berry, 3.
10. Isaac "King" Berry, letter to John R. Walden, February 20, 1941; letter from Isaac King, November 10, 1936. Archive.
11. *Tall Tales and Historic Adventures*, 10.
12. *Ibid.*
13. *Ibid.*, 2.
14. *Ibid.*, 12.
15. *Ibid.*, 11–12.
16. *Portrait and Biographical Record*, 898, n.d. Archive.
17. Camelia Berry, 2.
18. *Ibid.*, 4–6.
19. *Ibid.*, 8.
20. *Ibid.*, 12.
21. *Ibid.*
22. *Ibid.*, 19.
23. Churchill and Morris, 16.
24. *Mcclanahan V. Arizona Tax Commission* (1973), cited in Churchill and Morris, 19.
25. *Ibid.*
26. *Ibid.*, 15.
27. *Ibid.*, 15.
28. *Another Version of the First Opening of Old Oklahoma*, n.d., n.p. Archive.
29. John R. Walden, "Mosquitoes Got Scalps in Last Indian Scare," *Notes on Early Clark County Kansas*, vol. III (Ashland: Clark County Chapter of the Kansas State Historical Chapter, 1941). Archive.
30. *King Berry Reminisces 1850–1945*, n.d., n.p. Archive. The fear expressed was well-founded: as Lloyd suggests, the Osage rituals of death and mourning once required that "a scalp was taken to adorn the grave of the departed. These mourning ceremonies, a ritualization of grief and also a variant of the rite of war, were a cause of much bloodshed, since the relatives of the unwilling death-companion often sought revenge… Despite the efforts of government agents and missionaries it was practiced until this century." Lloyd, 29.
31. "Surprise! The Settlers Were Afraid of Cowboys!" n.d., n.p. Archive.
32. Linda Williams Reese, *Women of Oklahoma:1890–1920* (Norman: University of Oklahoma Press, 1997), 29.
33. Interview with Chrissie Childers, Hominy, OK, November 5, 2013.
34. John R. Walden, "Winfield Man," *Notes on Early Clark County Kansas*, by the Clark County Chapter of the Kansas State Historical Society, vol. III, September 1941-August 1942, edited by Dorothy Berrman and Melville Campbell Harper, reprinted from the Clark County Historical Society Column in the *Clark County Clipper*, Ashland, Kansas. Archive.
35. John R. Walden, *Short History of Berry Family*, n.d. n.p. Archive.
36. R. Neill Rahn, adjutant general chief of staff, Topeka, Kansas, letter to I.K. Berry, September 23, 1924. Archive.
37. Camelia Berry, 46.
38. Kenny A. Franks and Paul F. Lambert, *Pawnee Pride: A History of Pawnee County* (Oklahoma City: Western Heritage, 1994), 93.
39. For a history of black Indians in the Indian Territory, see William Loren Katz, *Black Indians: A Hidden Heritage* (New York: Simon and Schuster, 1986).

40. Wickett, xi.
41. *Ibid.*
42. Lloyd, 315.
43. *Ibid.*, 35.
44. Wickett, 99.
45. *Ibid.*, 107.
46. Katz, 149.
47. *Ibid.*
48. *Ibid.*
49. See Reese ("White women limited social contacts with blacks, and when friendships arose, they believed they had to explain them away or hide them. Under no circumstances would they condone intermarriage. They hired black women to cook and scrub, and they paid them wages far lower than those paid to white women ... in the one arena in which Oklahoma and Indian Territory women could vote and hold office, they restricted opportunities for black education."): 66.
50. Jimmie L. Franklin, "Black Oklahomans and a Sense of Place," in Davis D. Joyce, ed. *An Oklahoma I Had Never Seen Before": Alternative Views of Oklahoma History* (Norman: University of Oklahoma Press, 1994), 267.
51. *Ibid.*
52. *Ibid.*
53. *Ibid.*, 272.
54. *Ibid.*
55. Ellison, in Franklin, 274–75.
56. *Ibid.*, 269.
57. Dunjee, cited in Franklin, 277.
58. *Historical and Biographical History of Oklahoma*, 1901, n.p. Archive.
59. Interview with Thomas E. Berry, in *Legends of Oklahoma*, n.p., n.d. Archive.
60. "Among the Shawnees," Addie Lee Barker, in *Territorial Topic*, Purcell, Choctaw Nation, Indian Territory, 1890. Archive.
61. Camelia Berry, 43.
62. James B. Thoburn, *History of Oklahoma*, vol. 5 (Tulsa, OK: American Historical Society, 1916), p. 2135.
63. *Ibid.*
64. Camelia Berry, 206.
65. *Ibid.*, 44, 175.
66. *Ibid.*
67. William C. Davis, *The Illustrated Directory of the Old West* (Minneapolis, MN: Voyageur, 2002), 377.
68. *Ibid.*
69. *Ibid.*, 378.
70. *Ibid.*

71. "Biographical Sketch," in *Notes on Early Clark County Kansas*, vol. III (Ashland: Clark County Chapter of the Kansas State Historical Chapter: 1941). Archive.
72. Camelia Berry, 39. So dangerous were the wolves that snapped at the tendons of cattle that the Cherokee Strip Livestock Association offered bounties for wolf scalps. "Wolf Scalps Ranicky Bill." Archive.
73. Camelia Berry, 39.
74. *Ibid.*, 76.
75. Paul Laune, *Mustang Round Up*, n.p., n.d. Archive.
76. *Ibid.*
77. Franks and Lambert, 77.
78. "George M. Berry, Being Treated at Rochester, Has Had Long Experience With Redmen," unknown newspaper, January 22, 1939. Archive.
79. H.E. Chrisman, *Lost Trails of the Cimarron*, cited in Camelia Berry, 70.
80. Camilla Berry, 150.
81. *Ibid.*
82. "Out of the Past," reprinted from the *Files of the Cleveland American*, October 21, 2, p. 2a. Archive.
83. Gene Hill, "The Chisholm Trail," *Oklahoma Omnibus* (Oklahoma American Historical Society, 1986), 15. Archive.
84. *Ibid.*
85. Camelia Berry, 80.
86. "Out of the Past," p. 2a. Archive.
87. Lloyd, 105.

Chapter 4

1. Interview with Chrissie Childers, Hominy, OK, November 19, 2013.
2. Jackson, 16.
3. Bailey, *The Osage and the Invisible World*, 9.
4. As one Osage individual noted, "We do not believe that our ancestors were really animals, birds, etc., as told in the traditions. These things are only *Wa-We'-Ku-Ska-Ye*, 'symbols' of something higher." *Ibid.*, 40.
5. Bailey, 52.
6. Carter Revard, "Birdwatching in Wales and Indian Territory: Consecrations of Place in Osage and Pawnee Ceremonies and in Poems by Hopkins, Thomas, and Others," *European Review of Native American Studies* 20, issue 1 (2006): 47.
7. *Ibid.*

8. *Ibid.*
9. *Ibid.*
10. Bailey, 52.
11. *Ibid.*, 27.
12. Rollings, 19–20.
13. Hogan, 7–9.
14. George Sibley, cited in Rollings, *Unaffected by the Gospel: Osage Resistance to the Christian Invasion, 1673-1906: A Cultural Victory* (Albuquerque: University of New Mexico Press, 2004), 22.
15. Rollings, *Unaffected by the Gospel*, 16–20.
16. Alice Anne Callahan, *The Osage Ceremonial Dance I'n-Lon-Schka* (Norman: University of Oklahoma Press, 1990), 5.
17. Garrick Bailey, introduction, in Garrick A. Bailey, ed., *The Osage and the Invisible World: From the Works of Francis La Flesche* (Norman: University of Oklahoma, 1995), 19.
18. See Omer C. Stewart, *Peyote Religion: A History* (Norman: University of Oklahoma Press, 1987), Chapter 3.
19. *Ibid.*, 5.
20. Bailey and Swan, *Art of the Osage*, 3.
21. *Ibid.* For more information on the architecture of the Native American Church, see Daniel C. Swan, "Early Osage Peyotism," *Plains Anthropologist* 43, no. 163 (February 1998): 55–71.
22. Interview with Catherine Berry Hess, Lincoln, CA, April 10, 2014.
23. Bailey, 114.
24. *Ibid.*
25. *Ibid.*, 144.
26. Richard Gross, "Immaculate Conception Catholic Church: The Catholic Church of the Osage." *Stained* Glass *Quarterly*: 58–63.
27. *Ibid.*
28. Bailey, 145. "When the Osage settled on their Oklahoma reservation they maintained a tribal organization of several autonomous physical divisions. Today three of these divisions, or "Districts" as they are commonly referred to, remain: the Wah-xa Koh li, or 'Dwellers in the Thorny Thicket,' at Pawhuska, Oklahoma; the Pah Soli, or 'Dwellers Upon the Hill Top,' at Gray Horse, Oklahoma; [and] the Sa Soli, or 'Dwellers of the Forest' at Hominy, Oklahoma." Daniel Swan, "100 Years of Dancing: The Osages of Pawhuska District Observe an Anniversary," *Chronicles of Oklahoma* 63, issue 1 (1985): 96.
29. Bailey, *Art of the Osage*, 23–24.
30. *Ibid.*
31. *Ibid.*
32. Hogan, 24.
33. *Ibid.*
34. *Ibid.*
35. *Ibid.*
36. *Ibid.*, 34.
37. Callahan, 29.
38. *Ibid.*
39. Katy Holland, "Sustaining a Spirited Culture," *Bartlesville Magazine* (Spring 2014): pp. 6–17.
40. *Ibid.*, 161.
41. Michel Foucault, *Discipline and Punish: The Birth of the Prison* (New York: Random House, 1977).
42. Arrell M. Gibson, *The Oklahoma Story* (Norman: University of Oklahoma Press, 1986 [1971]): 48.
43. A second settlement was established at Hominy, and a third at Gray Horse. "When Oklahoma became a state in 1907 Pawhuska became the county seat of Osage County, the largest county in Oklahoma and the third largest county in the United States[.]" Hogan, 21, 22.
44. Mathews, 27.
45. *Ibid.*, 28.
46. *Ibid.*
47. *Ibid.*, frontispiece.
48. *Ibid.*
49. *Ibid.*
50. Bailey, 43.
51. Mathews, 320.
52. Baird, 84–85.
53. *Ibid.*, 321–322.
54. McAuliffe, 43.
55. Lloyd, 7.
56. McAuliffe, 190.
57. *Ibid.*, 190.
58. Bender, 307.
59. *Ibid.*
60. Goodson, *The Last Run*, 302.
61. Paper materials, n.d. 13. Archive.
62. Peavy and Smith, 50.
63. William C. Davis, *The Illustrated Directory of the Old West* (Minneapolis, MN: Voyageur, 2002), 216.
64. David Hess, 18.
65. Camelia Berry, 154.
66. "Biographical Sketch." Archive.
67. *Ibid.*
68. Mrs. John B. Smith, "Reminiscences." Archive.
69. *Ibid.*, 149.

70. "What Happened to the Headquarters of Berry Brothers Ranch?," n.d. Archive.
71. David Hess, *The Ancestors of the Hess Family of Anadarko* (published by the Hess family, 2004), 20.
72. Ibid.
73. Ibid., 17.
74. Interview with Thomas Berry in *Legends of Oklahoma*, n.d. Archive.
75. Franks and Lambert, 75–77, 133–135.
76. Ibid., 182.
77. "Death Claims E.C. Mullendore; Funeral Is Held Here Thursday," *The Cleveland American*, January 30, 1938, p.1.
78. Unidentified relative, letter, 2001. Archive.
79. Hogan, 46.
80. Ibid.
81. Helton and Robertson, 39.
82. Unidentified relative, letter, 2001. Archive.
83. Ibid.
84. Christmas card sent out by Everett Berry to family, n.d. Archive.
85. McAuliffe, 4.
86. Lloyd, 3.

Chapter 5

1. Garrick Bailey, "Introduction," in Bailey and Swan, ix.
2. Along with hundreds of bones in layers of hunts, archeologists have discovered spear points from the Beaver River floodplain in Harper County, Oklahoma, at an excavation known as the Cooper site. Archeologists theorize that American Indians gathered at the floodplain approximately 10,000 years ago, and in a massive kill forced hundreds of the now-extinct *Bison Antiquus* into a dead-end gully. In 1994, archeologist Leland Bement unearthed a bison skull in the Cooper site that had a bright red zigzag or lightning bolt. This flash, painted in hematite, is "the oldest painted artwork ever discovered in North America." Robert Dorman, *It Happened in Oklahoma* (Helena, MT: TwoDot, 2006), 1–4.
3. Robert Farris Thompson, *Flash of the Spirit: African and Afro-American Art and Philosphy* (NY: Vingage, 1983).
4. Ibid., 3.
5. Victor Turner, in Janet Berry Hess, 140.
6. Cited in Terry Wilson, "Osage Indian Women During a Century of Change, 1870–1980," 187.
7. Ibid.
8. William Least Heat-Moon and James K. Wallace, ed. and trans., *An Osage Journey to Europe, 1827–1830: Three French Accounts* (Norman: University of Oklahoma Press, 2013), 14, 36.
9. Ibid., 58.
10. Hogan, 19.
11. Heat-Moon and Wallace, 25.
12. Ibid.
13. Ibid., 27–29.
14. Arrell M. Gibson, *The Oklahoma Story* (Norman: University of Oklahoma Press, 1986 [1971]), 34.
15. Bailey, 7.
16. Ibid.
17. John Francis McDermott, ed., *Tixier's Travels on the Osage Prairies* (Norman: University of Oklahoma Press, 1940), 136.
18. Ibid., 137–38.
19. Heat-Moon and Wallace, 79.
20. Rollings, 17.
21. Burns, 209.
22. McMillen.
23. Rollings, 17.
24. Cited in Janet Berry Hess, *Art and Architecture in Postcolonial Africa*, 140.
25. Tixier, 137–38.
26. Rollings, 16.
27. Heat-Moon and Wallace, 80.
28. Bailey, 39.
29. Ibid., 11.
30. Ibid., 202, 72–73.
31. Ibid., 11.
32. Bailey and Swan, 14.
33. Bailey, 64.
34. "The Story of the Spider," Handout, Osage Tribal Museum, Pawhuska, OK, 2014.
35. Tixier, 137.
36. Burns, 209.
37. Bailey, 65.
38. Bailey, *The Osage and the Invisible World*, 197.
39. Nancy J. Parezo, "What's in a Name? The 1940s–1950s 'Squaw Dress,'" *American Indian Quarterly* 33, issue 3 (June 2009): 376.
40. *The Osage Indian Murders*, 45.
41. Unidentified relative, letter, 2001. Archive.
42. Ibid.
43. Interview with Catherine Berry Hess, Lincoln, CA, November 10, 2013.

44. Camilla Berry, 27.
45. Peavy and Smith, 44.
46. Ibid.
47. Photograph, Archive.
48. Parezo, 376.
49. *Pendelton Woolen Mills* (Albuquerque, NM: Avanyu, 1987 [1915]).
50. Ibid., p. 2.
51. Ibid., 4.
52. Ibid., 15.
53. Ibid.
54. Parezo, 374.
55. Lloyd, 338.
56. Ibid., 25.
57. Bailey, *The Osage and the Invisible World*, 5.
58. Ibid.
59. Bailey, 27.
60. Suzanne Blier, *African Vodun: Art, Psychology, and Power* (Chicago: University of Chicago Press, 1995), 9.
61. Ibid., 1, 20.
62. Ibid.
63. Rollings, 2–26.
64. La Flesche, cited in Bailey, *The Osage and the Invisible World*, 50.
65. Baird, 10.
66. Ibid., 30, 39.
67. Lloyd, 25.
68. Ibid.
69. Ibid., 27.
70. Ibid., 28.
71. Ibid.
72. Bailey, 51.
73. Heat-Moon and Wallace, 88.
74. Lloyd, 33.
75. Bailey, *The Osage and the Invisible World*, 18–21.
76. Ibid., 44.
77. Ibid., 51. According to Pbonchai Tallman, this complexity of medicine is common in other nations which continue to practice the old ways. Interview, Napa, CA, July 29, 2014.
78. Franks and Lambert, 23.
79. Ibid.
80. Blier, 2, 20.
81. Bailey, ed., *The Osage and the Invisible World: From the Works of Francis La Flesche* (Norman: University of Oklahoma Press, 1995), 82.
82. Ibid., 148.
83. Ibid.
84. Bailey, *The Osage and the Invisible World*, 281.

Chapter 6

1. John Joseph Matthews, *WAH'KON-TAH: The Osage and the White Man's Road* (Norman: University of Oklahoma Press, 1932), 47.
2. Stoller, xii.
3. Camelia Berry, 102–103, 105.
4. Ibid., 87.
5. David Mullendore, quoted in Camelia Berry, 114–115.
6. Camelia Berry, 116.
7. Ibid.
8. Lloyd, 296.
9. B.B. Chapman, *The Founding of Stillwater*, p. 182, n.d. Archive.
10. Omer C. Stewart, *Peyote Religion: A History* (Norman: University of Oklahoma Press, 1987), 109–110.
11. Lloyd, 308.
12. Daniel M. Cobb and Loretta Fowler, "Introduction," in Cobb and Fowler, ed., *American Indian Politics and Activism Since 1900* (Sante Fe: School for Advanced Research Press, 2007): xiii.
13. Cobb and Fowler, "Introduction," xiii; Taiawagi Helton and Lindsay G. Robertson, "The Foundations of Federal Law and Its Application in the Twentieth Century," in Cobb and Fowler, 40.
14. Helton and Robertson, in Cobb and Fowler, 36.
15. Lloyd, 329.
16. Mary Annette Pember, "Indian Assimilation: The Mystery of the Tiny Handcuffs, Solved," Indian Country Today, Media Network.com.
17. Helton and Robertson, 36.
18. Ibid.; see Churchill and Morris, 18.
19. Churchill and Morris, 17.
20. Baird, 63.
21. Mathews, cited in Lloyd, 330.
22. Mathews, 101.
23. *Osage Timeline*, 31.
24. Mathews, quoted in Lloyd, 328.
25. Lloyd, 308–09.
26. Ibid., 365. McAuliffe's research reveals the varied descriptions of white interlopers by historians: "riff-raff," "vagabonds, gamblers, whiskey peddlers, criminals," "sharpers, thieves, bandits," "lawbreakers, fugitives," "outcasts," "human predators, confidence men," "swearing illiterate men," "uneducated rough men," "unscrupulous white men," "low-down, sneaking, pillaging dogs," "horse

racers," "buzzards," "dishonest scamps," "schemers, crooks, floaters," "backwash," "convicts, bad men, card-sharps, former cow-punchers," "renegades, grafters," "petty thieves, barbarians, cutpurses, murderers, rapists, human rats," "half-savage frontiersmen," "ruthless men who would cut a baby's throat just to see if their blade was keen," and "the vile and the wicked from everywhere" (161).

27. Daniel M. Cobb, "Continuing Encounters: Historical Perspectives," in Cobb and Fowler, 58–59.

28. N.d, n.a. Archive.

29. James B. Thoburn, in *History of Oklahoma*, vol. 5 (American Historical Society, 6), 2134. Archive.

30. "George Berry, Pawnee Settler Had Interesting Career in this County," *Cleveland American*, January 26, 1939, n.p. Archive.

31. "Pioneer Banker Is an Authority On Indian Cookery," n.p., n.d. Archive.

32. Camelia Berry, 209.

33. Letter to Everett Berry, Jr., n.d. Archive.

34. Camelia Berry, 211.

35. Thoburn, 2134.

36. "George Berry, Pawnee Settler Had Interesting Career in this County," *Cleveland American*, January 26, 1939, n.p. Archive.

37. *Ibid.*

38. *Ibid.*

39. *Courier Dispatch*, n.d. Archive.

40. I.K. Berry, letter to George Berry, October 17, 1906. Archive.

41. C.J. Wrightsman, letter to George Berry, November 6, 1906, on letterhead from Wrightsman, Diggs & Houck. Archive.

42. F. S. Monnett, attorney in Columbus, Ohio, letter to George Berry, September 19, 1907. Archive.

43. *Times Democrat*, n.d., Oklahoma Press Clipping Bureau, Guthrie, Archive.

44. *Times Democrat*, December 27, 1906. Archive.

45. *Times Journal*, December 27, 1906, Oklahoma Press Clipping Bureau, Guthrie.

46. Mrs. H. Brim, letter to Hon. George Berry of Pawnee, January 23, 1907. Archive.

47. "On Parade," *Cushing Daily Citizen*, November 24, 1933, n.p. Archive.

48. Unattributed family account. Archive.

49. Franks and Lambert, 135.

50. Interview with Catherine Berry Hess, Lincoln, CA, January 9, 2014.

51. "George Berry, Being Treated at Rochester, Has Had Long Experience with Redmen." Archive.

52. *Ibid.*

53. "On Parade."

54. *Ibid.*

55. *Ibid.*

56. *Ibid.*

Chapter 7

1. *The Presbyterian Guild Cook Book* (Hominy, OK: 1st Presbyterian Guild, Dec. 1, 1927), 47, 49.

2. *Ibid.*, 5.

3. *Ibid.*, 7.

4. Reese, xvi.

5. *Ibid.*, xvii.

6. Camelia Berry, 42.

7. *Presbyterian Guild Cook Book*, 47.

8. Bertha Macky, letter to Mrs. Susan Harthur, July 15, 1915. Archive.

9. Camelia Berry, 169.

10. Martha ("Mattie") Brown Berry, letter to Juliet Sophia, March 20, 1881. Archive.

11. *Ibid.*

12. *Ibid.*

13. Camelia Berry, 63–65.

14. "Biographical Sketch." Archive.

15. *Ibid.*, 166.

16. Camelia Berry, 193.

17. Reese, 26.

18. Peavy and Smith, 31.

19. *Ibid.*, 167.

20. *Ibid.*, 97.

21. Camelia Berry, 158.

22. Berry Family Reunion notes, June 13, 1987. Archive.

23. Dora Berry Goodson, letter to her niece Dora Berry Snow, n.d. Archive.

24. *Ibid.*

25. Allen L. Farnum, *Pawnee Bill's Wild West: A Photo Documentary of the 1900–1905 Show Tours* (West Chester, PA: Schiffer, 1992), 20.

26. Genealogical record. Archive.

27. John T. Clark, letter to Martha Brown Berry, December 23, no year. Archive.

28. "Reminiscences," *Notes on Early Clark County Kansas*, vol. III (Ashland: Clark County Chapter of the Kansas State Historical Chapter, 1941). Archive.

29. Martha (Mattie) Brown Berry, letter to her mother-in-law, Juliet Sophia, March 20, 1881. Archive.

30. George Berry, letter to "Nell," from

Notes. Chapter 8

the Damon Hotel in Rochester, MN., n.d. Archive.
31. Peavy and Smith, 78.
32. Letter to Roy Berry from Pawnee, dated November 9, 1923. Archive.
33. David Hess, *Ancestors of the Hess Family of Anadarko*, 60–61.
34. Camelia Berry, 190.
35. Goodson, *The Last Run*, 302. Archive.
36. *Tall Tales and Historic Adventures*, 10.
37. *Ibid.*
38. *Ibid.*
39. *Ibid.*
40. *Ibid.*
41. *Ibid.*, 68.
42. Reese, 11.
43. *Presbyterian Guild Cook Book*, 11, 107.
44. *Ibid.*, 6.
45. Martha Brown, phone conversation with Virginia Harrison, spring 1987. Archive.
46. Camelia Berry, 217.
47. *Ibid.*, 159–160.
48. Interview with Catherine Berry Hess, Lincoln, CA, January 2, 2014.
49. Interview with Catherine Berry Hess, Lincoln, CA, February 9, 2014.
50. M. Annette Jaimes with Theresa Halsey, "American Indian Women: At the Center of Indigenous Resistance in Contemporary North America," in M. Annette Jaimes, *The State of Native America: Genocide, Colonization, and Resistance* (Boston: SouthEnd, 1992), 311.
51. *Ibid.*
52. *Ibid.*
53. *Ibid.*
54. *Ibid.*, 316–317.
55. *Ibid.*, 318.
56. *Ibid.*, 318–319.
57. *Ibid.*, 319.
58. Terry P. Wilson, "Osage Indian Women During a Century of Change, 1870–1980," 186–18.
59. *Ibid.*, 197.
60. *Ibid.*, 188.
61. *Ibid.*
62. Margot Ford McMillen, "Les Indiens Osages: French Publicity for the Traveling Osage," *Missouri Historical Review* 97, issue 4 (2003): 310, fn. 56.
63. *Ibid.*, 319, fn. 80.
64. *Ibid.*, 322.
65. Reese, 106.
66. Parezo, 375.
67. *Ibid.*, 376.
68. *Ibid.*
69. Wilson, 189.
70. *Ibid.*, 191.
71. *Osage Timeline*, 43, 45.
72. *Ibid.*, 61.
73. Swan, p. 97, fn. 8.
74. *Ibid.*, 95.
75. Reese, 148.
76. *Ibid.*, 148–149, 156.
77. *Ibid.*, 169–172.
78. *Ibid.*, 158.
79. *Ibid.*, 157.
80. *Ibid.*, 170.
81. *Ibid.*, 153.
82. Camelia Berry, 150.
83. Jackson, 16.
84. *Presbyterian Guild Cook Book*, 10.
85. *Ibid.*, 11.

Chapter 8

1. Jonathan Kwitny, *The Mullendore Murder Case* (New York: Warner, 1976), 33.
2. McAuliffe, 42.
3. C.B. Glasscock, *Then Came Oil: The Story of the Last Frontier* (New York: Bobbs-Merill, 1938), 157.
4. *Ibid.*
5. *Ibid.*
6. *Ibid.*, p. 263.
7. *Ibid.*, 174, 177.
8. W. David Baird, *The Osage People* (Phoenix: Indian Tribal Series, 1972), 73.
9. McAuliffe, 43.
10. Lloyd, 463.
11. Glasscock, 267.
12. Dennis McAuliffe, Jr., *Bloodland: A Family Story of Oil, Greed and Murder on the Osage Reservation* (San Francisco: Council Oaks, 1999), 42. One account describes the famous Osage John Stink checking into a hotel in Oklahoma City and sleeping on the floor. "Father's 300-Room Hobby," in Anne Hodges Morgan and Rennard Strickland, *Oklahoma Memories* (Norman: University of Oklahoma Press), 193.
13. Lloyd, 473; Hogan, 38.
14. Harmon, 180.
15. *Ibid.*, 172–73.
16. Tixier, 131.
17. Harmon, 180.
18. *Ibid.*, 207.
19. Unidentified relative, letter, 2001. Archive.

20. The humiliation of the guardianship system is still recalled by Osage today. Interview with Paula Farid, Pawhuska, OK, June 29, 2014.
21. Lloyd, 475.
22. *Ibid.*
23. *Ibid.*
24. *The Osage Indian Murders*, 41.
25. Hogan, 50.
26. Unidentified relative, letter, 2001. Archive.
27. *Osage Timeline*, 55.
28. Lloyd, 489.
29. *Ibid.*, 250–51.
30. *Ibid.*, 251.
31. McAuliffe, 229–230.
32. Burns, 474.
33. *Ibid.*, 474–475; Franks and Lambert, 216.
34. Wilson, "Historical Introduction," handout, Osage Tribal Museum.
35. Lloyd, 522.
36. *Ibid.*
37. Unidentified relative, letter, 2001. Archive.
38. Interview with Catherine Berry Hess, Lincoln, CA, November 1, 2013.
39. McAuliffe, 43.
40. "Out of the Past."
41. Kwitny, *The Mullendore Murder Case*, 23.
42. Interview with Thomas E. Berry, *Legends of Oklahoma*. Archive.
43. "Death Claims E.C. Mullendore; Funeral Is Held Here Thursday," *The Cleveland American*, January 20, 1938, p. 1. Archive.
44. Camelia Berry, 144.
45. Interview with Catherine Hess, Lincoln, CA, April 10, 2014.
46. Camelia Berry, 144.
47. *Ibid.*
48. Joseph Howell, n.p., n.d. Archive.
49. Kwitny, 33.
50. *Weekly Kansas Star*, June 27, 1945, n.p. Archive.
51. Interview with Catherine Berry Hess, Lincoln, CA, April 23, 2014.
52. Kwitny, 39.
53. "Mullendores Came Long Way from Shot to Shot," n.d, n.p. Archive.
54. Joseph E. Howell, in unidentified article, n.p. Archive.
55. *Ibid.*
56. Interview with Catherine Hess, Lincoln, CA, April 10, 2014.
57. Kwitny.
58. Interview, Arlena Trumbly, Pawhuska, OK, June 28, 2014.

Chapter 9

1. Joe Williams, *Woolaroc* (Bartlesville, OK: Frank Phillips Foundation,1991), 34.
2. *Ibid.*, 34–35.
3. *Ibid.*
4. *Ibid.*
5. National Cowboy & Western Heritage Museum website, Monumental Sculpture.
6. Ken Johnson, "Manifest Destiny, at the Point of a Gun," *New York Times*, December 19, 2013.
7. *Ibid.*
8. Richard W. Hill, Sr., "Developed Identities: Seeing the Stereotypes and Beyond," in Tim Johnson, ed., *Spirit Capture: Photographs from the National Museum of the American Indian* (Washington: Smithsonian Institution Press, 1998), 141.
9. *Ibid.*, 147.
10. *Ibid.*, 149.
11. *Ibid.*, 147–48.
12. Hill, in Johnson, 141.
13. *Ibid.*, 157.
14. *Ibid.*
15. *Ibid.*
16. Baird, 75.
17. Swan, in Bailey, 166.
18. *Ibid.*
19. Baird, 16–17.
20. *Ibid.*, 80–81.
21. Janet C. Berlo and Ruth B. Phillips, *Native North American Art* (New York: Oxford University Press, 1998), 9.
22. *Ibid.*, 212.
23. *Ibid.*
24. *Ibid.*
25. Ivan Karp, "Introduction: Museums and Communities: The Politics of Public Culture," in Ivan Karp, Christine Mullen Kreamer, and Steven D. Lavine, *Museums and Communities: The Politics of Public Culture* (Washington, DC: Smithsonian Institution, 1992): 1.
26. *Ibid.*, 20.
27. *Ibid.*, 13.
28. Lloyd, 65.
29. *Ibid.*
30. Berlo and Phillips, 221.
31. *Ibid.*, 221.

32. Rick Glazer-Danay, in Lawrence Abbott, ed., *I Stand in the Center of the Good: Interviews with Contemporary Native American Artists* (Lincoln: University of Nebraska Press), 9.
33. Glenn Shirley, *Pawnee Bill: A Biography of Major Gordon W. Lillie* (Stillwater, OK: Western, 1993), 228.
34. *Ibid.*
35. Camilla Berry, 169, 176.
36. Duane H. King, "The Legacy of a Visionary," in *Thomas Gilcrease* (Tulsa, OK: University of Tulsa, 2009): 9–10.
37. Daniel Swan, "The Anthropology Collection," in Anne Morand, Kevin Smith, Daniel C. Swan, and Sarah Erwin, *Treasures of Gilcrease: Selections from the Permanent Collection* (Tulsa, OK: Gilcrease Museum, 2003), 123.
38. *Ibid.*, 124.
39. Eric Singleton, "Collecting Antiquity: Masterpieces from the Ancient Past," in *Thomas Gilcrease*, 137.
40. Anne Morand, "Masterworks of a Master Collector," in *Thomas Gilcrease*.
41. Edwin Wade, "The Ethnic Art Market in the American Southwest 1880–1980," in George W. Stocking, ed., *Objects and Others: Essays on Museums and Material Culture*, History of Anthropology, vol. 3 (Madison: University of Wisconsin, 1985), 167.
42. Carole Klein, "Patron, Friend, and Collector," in *Thomas Gilcrease*, 101.
43. Wiley Steve Thornton, "Indian in a Strange Land," in MariJo Moore, ed., *Genocide of the Mind: New Native American Writing* (New York: Nation, 2003), 34.
44. Postcard of color lithograph, "Princess Wenona and Edith Tatlinger 101 Ranch Promotional Poster," Gilcrease Museum, Tulsa, OK.
45. Franks and Lambert, 107.
46. *Ibid.*, 106.
47. *Ibid.*
48. Franks and Lambert, 98.
49. *Ibid.*
50. *Ibid.*
51. *Ibid.*, 102.
52. *Ibid.*, 103.
53. *Ibid.*, 105.
54. *Ibid.*, 106.
55. *Ibid.*
56. Allen L. Farnum, *Pawnee Bill's Wild West*, 24.
57. *Ibid.*, 32.
58. Richard W. Hill, Sr., "Developed Identities: Seeing the Stereotypes and Beyond," in Johnson, *Spirit Capture*, 148.
59. Dee Brown, *Bury My Heart at Wounded Knee: An Indian History of the American West* (New York: Henry Holt, 2007 [1970]), 443.
60. Hill, 148.
61. Farnum, 33.
62. *Ibid.*, 33, 36.
63. *Ibid.*
64. Heat-Moon and Wallace, 4.
65. *Ibid.*, 17.
66. *Ibid.*, 5.
67. *Ibid.*, 20.
68. *Ibid.*, 21.
69. *Osage Timeline*, 57.
70. In Janet Berry Hess, *Art and Architecture in Postcolonial Africa*, 17.
71. Edwin Wade, "The Ethnic Art Market in the American Southwest 1880–1980," in George W. Stocking, ed. *Objects and Others: Essays on Museums and Material Culture*, History of Anthropology, vol. 3 (Madison: University of Wisconsin, 1985): 167.

Chapter 10

1. Momaday, 166.
2. Jaimes, 127.
3. *Ibid.*, 128.
4. *The Osage Timeline*, 54.
5. *Ibid.*, 38. Curtis would also witness the termination of the tribe in which he was enrolled, the Kaw, during his vice presidency.
6. Rebecca L. Robbins, "Self-Determination and Subordination: The Past, Present, and Future of American Indian Governance," in Jaimes, *The State of Native America*, 98.
7. Donald L. Fixico, "Witness to Change: Fifty Years of Indian Activism and Tribal Politics," in Cobb and Fowler, *Beyond Red Power*, 4.
8. Burns, 478–479.
9. *Ibid.*
10. Churchill and Morris, 15.
11. Burns, 478.
12. McAuliffe, 179.
13. Rebecca Robins, "Self-Determination and Subordination," in Jaimes, 90.
14. Ward Churchill, *From a Native Son: Selected Essays on Indigenism 1985-1995* (Boston: South End, 1996), 34.
15. Churchill and Morris, 16.

16. *Ibid.*, 19.
17. *Ibid.*
18. Fixico, 5.
19. William O'Barr, "Images of Native Americans in Advertising," p. 2, 9.
20. *Osage Indian Tribe Centennial Celebration: 1872-1972.*
21. *Ibid.*
22. *Ibid.*
23. *Ibid.*
24. *Ibid.*
25. *Ibid.*
26. Jaimes, 126.
27. Ross Hess, "The View from Persimmon Hill," *Sunday Oklahoman*, n.d. Archive.
28. *Ibid.*
29. *Ibid.*
30. *Ibid.*
31. *Ibid.*
32. *Ibid.*
33. *Ibid.*, January 9, 1966.
34. Callahan, 20.
35. *Ibid.*, 135.
36. *Ibid.*, 136.
37. *Ibid.*, 21.
38. Burns, 158-25.
39. Charlotte Heth, *Native American Dance: Ceremonies and Social Traditions* (Washington, DC: National Museum of the American Indian, Smithsonian Institution, with Starwood, 1992), 109.
40. *Ibid.*
41. For an outstanding account of the history of the *I'n-lon-schka*, see Alice Anne Callahan, *The Osage Ceremonial Dance I'n-Lon-Schka* (Norman: University of Oklahoma Press, 1990).
42. Daniel C. Swan, "100 Years of Dancing: The Osages of Pawhuska District Observe an Anniversary," *Chronicles of Oklahoma* 63, issue 1 (1985): 90.
43. *Ibid.*; *Osage Timeline*, 34.
44. Swan, in Bailey and Swan, 158.
45. Heth, 109.
46. *Ibid.*, 111.
47. *Ibid.*, 107.
48. Callahan, 88.
49. *Ibid.*, 27.
50. Swan, in Bailey and Swan, 158.
51. *Ibid.*, 159.
52. *Ibid.*, 158.
53. *Ibid.*, 159.
54. Bailey, 148-49.
55. Callahan, 21.
56. *Ibid.*, 84; 89-91.
57. *Ibid.*, 45.
58. *Ibid.*, 21.
59. *Ibid.*
60. *Ibid.*, 29, 32.
61. *Ibid.*, 97-98.
62. *Ibid.*, 98.
63. These descriptions are based upon personal observation. According to Callahan, the hierarchy of participants include the drumkeeper, the chairman of the dance committee and committeemen, advisors, tail dancers, whipmen, water boys, cooks, a drum warmer, a head singer and supporting singers, and a town crier, each with specified and elaborate roles and on the account offered. Callahan, Chapter Three, "Traditions of the I'n-Lon-Schka," 33-72. The Five Woman Council in Pawhuska also played an active role.
64. Daniel C. Swan, "Osage Dancing Societies and Organizations," in Bailey. "The position of Drum Keeper is one of great honor and responsibility. The most important duties of the Drum Keeper are the protection and care of the dance drum and sponsorship of the I Lon Shka dance in his district." Swan, "100 Years of Dancing," p. 97, fn. 6.
65. *Ibid.*
66. Carolyn Steedman, *Dust: The Archive and Cultural Memory*, p. 2.
67. Swan, "100 Years of Dancing," 96.
68. Interview with Pbonchai Tallman, Napa, CA, June 10, 2014.
69. Cited in Ward Churchill, *Fantasies of the Master Race: Literature, Cinema and the Colonization of American Indians* (San Francisco: City Lights, 1998), 101.
70. *Ibid.*, 102.
71. George E. Tinker, "American Indian Religious Traditions, Colonialism, Resistance, and Liberation," in Richard A. Grounds, George E. Tinker, and David E. Wilkins, *Native Voices: American Indian Identity and Resistance* (Lawrence: University Press of Kansas, 2003), 225.
72. *Ibid.*, 236.
73. *Ibid.*, 237.
74. Callahan, 137-138.
75. Joy Harjo, "There Is No Such Thing as a One-Way Land Bridge," in Richard Grounds, George E. Tinker, and David E. Wilkins, *Native Voices: American Indian Identity and Resistance* (Lawrence: University Press of Kansas), 243.
76. Hogan, 3.

77. *Ibid.*
78. Lloyd, 22, 24.
79. Lloyd, 24.
80. Callahan, 19.

Chapter 11

1. Momaday, 47.
2. Camila Berry, 110.
3. Mathews, 19.
4. *Ibid.*, 25–26.
5. Jackson, 132.
6. Carter Revard, *Family Matters, Tribal Affairs* (Tucson: University of Arizona Press, 1998), 6, 8–19.
7. *Ibid.*, 133.
8. *Ibid.*
9. *Ibid.*, 133–34.
10. Hogan, *The Osage Indian Murders*, 1.
11. *Ibid.*, 2. In 1802 a third division, "the 'Arkansas Band,' was created by the migration of nearly half of the Great Osage to the Arkansas River" (Hogan).
12. *Ibid.*, 1; Revard, 138.
13. Black Dog, "Children of the Sun and Moon," in John T. Price, ed., *The Tallgrass Prairie Reader* (Iowa City: University of Iowa Press, 2014): 1–2.
14. John Joseph Mathews, "Planting Moon," in Price, 147.
15. *Ibid.*, 148–49.
16. N. Scott Momaday, *The Man Made of Words: Essays, Stories, Passages* (New York: St. Martin's Griffin, 1997).
17. Revard, "Birdwatching," 47.
18. *Ibid.*
19. *Ibid.*, 51.
20. "Death Claims E.C. Mullendore; Funeral Is Held Here Thursday," *The Cleveland American*, January 20, 1938, p. 1. Archive.
21. Bailey, 56–57.
22. "E.C. Mullendore IV Given Tribal Name."
23. Goodson, *The Last Run*, 294.
24. Katie Hess, "Old Fashioned Thrift," *Des Moines Register*, 1975. Archive.
25. Lloyd, 3.
26. *Ibid.*
27. *Ibid.*
28. Price, xv.
29. McAuliffe. Stewart Beekman bribed agents to obtain the names of Allottees, and then purchased from many Osage their northern holdings, ultimately sold to white ranchers and then in 1983 to the Nature Conservancy.
30. John May, "Osage County," *Oklahoma Historical Society's Encyclopedia of Oklahoma History and Culture*. N.p., n.d. Archive.
31. Franks and Lambert, 135–36.
32. *Ibid.*
33. Interview with Catherine Berry Hess, November 1, 2013, Lincoln, CA.

Conclusion

1. Jackson, 17.
2. Lloyd, 35.
3. *Ibid.*
4. Jackson, 2, 10, 137.
5. Jackson, 27.
6. *Ibid.*, 208.
7. *Ibid.*

Appendix

1. N.d. Archive.

Bibliography

Abbott, Lawrence, ed. *I Stand in the Center of the Good: Interviews with Contemporary Native American Artists.* Lincoln: University of Nebraska Press, 1994.
Alexie, Sherman. *Old Shirts and New Skins.* Los Angeles: University of California Press, 1993.
Another Version of the First Opening of Old Oklahoma. N.d., n.p. Archive.
Bailey, Garrick A. *The Osage and the Invisible World: From the Works of Francis La Flesche.* Norman: University of Oklahoma Press, 1995.
Bailey, Garrick, and Daniel C. Swan. *Art of the Osage.* St. Louis: St. Louis Art Museum in Association with University of Washington Press, 2004.
Baird, W. David. *The Osage People: Centennial Commemorative Issue.* Phoenix: Indian Tribal Series, 1972.
Barker, Addie Lee. "Among the Shawnees." In *Territorial Topic.* Purcell: Choctaw Nation, Indian Territory, 1890. Archive.
Bender, Barbara. "Place and Landscape." In Christopher Tilley, Webb Keane, Susanne Kuechler-Fogden, Mike Rowlands, and Patricia Spyer, *Handbook of Material Culture,* London: Sage, 2006: 303–314.
Berlo, Janet C., and Ruth B. Phillips. *Native North American Art.* New York: Oxford University Press, 1998.
Berry, Camelia Uzzell. *Oklahoma Prairie Plowed Under: The Story of Berry Bros. in Indian Territory.* Cortez, CO: Mesa Verde, 1988.
Berry, George. Letter to "Nell," from Damon Hotel in Rochester, MN. N.d. Archive.
Berry, Isaac "King." Letter to George Berry, October 17, 1906. Archive.
———. Letter to John R. Walden, February 20, 1941. Archive.
Berry, Hobert T. "The Berry Family of Augusta & Washington Co VA. July 1993 Update." Archive.
Berry, Martha Brown. Letter to Juliet Sophia Berry, March 20, 1881. Archive.
Berry, T.N. "Father and Son Made the Run," *The Last Run.* N.p., n.d. Archive.
Berry, Thomas Edward, interview in *Legends of Oklahoma*, rearranged for clarity by Camelia Berry. N.p., n.d. Archive.
Berry, W. E. N.d. Archive.
Berry Family Reunion notes. June 13, 1987. Archive.
"Biographical Sketch," in *Notes on Early Clark County Kansas*, vol. III. Ashland: Clark County Chapter of the Kansas State Historical Chapter, 1941. Archive.
Black Dog. "Children of the Sun and Moon." In John T. Price, *The Tallgrass Prairie Reader.* Iowa City: University of Iowa Press, 2014.
Blier, Suzanne. *African Vodun: Art, Psychology, and Power.* Chicago: University of Chicago Press, 1995.

Brim, Mrs. H. Letter to Hon. George Berry of Pawnee, January 23, 1907. Archive.
Brock, Lou. *The Osage Timeline*. Pawhuska: Osage Tribal Museum, 2013.
Brown, Dee. *Bury My Heart at Wounded Knee: An Indian History of the American West*. New York: Henry Holt, 2007 (1970).
Burns, Louis F. *A History of the Osage People*. Tuscaloosa: University of Alabama Press, 2004.
Burrill, Robert M. "The Establishment of Ranching on the Osage Reservation." *Geographical Review* 62, no. 4 (1972): 524–543.
_____. "The Osage Pasture Map." *The Chronicles of Oklahoma* 53, issue 2 (1975): 204–211.
Burton, Antoinette, ed. *Archive Stories: Facts, Fictions, and the Writing of History*. Durham, NC: Duke University Press, 2005.
Callahan, Alice Anne. *The Osage Ceremonial Dance I'n-Lon-Schka*. Tulsa: Civilization of the American Indian Series, 1993.
Chapman, B.B. *The Founding of Stillwater*. N.d. Archive.
Childers, Chrissie. Interview. November 19, 2013, Hominy, Oklahoma.
Churchill, Ward. *Fantasies of the Master Race: Literature, Cinema and the Colonization of American Indians*. San Francisco: City Lights, 1998.
_____. *From a Native Son: Selected Essays on Indigenism*. Boston: South End, 1996.
_____, and Glenn T. Morris, "Key Indian Laws and Cases." In *The State of Native America: Genocide, Colonization, and Resistance*. Boston: South End, 1992: 13–21.
Clark, John T. Letter to Martha Brown Berry, December 23, no year. Archive.
Cobb, Daniel M., and Loretta Fowler, ed. *Beyond Red Power: American Indian Policies and Activism Since 1909*. Sante Fe, NM: School for Advanced Research Press, 2007.
Courier Dispatch. N.d. Archive.
Davis, William C. *The Illustrated Directory of the Old West*. Minneapolis: Voyageur, 2002.
"Death Claims E.C. Mullendore; Funeral Is Held Here Thursday." *The Cleveland American*, January 20, 1938, p. 1. Archive.
Dorman, Robert. *It Happened in Oklahoma*. Helena, MT: TwoDot, 2006.
Dyer, Richard. *White*. New York: Routledge, 1997.
"E.C. Mullendore IV Given Tribal Name at Ceremony." *Pawhuska Journal-Capital*. February 18, 1970. N.p. Archive.
Farge, Arlette. *The Allure of the Archives*. New Haven, CT: Yale University Press, 2013.
Farid, Paula. Interview. Pawhuska, OK, November 20, 2013.
Farnum, Allen L. *Pawnee Bill's Historic Wild West: A Photo Documentary of the 1900–1905 Show Tours*. West Chester, PA: Schiffer, 1992.
Foucault, Michel. *Discipline and Punish: The Birth of the Prison*. New York: Random House, 1977.
Franklin, Jimmie L. "Black Oklahomans and a Sense of Place," in Davis D. Joyce, ed. *"An Oklahoma I Had Never Seen Before": Alternative Views of Oklahoma History*. Norman: University of Oklahoma Press, 1994: 265–279.
Franks, Kenny A., and Paul F. Lambert. *Pawnee Pride: A History of Pawnee County*. Oklahoma City: Western Heritage, 1994.
"George Berry, Pawnee Settler Had Interesting Career in This County," January 26, 1939, n.p. Archive.
"George M. Berry, Being Treated at Rochester, Has Had Long Experience with Redmen." Unknown newspaper, January 22, 1939. Archive.
Gibson, Arrell M. *The Oklahoma Story*. Norman: University of Oklahoma Press, 1986 [1971].
Glaberson, William. "Who Is a Seminole, and Who Gets to Decide?" *New York Times*, January 29, 2001, p. A1.
Glasscock, C. B. *Then Came Oil: The Story of the Last Frontier*. New York: Bobbs-Merill, 1938.
Goodson, Dora Berry. *The Last Run*. Ponca City Chapter of the Daughters of American Revolution, 1939. Archive.
_____. Letter to Dora Berry Snow. N.d. Archive.
Gross, Richard. "Immaculate Conception Catholic Church: The Catholic Church of the Osage." *Stained Glass Quarterly* Vol. 105, No. 1 (2010): 58–63.

Grounds, Richard A., George E. Tinker, and David E. Wilkins. *Native Voices: American Indian Identity and Resistance.* Lawrence: University of Kansas, 2003.
Harjo, Joy. *How We Became Human.* New York: W.W. Norton, 2002.
———. "There Is No Such Thing as a One-Way Land Bridge." In *Native Voices: American Indian Identity and Resistance.* Topeka: University Press of Kansas, 2003.
Harmon, Alexandra, "Osage Oil Owners," in *Rich Indians: Native People and the Problem of Wealth in American Society.* Chapel Hill: University of North Carolina Press, 2010: 171-208.
Heat-Moon, William Least, and James K. Wallace, ed. and trans. *An Osage Journey to Europe, 1827-1830: Three French Accounts.* Norman: University of Oklahoma Press, 2013.
Hess, Catherine Berry. Interviews. Lincoln, CA, November 1, 2013, December 4, 29, 2013; January 9, 2014; April 10, 2014.
———. "Old Fashioned Thrift." *Des Moines Register*, 1975. Archive.
Hess, David. *The Ancestors of the Hess Family of Anadarko.* Published by the Hess family, 2004.
Hess, Janet Berry. *Art and Architecture in Postcolonial Africa.* Jefferson, NC: McFarland, 2006.
Hess, Ross. "The View from Persimmon Hill." *Sunday Oklahoman*, 1965. Archive.
Heth, Charlotte. *Native American Dance: Ceremonies and Social Traditions.* Washington, DC: National Museum of the American Indian, Smithsonian Institution, with Starwood, 1992.
Hill, Gene. "The Chisholm Trail." *Oklahoma Omnibus.* Oklahoma Historical Society, 1986. Archive.
Hill, Richard W., Sr. "Developed Identities: Seeing the Stereotypes and Beyond," in Tim Johnson, ed., *Spirit Capture: Photographs from the National Museum of the American Indian.* Washington: Smithsonian Institution, 1998: 139-160.
Historical and Biographical History of Oklahoma. 1901. N.p. Archive.
Hogan, Lawrence J. *The Osage Indian Murders: The Story of a Multiple Murder Plot to Acquire the Estates of Wealthy Osage Tribal Members.* Frederick, MD: Amlex, 1998.
Holland, Katy. "Sustaining a Spirited Culture: Board Promotes Pawhuska Indian Village." *Bartlesville Magazine* 7, no. 4 (Spring 2014), n.p.
Howell, Joseph E. Unidentified article, n.p. Archive.
Hoxie, Frederick E. "Missing the Point: Academic Experts and American Indian Politics," in Daniel M. Cobb and Loretta Fowler, ed., *Beyond Red Power: American Indian Policies and Activism Since 1909.* Sante Fe, NM: School for Advanced Research Press, 2007: 16-32.
Jackson, Michael. *Minima Ethnographica: Intersubjectivity and the Anthropological Project.* Chicago: University of Chicago Press, 1998.
Jaimes, Annette M., ed. *The State of Native America: Genocide, Colonization, and Resistance.* Boston: South End, 1992.
Johnson, Ken. "Manifest Destiny, at the Point of a Gun." *New York Times*, December 19, 2013.
Johnson, Tim. *Spirit Capture: Photographs from the National Museum of the American Indian.* Washington, DC: Smithsonian Institution Press, 1998.
Joyce, David D. *"An Oklahoma I Had Never Seen Before": Alternative Views of Oklahoma History.* Norman: University of Oklahoma Press, 1994.
Karp, Ivan, Christine Mullen Kreamer and Steven D. Lavine, ed. *Museums and Communities: The Politics of Public Culture.* Washington, DC: Smithsonian Institution Press, 1992.
Katz, William Loren. *Black Indians: A Hidden Heritage.* New York: Simon and Schuster, 1986.
Kavanagh, Thomas W. "Southern Plains Dance: Tradition and Dynamism," in Charlotte Heth, ed. *Native American Dance: Ceremonies and Social Traditions.* New York: Smithsonian Institution, 1992.
Kaye, Frances W. "Little Squatter on the Osage Diminished Reserve: Reading Laura Ingalls Wilder's Kansas Indians." *Great Plains Quarterly* 20, issue 2 (2000): 123-140.
King Berry Reminisces 1850-1945. N.p., n.d. Archive.
Krisch, Joshua A. "When Racism Was a Science." *New York Times*, October 14, 2014, p. D6.
Kwitny, Jonathan. *The Mullendore Murder Case.* New York: Warner, 1976.

La Chapelle, Peter. *Proud to Be An Okie: Cultural Politics, Country Music, and Migration to Southern California.* Berkeley: University of California Press, 2007.
Laune, Paul. *Mustang Round-Up.* N.p., n.d. Archive.
Letter to Everett Berry, Jr., n.d. Archive.
Letter to Roy Berry from Pawnee, November 9, 1923. Archive.
Lloyd, Roger Hall. *Osage County: A Tribe and American Culture, 1600-1934.* Lincoln, NE: iUniverse, 2006.
Macky, Bertha. Letter to Mrs. Susan Harthur, July 15, 1915. Archive.
Mathews, John Joseph. "Planting Moon." In John T. Price, *The Tallgrass Prairie Reader.* Iowa City: University of Iowa Press, 2014: 147–155.
_____. *Wah'Kon-Tah: The Osage and the White Man's Road.* Norman: University of Oklahoma Press, 1932.
McAuliffe, Dennis Jr. *Bloodland: A Family Story of Oil, Greed and Murder on the Osage Reservation.* New York: Random House, 1994.
McMillen, Margot Ford. "'Les Indiens Osages': French Publicity for the Traveling Osage." *Missouri Historical Review* Vol. 97, no. 4 (July 2003): 295–333.
Minges, Patrick. *Black Indian Slave Narratives.* Winston-Salem, NC: John F. Blair, 2004.
Momaday, N. Scott. *The Man Made of Words: Essays, Stories, Passages.* New York: St. Martin's Griffin, 1997.
Monnett, F. S. Letter to George Berry, September 19, 1907. Archive.
Moore, MariJo, ed. *Genocide of the Mind: New Native American Writing.* New York: Nation, 2003.
Morand, Anne, Kevin Smith, Daniel C. Swan, and Sarah Erwin. *Treasures of Gilcrease: Selections from the Permanent Collection.* Tulsa: Gilcrease Museum, 2003.
"Mullendores Came Long Way from Shot to Shot." N.p., n.d. Archive.
National Cowboy & Western Heritage Museum website, Monumental Sculpture.
O'Barr, William. "Images of Native Americans in Advertising." *Advertising and Society Review* 14, issue 1 (30 November 2012): 1–51.
Oguibe, Olu, and Okwui Enwezor, ed. *Reading the Contemporary: African Art from Theory to the Marketplace.* Cambridge: MIT Press, 1999.
Oklahoma Press Clipping Bureau, Guthrie, Oklahoma, *Times Journal.* December 27, 1906. N.p. Archive.
"On Parade," *Cushing Daily Citizen*, November 24, 1933. N.p. Archive.
Osage Agency. *1872-1972 Osage Indian Tribe Centennial Celebration.* Tulsa: Acorn, 1972.
"Out of the Past." Reprinted from the files of the *Cleveland American*, October 21, 1982, p. 2a. Archive.
Parezo, Nancy J. "What's in a Name? The 1940s-1950s 'Squaw Dress.'" *American Indian Quarterly* 33, issue 3 (June 2009): 373–404.
Peavy, Linda, and Ursula Smith. *Pioneer Women: The Lives of Women on the Frontier.* Norman: University of Oklahoma Press, 1996.
Pember, Mary Annette. "Indian Assimilation: The Mystery of the Tiny Handcuffs, Solved." Indian Country Today Media Network.com.
Pendleton Woolen Mills. Albuquerque: Avanyu, 1987 [1915].
"Pioneer Banker Is an Authority on Indian Cookery." N.p., n.d. Archive.
"Portrait and Biographical Record," p. 898. N.d. Archive.
Postcard of color lithograph. "Princess Wenona and Edith Tatinger 101 Ranch Promotional Poster." Gilcrease Museum, Tulsa, Oklahoma.
Presbyterian Guild. *The Presbyterian Guild Cook Book.* Hominy, OK: 1st Presbyterian Guild, Dec. 1, 1927.
Rahn, R. Neill. Letter to Isaac "King" Berry, Topeka, Kansas, September 23, 1924. Archive.
Reese, Linda Williams. *Women of Oklahoma: 1890-1920.* Norman: University of Oklahoma Press, 1997.
Revard, Carter. "Birdwatching in Wales and Indian Territory: Consecrations of Place in Osage and Pawnee Ceremonies and in Poems by Hopkins, Thomas, and Others." *European Review of Native American Studies* 20, issue 1 (2006): 47–51.

_____. *Family Matters, Tribal Affairs.* Tucson: University of Arizona Press, 1998.
Robbins, Rebecca L. "Self-Determination and Subordination: The Past, Present, and Future of American Indian Governance," in Annette M. Jaimes, ed., *The State of Native America: Genocide, Colonization, and Resistance.* Boston: South End, 1992: 87–122.
Rollings, Willard Hughes. *The Osage: An Ethnographical Study of Hegemony on the Prairie-Plains.* Columbia: University of Missouri Press, 1992.
_____. *Unaffected by the Gospel: Osage Resistance to the Christian Invasion 1673-1906: A Cultural Victory.* Albuquerque: University of New Mexico Press, 2004.
Shirley, Glenn. *Pawnee Bill: A Biography of Major Gordon W. Lillie.* Stillwater, OK: Western, 1993.
Smith, Mrs. John B. "Reminiscences." N.d., n.p. Archive.
Steedman, Carolyn. *Dust: The Archive and Cultural History.* New Brunswick, NJ: Rutgers University Press, 2001.
Stewart, Omer C. *Peyote Religion: A History.* Norman: University of Oklahoma Press, 1987.
Stocking, George W., Jr, ed. *Objects and Others: Essays on Museums and Material Culture.* History of Anthropology, vol. 3. Madison: University of Wisconsin Press, 1985.
Stoler, Ann Laura. *Along the Archival Grain: Epistemic Anxieties and Colonial Common Sense.* Princeton, NJ: 2009.
Stoller, Paul. *Sensuous Scholarship.* Philadelphia: University of Pennsylvania Press, 1997.
"The Story of the Spider." Handout, Osage Tribal Museum, Pawhuska, OK, 2014.
"Surprise! The Settlers Were Afraid of Cowboys!" N.d., n.p. Archive.
Swan, Daniel. "Early Osage Peyotism." *Plains Anthropologist* 43, no. 163 (February 1998): 51–71.
_____. "100 Years of Dancing: The Osages of Pawhuska District Observe an Anniversary." *Chronicles of Oklahoma* 63, issue 1 (1985): 90–97.
Tall Tales and Historic Adventures: David Duncan Legendary Longhunter. N.d., p. 6. Archive.
Tallman, Pbonchai. Interview. Napa, CA, 2014.
Thoburn, James B. *History of Oklahoma*, vol. 5. American Historical Society, 1916. Archive.
Thomas Gilcrease. Tulsa: Gilcrease Museum, 2009.
Times Democrat, Oklahoma Press Clipping Bureau, Guthrie, Oklahoma. December 27, 1906. N.p. Archive.
Tixier, Victor, John Francis McDermott, ed., Albert J. Salvan, trans. *Tixier's Travels on the Osage Prairies, 1839-40.* Norman: University of Oklahoma Press, 1940 (France: Clermand-Ferrand, 1844).
Transcription of phone call between Martha Brown and Virginia Berry Harrison, 1987. Archive.
Trumbly, Arlena. Interview. Pawhuska, OK, June 28, 2014.
Vizenor, Gerald. *Fugitive Poses: Native American Indian Scenes of Absence and Presence.* Lincoln: University of Nebraska Press, 1998.
Walden, John R. *Short History of Berry Family.* N.d., n.p. Archive.
_____. "Winfield Man." *Notes on Early Clark County Kansas*, vol. III, by Clark County Chapter of the Kansas State Historical Society, Dorothy Berrman and Melville Campbell Harper, ed., September 1941–August 1942, reprinted from the Clark County Historical Society Column in the *Clark County Clipper*, Ashland, Kansas. Archive.
Weekly Kansas Star, June 27, 1945. N.p. Archive.
Wickett, Murray R. *Contested Territory: Whites, Native Americans and African Americans in Oklahoma, 1865–1907.* Baton Rouge: Louisiana State University Press, 2000.
Williams, Joe. *Woolaroc.* Bartlesville, OK: Frank Phillips Foundation, 1991.
Wilson, Terry P. "Osage Indian Women During a Century of Change, 1870-1980." *Prologue* 14, issue 4 (1982): 185–201.
"Wolf Scalps Ranicky Bill." N.p., n.d. Archive.
Wrightsman, C.J. Letter to George Berry, November 6, 1906. Archive.

Index

Numbers in ***bold italics*** indicate pages with photographs.

African American freedmen 34, 46–48
African American women 124–126, 204*ch*3*n*49
Alexie, Sherman 29
allotment 11, 18, 23, 25, 34, 155
archive 1–7, 11, 38–40, 42, 52, 67–69, 114, 133, 189

Bailey, Garrick 12–13, 57–58, 60, 64, 76, 90–92
Barnsdall 60, 168
Berry, Camelia vi, 9, ***30***–31, 35, 40–***41***, 45–46, 49, ***51***, 69, 84, 94, ***105***, 110–***112***, 115–116, 125, 179
Berry, Everett, Jr. v, 55, 71–72, 85–***86***, 104, 106, 125, 147, 184, 187, 189
Berry, Everett, Sr. 85–***86***, 96, 130–***131***, 137, 187
Berry, George Madison 5, 47–49, 93, 102–104, ***105***–107, 114, 125, 127, 135, 148
Berry, Harriet 113, 125
Berry, Isaac King 44–45, 48–49, 52, 70, 95, 104
Berry, Jack 30, 37, 49, 69
Berry, James 183–84
Berry, Juliet Sophia 30, 49, 111, 113, 116
Berry, Louella ("Grandmother") 55, 61, 70, 85, 108–***109***, 110, 117, 125, 130–***131***, 168, 187, 189
Berry, Nancy Jane 30–31, 42–43, 110–112
Berry, Sarah 41–42
Berry, Thomas E. 6, 30, 42, 48–49, 52, 69, 95, 115, 135
Berry, William E. 29, 37, 49, 51–52, 85, 95, 113

Berry Brothers 49, 51, 53, 68, 94, 104, 113
Bigheart, James, Chief 22, ***23***–25, 143, 157–158
Black Dog (*Shon-ton-ca-be*) ***78***, 181–182
blackjack trees ***24***, 66, 74, 180, 184, 187
Blier, Suzanne 88–89, 91
Bureau of Indian Affairs 155–156
Burns, Louis 12–13, 23
Burton, Antoinette 39

Callahan, Alice Anne 166, 171, 177
cattle drive 192, 194, 196
Cherokee 5, 18–20, 23, 32–33, 40, 44, 48, 52, 68, 72, 93, 94, 101, 120, 134, 155, 139, 191; *Cherokee Nation v. Georgia* 43–44; Cherokee Strip 93–94, 101
Cheyenne 32
Chickasaw 18–20, 32, 46, 155
Childers, Chrissie vi, 44, 55
Chisholm Trail 48, 53, 68, 191
Choctaw 18–20, 32, 46, 155
Churchill, Ward 31, 43, 157
Civil War 43, 51
commercial representations of American Indians 157–159
constitution: and Oklahoma 6, 47, 74, 102, 104–107; Oklahoma Territory 102; Osage 24–25; and statehood 102, 205*ch*4*n*43
Council of the Osage 22–23, 143
cowboy 50–54, 68, 149–150, 159, ***160–162***, 163, 191, 193–94
Cross Bell brand 52–53, 137, 186
Curtis, Charles 139, 155, 211*ch*10*n*5; and Curtis Act 155
Custer, George 28–29, 83

219

Index

Dawes (General Allotment) Act 11–12, 23–24, 33, 122, 155
Derrida, Jacques 3, 7
Dreadfulwater, Nathan *170*, *175*
Drummond, Ree 67, 108
Drummond family 67, 70, *71*, 86, 108, 111
Dust Bowl 35, 134
Dyer, Richard 27–28

Echohawk, Brummett 72
"End of the Trail" 141–*142*
expositions: exhibitions of Osage 77, 79, 145, 151–152; Pawnee Bill 148–151

Farge, Arlette 3, 7, 39
Farid, Amy 172–173, *174*
Farid, Paula 16, 122–*123*, 172–173, *174*, 177, 210*ch8n*20
femininity 87, 115–119, 124–125
Five Woman Council 16, 122, 173
Foucault, Michel 3, 63
France 12, 14, 16–17

genocide 12
Gilcrease Museum 104, 147–148
Goodson, Dora Berry 52, 69, 113
Grant, Ulysses 21, 93, 96
Gray Horse *4*, 58, 60–*61*, 99, 168, *171*
guns 18, 51–52, 192–193
Guthrie, Woody 187

Harjo, Joy v, vi, 177
Harmon, Alexandra 13, 132
Hess, Catherine Berry (mother) v, 38, 71–72, *73*, *74*, *75*, *86*, 106, 114, 118, 134–135, 137, *184*–185, 187, 189
Hess, Janet Berry 16, 55, 81, 106–107, *72*, 176–177, 185–*186*, 187, 189
Hess, Julia 35, 69–70, 115
Hess, Otto 35, 53, 69–70
Hess, Ross (father) v, 106, 138, 141, 146, 153–*154*, 159, *160*–*162*, 163–164, 189, 191–197
Hickock, "Wild Bill" 192–193
hominy 7, 45, 55–56, 58–*59*, 60–*62*, *67*, 70, *71*, 72, *74*, 74, 86, 96, 111, 116, 117, 134, 135, 166, 168, *170*, 184

illness: African American women 124; Osage 58, 60; white settlers 114–115
Indian Citizenship Act 155
"Indian Territory" 1, 5, 11, 13, 19, 23, 29, 43–45, 48, 50, 52–53, 56, 63, 68, 102
industrialization 86–87
I'n-lon-schka *4*, 7–*8*, 16, 62, 81, 86–87, 92, 123, 155, 164–165, *166*–*170*, *171*–178, 212*n*63–64; *see also* Osage spirituality

Jackson, Pres. Andrew 19–20
Jackson, Michael 1, 5, 7, 9, 26–27, 29, 36–38, 47, 72, 125–126, 180, 188–189, 192
Jefferson, Pres. Thomas 17, 29–30

Kansas 4, 11, 13, 19–21, 23–24, 33, 43–45, 49, 68–69, 94, 98, 99, 111, 113, 132, 148, 191–192
Kentucky 4–5, *30*–31, *41*–43, 111, 113, 118
Kiowa 14, 20, 36, 49, 58, 120
"Kiowa Five" 146–147
Ku Klux Klan 43, 45–47

LaFlesche, Francis 34, 83, 90–91
land auctions 25, 202
Land Ordinance of 1787 17, 68, 96, 101, 152
Land Run 5, 48, 52, 68, 93, *94*–96, 101, 124, 135, 184
Lloyd, Roger Hall 9, 12–14, 20, 29, 53–54, 75, 88, 90, 98, 185, 188, 192
Lookout, Fred, Chief 139–140, *149*, 183
loss of territory 11, 18–21, 33, 102
Louisiana 16–18

Madden, Daniel *170*, *175*
Madden, David *169*–*170*
Madden, Tara *169*–*170*, *175*
masculinity 29, 53
Mathews, John Joseph 9, 12–13, 21, 23, 64, 66, 77, 93, 99, 101, 134, 180
McAuliffe, Dennis 12, 17, 20, 67, 74, 134, 185
Miller, Zach and the "101 Ranch" 140, 148–*149*, 164, *165*
"Million Dollar Elm" 25, 128, 130, 135
mineral wealth 11–13, 24–25, 52, 70–71, 128, 130, 132–133, 202*ch1n*84; and "Reign of Terror" 133–134
Mississippi 15–16, 19–20, 93
Mississippi River 13–14, 16–17, 20, 93
Missouri 13–14, 15, 19–20, 43, 111, 113
Momaday, N. Scott 9, 36, 153, 179, 182
Mullendore, E.C. 106, 127, 135, *136*–137, 183
Mullendore, Jennie Berry 69, 95, 114, 135, *136*–37
Mullendore family 6, 53, 70, 95–96, 101, 135–138, 183
museum collections 12, 16, 81, 145–146, 149

National Cowboy and Western Heritage Museum 141, 159; and "End of the Trail" 141–142
Native American Church 58, *59*, 60–61, 88, 91, 98, 147, 168, 177

Index

oil wells 65–67, **72**, **129**, 135, 186
Osage Allotment Act of 1906 25, 60, 122
Osage and "social reconstruction" **97**–101
Osage architecture 56–62
Osage art 14, 16, 64, 76–77, 81, 143–48
Osage boarding school 6, 63, 80, 83, 98–**99**, **100**, 122
Osage body ornamentation 76–84, 128, 130
Osage chiefs 11, **15**, **19**, 22–**23**, 78, 81
Osage Council **22**–23, 33, 122, 156–157; Council House 63–64, **65**, 143
Osage grass leasing 24–25, 52, 128, 130
Osage spirituality 14, 56–58, 76, 81–83, 204*ch*4*n*4; and Catholicism 58, 60, 91, 98–99, 180–183; Immaculate Conception Catholic Church 60; Medicine Men 58, 90–92, 173–174; sacred objects (*wa-xo-be*) 87–**88**, 89–92, 145; *see also I'n-lon-schka*; Native American Church
Osage trade 14, 16
Osage Tribal Museum 5, 11–12, 25–26, 128, 143, 147–48, 185
Osage women 14, 80–81, **82**, 83–84, 119–123, **130**, 171–72, 182; Mrs. Arthur Bonnicastle **121**
outlaws 133, 195–196, 207–208*ch*6*n*26

Paiute 167, 172, 174
Parker, Ely 21
Parker, Quanah 58, 88, 147
Pawhuska 5, 7, 11–12, 38, 45, 49, 52, 60, 62–64, 70, 76–77, 74, 98, 100, 102, 116, 128, 138, 144, 157, 159, 167–168, 177; architecture 25, 60–64, **65–66**, 67
Pawhuska, Chief (*Pah-hui-skah*) 6, 17, 23, 79, 201*ch*1*n*35
Pawnee 5, 15, 44–46, 49–50, 52, 70, 74, 91, 93, 102–105, 107, 115, 144, 146, 148–149, 153, 167; city of 46, 63, 70, 105–106, 135, 184; Trading Post 48–50, 102
Pawnee Bill (Gorden Lillie) 106, 146, 148, **149**–152, 173
Pendleton blanket 70, 86–87, 143, 166
Phillips, Frank 128, 139-**140**, **144**, **149**
photography 141–144
Pickett, Bill 163–164, **165**
Ponca 13, 68
precolonial contact 12–14, 16

Quakers 21, **62**, 98

"racial" categories 18, 24, 46, 27–34, 124, 132–133, 201*ch*1*n*74; eugenics 13, 33–36, 143, 145, 159
recipes 108, 110, 126
Reese, Linda Williams 109, 116–117, 124
removal to reservations 11–12, 18, 20–24, 205*ch*4*n*28
Revard, Carter 57, 180–183, 185
Rogers, Will 106, 139, **149**
Rollings, Willard 13, 57–58, 80
roundhouse **4**, 6, 55–**56**, 60, **61–62**, 67, **170**

Seminole 32, 34–35, 46, 146, 155
settler architecture 68–72
settler dress 84–86
slavery 20, 27, **30**–36, 42, 46
Spain 16–17
Steedman 172
Stoler, Ann Laura 3–4
Stoller, Paul 1, 6, 36–37, 93

Tallgrass Prairie Reserve 81, 185–**186**, 213*ch*11*n*29
Tallman, Pbonchai vi, **59**, **66–67**, 172–173, 176, 207*ch*5*n*76
Tennessee 41–42
Termination Act of 1953 156–157
Tixier, Victor 79–83, 132
"Trail of Tears" (Indian Removal Act) 19–20, 34, 93–94
treaties 16–25, 71, 94, 98

United States Supreme Court decisions 19, 43, 98, 157

"The View from Persimmon Hill" 153, 159, **160–162**, 163–164

Walters, Col. E. 25, 128
Washington, George 40–41, 116
whiteness 27–28
Wilder, Laura Ingalls 21
Woolaroc 139–**140**
Wynona 67, **72**, **74**, 87, 96, **144**, 187